Roadside History of
COLORADO

Roadside History of
COLORADO

CANDY MOULTON

2006
MOUNTAIN PRESS PUBLISHING COMPANY
MISSOULA, MONTANA

Cover image: *Main Street of Telluride, Colorado.* Courtesy Center of Southwest Studies, Fort Lewis College, Nina Heald Webber Southwest Colorado Collection

Photos not otherwise credited are by the author.

Maps by Tony Moore, Moore Creative Designs

Library of Congress Cataloging-in-Publication Data

Moulton, Candy Vyvey, 1955–
  Roadside history of Colorado / Candy Moulton
    p. cm. — (Roadside history series)
  Includes bibliographical references and index.
  ISBN-13: 978-0-8-97842-520-4 (pbk. : alk. paper)
  1. Colorado—Guidebooks. 2. Colorado—History, Local.
3. Automobile travel—Colorado—Guidebooks. I. Title. II. Series.
  F774.3.M68 2006
  917.880434—dc22
                    2006003999

PRINTED IN THE UNITED STATES

MOUNTAIN PRESS PUBLISHING COMPANY
P.O. Box 2399 • Missoula, MT 59801
406-728-1900

To the Herrings

Contents

Preface and Acknowledgments _____

Since I was a child, my home has always been only about a thirty-minute drive north of the Colorado-Wyoming border. With my family I have ridden over Colorado's mountain passes on the way to Denver, where I had numerous aunts, uncles, and cousins. From our Wyoming ranch we shipped livestock to markets in Brush and Fort Collins and sold grain to ranchers in North Park. Even today, I often jump in the car and drive to Walden to buy lottery tickets. For me, Colorado has always been filled with wonderful sights, from mountain peaks to Denver theater. Visiting Colorado again while researching this book was great fun. I hope you enjoy the stories I found along the way.

Conducting the research for a Roadside History can be daunting. Any major project, and particularly one like this, requires a great deal of assistance. I want to extend my thanks to several people who have been particularly helpful. In addition to the entire staff at Mountain Press in Missoula, Montana, I am indebted to various friends and family members. Among them are Orville and GeGe Herring, Betty and Fox Vyvey, Bob Lovato, Elaine Long and the late Arthur Long, Rita Cleary, Nell Brown Propst and the late Keith Propst, Dorothy and Nick Jamison, Jim Smith, and of course Steve, Shawn, and Erin Moulton. I am especially grateful to James A. Crutchfield, Lori Van Pelt, and Terry A. Del Bene, who shared research materials and always found answers for me when I had a Colorado question.

This book would not have been possible without the pioneering research and writing of historians who have left behind volumes on Colorado's history. I cannot name all of them, but I would like to acknowledge the work of LeRoy Hafen, Virginia Simmons, Ken Reyher, P. David Smith, Duane A. Smith, David Lavender, and Ron Kessler. I am particularly indebted to the work of David A. White, editor of the nine-volume *News of the Plains and Rockies*, which includes reproductions of many primary documents related to Colorado and the West, published by the Arthur H. Clark Company. Another valuable resource was the *Encyclopedia of Frontier Biography*, by Dan L. Thrapp, published by the University of Nebraska Press.

As I traveled, I had the tremendous support of many Colorado visitor bureaus and chambers of commerce, whose staff helped me arrange tours and interviews and in many cases provided lodging and meals. Special thanks to Distinctive Inns of Colorado; the Sterling Convention and

Visitor's Bureau; the Lightner Creek Inn in Durango; Romantic River Song in Estes Park; the Wyman Hotel & Inn in Silverton; the Old Library Inn in Sterling; Lynn Dyer of the Mesa Verde Country Visitor Information Bureau in Cortez; the Turquoise Inn in Cortez; the Fort Sedgwick Historical Society, particularly Mary McKinstry; the staff of the Colorado Historical Society and its affiliates; the public relations division of the Colorado Tourism Office, especially Christy Nielson; and the staff and volunteers at museums and historic sites all across Colorado.

Colorado Facts_____

Nickname: Centennial State

State motto: Nil sine numine, "Nothing Without the Deity"

State animal: Rocky Mountain bighorn sheep

State bird: Lark bunting

State fish: Greenback cutthroat trout

State insect: Colorado hairstreak butterfly

State tree: Colorado blue spruce

State flower: White and lavender columbine

State grass: Blue grama grass

State fossil: Stegosaurus

State mineral: Rhodochrosite

State Rock: Yule marble

State gemstone: Aquamarine

State folk dance: Square dance

State song: "Where the Columbines Grow" by A. J. Fynn, 1915

(VERSE 1)
Where the snowy peaks gleam in the moonlight,
Above the dark forests of pine,
And the wild foaming waters dash onward,
Toward lands where the tropic stars shine;
Where the scream of the bold mountain eagle
Responds to the notes of the dove
Is the purple-robed West, the land that is best,
The pioneer land that we love.

(CHORUS)
'Tis the land where the columbines grow,
Overlooking the plains far below,
While the cool summer breeze in the evergreen trees
Softly sings where the columbines grow.

(VERSE 2)
The bison is gone from the upland,
The deer from the canyon has fled,
The home of the wolf is deserted,

The antelope moans for his dead,
The war whoop re-echoes no longer,
The Indian's only a name,
And the nymphs of the grove in their loneliness rove,
But the columbine blooms just the same.

(VERSE 3)
Let the violet brighten the brookside,
In sunlight of earlier spring,
Let the fair clover bedeck the green meadow,
In days when the orioles sing,
Let the goldenrod herald the autumn,
But, under the midsummer sky,
In its fair western home, may the columbine bloom
Till our great mountain rivers run dry.

National Parks, Monuments, Recreation Areas, and Historic Sites:

Bent's Old Fort National Historic Site, near La Junta (established June 3, 1960)

Black Canyon of the Gunnison National Park, west of Gunnison (established as national monument March 2, 1933; became a national park October 21, 1999)

Canyon of the Ancients National Monument, near Cortez (established June 9, 2000)

Colorado National Monument, near Grand Junction (established May 24, 1911)

Curecanti National Recreation Area, west of Gunnison (established February 6, 1965)

Dinosaur National Monument, on the Yampa Plateau in Moffat County (established July 14, 1938; later expanded)

Florissant Fossil Beds National Monument, near Florissant (established August 20, 1969)

Great Sand Dunes National Park and Preserve, San Luis Valley (established as national monument March 17, 1932; became a national park and preserve November 22, 2000)

Hovenweep National Monument, Montezuma County (established March 2, 1923)

Mesa Verde National Park, near Mancos (established June 29, 1906)

Rocky Mountain National Park, near Estes Park (established January 26, 1915)

Sand Creek Massacre National Historic Site, near Chivington (authorized November 7, 2000; not yet established)

Yucca House National Monument, near Cortez (established December 19, 1919)

Chronology _____

c. 8000 BC
or earlier   First known human occupation of Colorado, Cortez area

c. AD 450   Farming begins in Cortez area

Ancestral Puebloans in Mesa Verde area develop bow and arrow, pottery, and pit houses

c. AD 750   Pueblo building begins in Mesa Verde area

c. 1100   First cliff dwellings built in Mesa Verde area

c. 1120   Escalante Pueblo built

c. 1300   Cliff dwellings in Mesa Verde area abandoned

1598   Juan de Oñate enters Colorado near the San Luis Valley

1682   Sieur de la Salle claims Louisiana Territory, which includes the eastern half of future Colorado, for France

1706   Searching for runaway Pueblo Indians, Spaniards march from New Mexico to Pueblo area and claim region for Spain

1762   France cedes all lands west of Mississippi River to Spain

1776   Spanish priests Francisco Atanasio Domínguez and Silvestre Vélez de Escalante explore western Colorado and create first written record of the area

1800   Spain retrocedes Louisiana Territory to France

1803   Louisiana Purchase made; eastern Colorado now U.S. territory

1806–07   Explorer Zebulon Pike traverses Colorado; builds first American structure in Colorado near Pueblo

1820   Maj. Stephen Long leads first U.S. military expedition to northeastern Colorado

Dr. Edwin James makes first known ascent to summit of Pikes Peak

1821	William Becknell forges Santa Fe Trail through southeastern Colorado
1833	Bent, St. Vrain Company establishes Bent's Fort, the first successful business in Colorado
	Mexican government establishes first land grants in Colorado, in the San Luis Valley
1836	Texas declares its independence and claims a narrow strip of land in Colorado
1842	Expedition of John C. Frémont, led by Kit Carson, explores northeast Colorado
1846	Stephen Watts Kearny leads Army of the West through Colorado to Santa Fe
1848	Treaty of Guadalupe Hidalgo signed; United States acquires territory that includes western Colorado
1849	First settlement in Colorado established, in present Garcia Cherokee Indians and others forge Cherokee Trail
1850	U.S. government purchases Texas claims in Colorado
1852	Fort Massachusetts, the first U.S. Army post in Colorado, established
1853	Capt. John Gunnison and the U.S. Corps of Topographical Engineers survey route through Rocky Mountains in southwestern Colorado
1858	Gold discovered in mountains west of Denver, leading to Pikes Peak gold rush; Montana City, St. Charles, Auraria and Denver City are founded, all of which eventually become part of Denver
1859	First newspaper in Colorado, the *Rocky Mountain News*, begins publication
1861	Colorado Territory established; William Gilpin named first territorial governor
	Cheyennes and Arapahos cede most of their remaining lands in Colorado to United States in Fort Wise Treaty
1862	First Colorado Territorial Legislature convenes in Colorado City; Golden chosen as new capital; Homestead; Act fosters settlement of land in Colorado and throughout the West

1863	Council for Treaty of 1863 meets; several Ute bands agree to allow white development on their land in Colorado
1864	Plains Indian wars begin: An upsurge in Indian raids against settlers on the Great Plains leads to army campaign to subjugate natives. Several significant battles occur, culminating in the Sand Creek Massacre, which sets off a series of Indian retaliations.
1865	"Bloody Year on the Plains": Indian wars heat up with Cheyenne and Arapaho attacks on soldiers, settlers, and travelers
1866	Charles Goodnight and Oliver Loving drive first cattle into Colorado from Texas
1867	Denver becomes new territorial capital
	Violence erupts in December between whites and Mexicans in Trinidad; in January 1868, federal troops are called in to quell the conflict
1868	Treaty of 1868 establishes a Ute reservation encompassing nearly one-third of Colorado Territory; the territorial governor and other whites protest its terms
	Cheyenne leader Roman Nose is killed in Battle of Beecher Island
1869	U.S. troops kill Cheyenne leader Tall Bull and defeat the Cheyenne Dog Soldiers in the Battle of Summit Springs, leading to the final subjugation of the Plains Indians in Colorado
	First known rodeo held in Deer Trail
1873	Brunot Treaty concentrates Utes in western Colorado, opening additional Indian lands to mining and settlement
1874	First scientific investigation of pueblo ruins in Mesa Verde area
1876	Colorado becomes thirty-eighth state; John L. Routt elected governor
1878	Railroads vie for right to build through Royal Gorge, leading to strife in "Royal Gorge War"
1879	Ute uprising at White River Agency, known as the Meeker Massacre, occurs, leading to the Utes' permanent removal from Colorado

1883	Prospector Alfred Packer convicted of murdering and cannibalizing five companions in the San Juan Mountains
1896	Western Federation of Miners leads strike in Leadville; strikers destroy Coronado Mine; state militia called in to quell riot
1901	Riot during mining strike in Telluride leaves three dead
	First ascent of Pikes Peak by automobile
1903	Mining strikes occur in Victor, Colorado City, Idaho Springs, and Cripple Creek; several turn violent
1905	Construction begins on the Gunnison Tunnel, the first U.S. Bureau of Reclamation project in Colorado
1906	First national park in Colorado, Mesa Verde National Park, established
	Denver Mint issues its first coins
1913–14	"Southern Coal Field War": Miners' strike in Trinidad area leads to numerous deaths, including those of eighteen men, women, and children in "Ludlow Massacre" of April 1914
1915	Pikes Peak Highway built
1917	Construction of Durango-Silverton-Ouray Highway (Million Dollar Highway) begins
1928	Moffat Tunnel opens, providing the first rail link through the Continental Divide
1929	Prison riot at the state penitentiary in Canon City leaves thirteen dead and ten wounded
1935	In response to the Dust Bowl, President Franklin D. Roosevelt establishes Resettlement Administration to buy back homesteads of destitute farmers in Colorado and elsewhere
1941	First unit of alpine ski troops, the Eighty-seventh Infantry Mountain Regiment, activated at Camp Hale
1942	Camp Amache, a World War II Japanese American relocation camp, established near Granada
1968	Funding approved for Dolores Project, an archaeological excavation to salvage artifacts prior to building of McPhee Dam

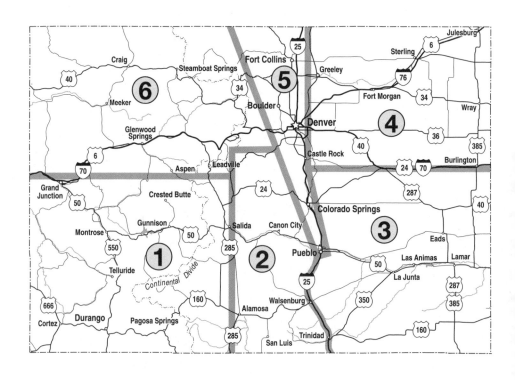

Introduction
TOP OF THE ROCKIES

The news reached Hahns Peak in early August of 1876: "Colorado Admitted to the Union of States." The dozen or so prospectors, freighters, and miners in the only saloon in camp raised their glasses and gave three cheers for the new state. The saloon owner, Charley Miller, declared, "All hands have a drink on the house to the success of the newborn state." The miners drank Miller's offering, then bought rounds of drinks for each other. Soon, according to one man present, "[The] celebration of the new state of Colorado was in full blast with card games, drinks, and much hilarity, continuing until late morning hours."

The residents of this remote mountain camp were celebrating an event that had been years in the making. In September 1859, Jefferson Territory was formed from the western half of Kansas Territory, although it was not acknowledged by the U.S. Congress. Finally, in February 1861, Congress authorized the new territory, redubbed Colorado. The first statehood bill was drafted in 1863, but it was not until 1874 that Congress proposed a provisional bill. Then, it took another two years to draft a constitution and have it approved by the people. President Ulysses S. Grant issued the proclamation authorizing statehood for Colorado on August 1, 1876.

Colorado was admitted to the Union as the United States celebrated its 100th birthday, giving it the nickname the "Centennial State." Katharine Lee Bates eloquently described the stunning landscapes of Colorado in the words to "America the Beautiful," a song inspired by a trip she made to Pikes Peak in 1893: "O beautiful for spacious skies, for amber waves of grain, for purple mountain majesties above the fruited plain."

Early Colorado

Colorado's human story goes back tens of thousands of years to the Clovis, Folsom, and Fremont people who roamed the land, leaving behind spear points and other artifacts. Paleo-Indians hunted mammoths in the San Luis Valley and camped along the Front Range, where scientists discovered the very first Folsom-era artifacts at the Lindenmeier archaeological site.

1

*This four-story build-
ing in Mesa Verde
National Park is one
of many elaborate
sandstone struc-
tures the Ancestral
Puebloans built in the
canyons of southwest-
ern Colorado.*

The Ancestral Pueblo, or Anasazi, people came to the region about
1000 BC. They constructed elaborate, multilevel homes in villages
throughout the Southwest, such as those at Mesa Verde National Park,
in the southwestern corner of Colorado. The Ancestral Puebloans abandoned their structures at Mesa Verde about AD 1270, likely because of
severe climate changes. The Fremont cultural period followed, eventually giving way to the historic tribes, including the Utes, who considered
most of western Colorado their homeland. The Apaches, Comanches,
Cheyennes, and Arapahos also lived in Colorado, and the Kiowas, Sho-
shones, and Sioux spent time here as well.

In 1595, Spanish explorer Juan de Oñate crossed into what is now
Colorado searching for gold. Other Spanish explorers saw portions of
Colorado, too, including Juan María Rivera in 1765 and Juan Bautista
de Anza in 1779. Eleven years later, two Franciscan friars, Francisco
Atanasio Domínguez and Silvestre Vélez de Escalante, crossed south-
ern and western Colorado while forging a trade route from Santa Fe to
Monterey, California. The route they established became known as the
Old Spanish Trail.

American explorations began in 1806, when Zebulon Pike came to Colorado on a mission to follow the Arkansas River to its source. On that expedition he spied the great peak that now bears his name. He also built two structures, a temporary camp near Pueblo and a stockade in the San Luis Valley, which are the first known American constructions in the state.

By 1819, a portion of Colorado north of the Arkansas River and east of the Continental Divide was under control of the United States, opening the region to further American exploration. Maj. Stephen Long led an American expedition through the Platte River Valley and crossed into Colorado, where a few members of his party made the first known ascent of Pikes Peak. In 1821 the American William Becknell took the first freight over the Santa Fe Trail, which linked the trading centers of eastern Kansas with Santa Fe. This trail became the primary commercial route into the West and served a steady stream of traffic for twenty years before the Oregon Trail eclipsed it.

A major stopping point and gathering area for trappers, traders, Indians, and travelers on the Santa Fe Trail was Bent's Fort in southeastern Colorado. Fur traders Charles and William Bent and Ceran St. Vrain built the trading post in 1833, and most of the legendary figures of the era spent time there, including Kit Carson, "Old Bill" Williams, Thomas "Broken Hand" Fitzpatrick, "Uncle Dick" Wootton, and James Beckwourth.

Among the first to settle in the southern part of present-day Colorado were people from New Mexico who had received land grants from the Mexican government after 1843. Around the same time, during the Mexican-American War, Stephen Watts Kearny and his Army of the West marched through southeastern Colorado en route to New Mexico in 1846.

The northern half of the state was hardly explored until 1858, when William Green Russell and his brothers Oliver and Levi, along with a party of Cherokee miners, found placer gold deposits near the confluence of Cherry Creek and the South Platte River. Communities quickly sprang up along Cherry Creek. Among them were St. Charles, Auraria, and Denver City, which later combined into Denver. Horace Greeley, editor of the *New York Tribune*, helped spread the word, inciting the Pikes Peak gold rush.

Later, discovery of silver deposits at such places as Gregory Gulch, Black Hawk, Cripple Creek, and Leadville added silver mania to the gold fever. Before long, pressure mounted for the government to survey public land in the region and make it available for purchase, which in many cases meant revoking Indian land titles. Settlers also petitioned Washington for territorial status for Colorado, which it received on February 26, 1861. Once Colorado Territory was established, both mining

An old prospector panning for gold (date unknown) —Courtesy Wyoming State Archives

and settlement increased rapidly. But of the estimated 100,000 people who streamed into the area during the Pikes Peak gold rush, about 90 percent of them turned around and went home, giving them the nickname "go-backs."

Colorado in the Civil War

Colorado Territory was born during the most tense time in the nation's history—the beginning of the Civil War. The riches buried in the western mountains were resources for the Union to defend, raising the stakes. Most of the newcomers to the territory were Union sympathizers, but there were Confederate supporters as well.

Colorado troops played an important role in the Civil War. The Union recruited infantry and cavalry volunteers throughout the region. These troops provided support and leadership during the New Mexico campaign, particularly at the Battle of Glorieta Pass, which became known as the "Gettysburg of the West." In this fight, federal soldiers under the command of Maj. John Chivington rebuffed Confederates who were making their way toward Fort Union. If the rebels controlled the fort, they would secure an open route to Colorado and the potential riches there. A key component in the Union's success at Glorieta Pass was the capture of Confederate supplies at Pigeon's Ranch by Chivington's Colorado troops.

In 1863, the Civil War was still raging when the first Indian depredations started along the Overland Trail in northeastern Colorado. Most of the Civil War–era engagements fought on Colorado soil involved conflicts with Indians. Throughout 1863 and the summer of 1864, soldiers fought isolated skirmishes with raiding Indians around the South Platte and Arkansas Rivers. Then, on November 29, 1864, Colonel Chivington's Colorado troops attacked an Arapaho and Cheyenne village on Sand Creek, brutally slaying hundreds of Indian men, women, and children. It was the match that set off a powder keg of Indian retaliation. The first raid occurred in January of 1865, launching what became known as the "Bloody Year on the Plains." The hostilities swept from Colorado through Wyoming, Nebraska, and Montana and continued for many more years.

Expanding Settlement

Even during the trying years of the Civil War and the Plains Indian Wars, prospectors and miners continued exploring Colorado's mountains. The mining and processing of gold and silver spawned communities all across the region. Soon, new Indian treaties negotiated in the 1860s forced the Cheyennes and Arapahos out of Colorado. With fears about Indians abated, homesteaders started arriving in the territory in the 1870s. Ethnic Germans from Russia and Japanese immigrants claimed land along the South Platte from Sedgwick to Greeley and began farming. As railroads were built, homesteaders spread across the eastern plains as well.

An economic depression in the 1890s caused gold and silver prices to plummet, leaving many miners out of work. Some moved into urban areas, such as Denver, to seek employment. For those who remained in the mining industry, the late 1890s and early 1900s brought numerous labor disputes, many of which turned violent.

In the twentieth century, new technologies brought more change to Colorado. In the 1920s a massive rail tunnel through the Continental Divide—the Moffat Tunnel—provided the first transportation link between the Front Range and the Western Slope. Before long, a new industry started to develop in Colorado based on the state's natural attributes of mountains and snow: skiing.

Skiers had been swooshing down the mountains near Steamboat Springs since before World War I, but the first ski areas in Colorado opened in the 1940s. During the 1960s and 1970s, resorts opened on seemingly every steep-sloped mountainside in the western half of the state. Aspen, Vail, Winter Park, Breckenridge, Telluride, Steamboat

Men, women, and children harvesting crops in a potato field near Ovid (date unknown) —Courtesy Fort Sedgwick Historical Archives, Julesburg

Springs, Copper Mountain, and Beaver Creek attracted an international clientele. Eventually winter tourism spilled over into other seasons, as hiking and mountain biking became major draws.

Besides attracting tourists, Colorado has also drawn new residents. During the 1980s and 1990s, the population exploded with newcomers seeking a mountain lifestyle. The Front Range communities of Fort Collins, Greeley, Boulder, Denver, and Colorado Springs saw the greatest impact, but the surrounding communities expanded as well. The state had to build new roads capable of handling four or five lanes of traffic and provide essential services such as water and sewer.

As developers bought up ranches along the Front Range and turned them into subdivisions, golf courses, and condominium complexes, conservation groups such as the Open Space Alliance and the Nature Conservancy worked to counter unruly development. These groups bought up land or arranged conservation easements to preserve open space and wildlife habitat and to maintain working ranches.

Colorado's urban sprawl was never more evident than during the summer of 2002, when massive wildfires broke out. After a three-year drought that climatologists said was the worst in 100 years, hundreds of thousands of acres burned, including many homes built in forested areas. People have begun to see that reductions in timber harvesting can sometimes cause fuels to build up and lead to devastating, widespread fires.

Journey through Changing Times and Landscapes

Since Colorado is the nation's highest state, you might say everything is downhill once you leave there. While Colorado is the "Top of the Rockies," it's made up of diverse landscapes ranging from fourteen-thousand-foot peaks, to the spectacular Royal Gorge of the Arkansas River, to the mesas and buttes of the Western Slope, to the rolling plains of the east. We'll begin our exploration of Colorado in the Four Corners country, where Paleo-Indian civilizations established impressive communities. From there we'll travel east to the fertile San Luis Valley, where the first Mexican settlers forged homes and towns, then make our way to the southeastern plains, over which Americans once traveled on the Santa Fe Trail. Next, we'll move to the northeastern corner of the state; though it was one of the last areas to be settled, major travel routes passed through this region during the gold rush. The fifth part of this book explores the Front Range, where most of the state's biggest urban areas are concentrated. Finally, venturing west over the mountains, we'll visit the parks and valleys of northwestern Colorado. I hope you enjoy the journey.

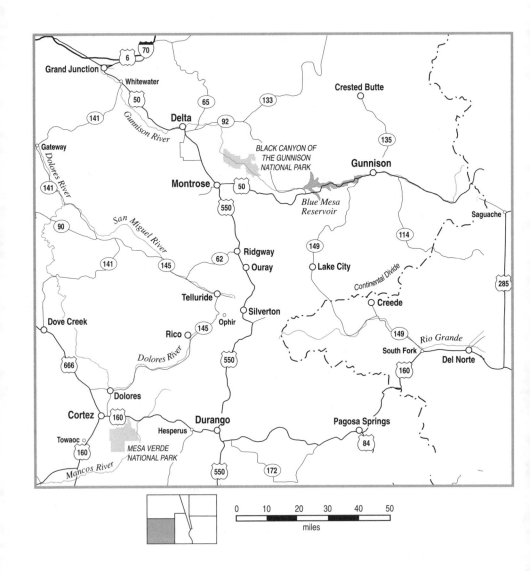

PART ONE

Southwest
FOUR CORNERS COUNTRY

When you look at a map of the United States and see the only point where four states adjoin—Colorado, New Mexico, Utah, and Arizona—it is easy to get the impression that the Four Corners area is a smooth, flat place where straight lines naturally converge. But that is not the case at all. Although the round stone marker at Four Corners is on a relatively flat site, the country surrounding it is rough, broken by hills and dominated in southwestern Colorado by Sleeping Ute Mountain. Traditionally the land of the Utes, and even earlier the homeland of the people usually referred to as the Anasazi or Ancestral Puebloans, the region is characterized by mountains to the east and high desert to the west and south.

In this book, the region designated Four Corners Country includes both the area around the Four Corners Monument—where visitors can touch four states at once, have a piece of Indian fry bread, and buy goods from Navajo traders—and the southwestern part of Colorado. For our purposes, the borders are New Mexico on the south, Utah on the west, Grand Mesa and Gunnison National Forests on the north, and the Continental Divide (but incorporating Mineral County) on the east. The region includes much of the mountainous area known as the Western Slope, comprising the San Juan Mountains, the Uncompahgre (un-CUM-pa-gray) Plateau, Grand Mesa, Battlement Mesa, and the Sawatch Range, plus other lesser-known ranges such as the San Miguel Mountains.

Domínguez-Escalante Expedition

This part of Colorado is the area explored by the Domínguez-Escalante expedition. In 1776, as the American colonies announced their independence from England, Spanish priests Francisco Domínguez and Silvestre Vélez de Escalante traveled across what would become western Colorado, providing the first written record of this area. Escalante kept a journal of the trip, which has been translated and published in several versions. Some scholars believe the work was in fact a collaborative effort of both priests.

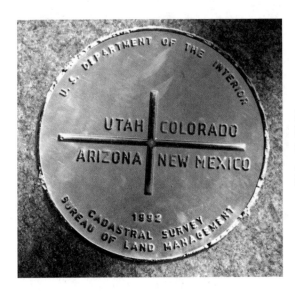

Marker at Four Corners, where Colorado, Utah, Arizona, and New Mexico meet

The padres embarked on their journey hoping to develop a supply route between the Spanish settlements at Santa Fe and Taos and Spanish missions in California. Some of their route later became part of the Old Spanish Trail, over which pack trains hauled woolens such as serapes, rugs, blankets, yard goods, and leggings from the Upper Rio Grande settlements to Mexican pueblos and missions in southern California, particularly those around Monterey.

Their route passed southwest of Durango and continued west, roughly along the route of US 160. Near today's Mancos, they turned northwest and made their way to El Río de los Dolores (Our Lady of Sorrows River), the present Dolores River. Camped near the river on August 13, 1776, Escalante noted, "Upon an elevation on the river's south side, there was in ancient time a small settlement of the same type as those of the Indians of New Mexico, as the ruins which we purposely inspected show." This "settlement" was likely the ruins now called the Escalante and Domínguez Pueblos, near Dolores (see Domínguez and Escalante Ruins, later in this section).

Past the ruins, the Domínguez-Escalante expedition traveled primarily north along the Dolores River. On the benchland above the river canyon, the party had trouble finding water. The first source they found was a small spring that was adequate for the men but did not have enough water for the livestock. From a point near today's Egnar, the party turned east, striking the Dolores River. They called one canyon El Laberinto de Miera (Miera's Labyrinth) for the expedition's cartographer, Bernardo

Miera y Pacheco, noting its "pleasing scenery of rock cliffs which it has on either side and which, for being so lofty and craggy at the turns, makes the exit seem all the more difficult the farther one advances."

Along the way, the expedition hired a Ute Indian guide, paying him "two big all-purpose knives and sixteen strings of white glass beads." On August 26 they descended to the valley of the river the Utes called Ancapagari, or Red Lake, today's Uncompahgre River. The explorers followed the Uncompahgre north, roughly along the route of US 50 and US 550, to the north fork of the Gunnison River, which they followed northwest. They then continued north, basically along the route of CO 139, and crossed what is now the state line south of the present town of Dinosaur.

Ute Indians

The only Indian reservations in Colorado, the Ute Mountain and Southern Ute Reservations, are both in the southwestern part of the state. Most of the native tribes who had territory in what is now Colorado, including many Utes, were moved to reservations in other western states.

The Utes were among several tribes once living or roaming in Colorado. At one time or another, they ranged across most of the state and into Utah, New Mexico, and Wyoming. Collectively known as the Yutas, the Utahs, or the Blue Sky People, by the late 1700s the Utes had divided into seven distinct bands. The Uintah Utes lived primarily in Utah's Uintah Basin. The Yampa Utes occupied lands in the Yampa River valley of northwestern Colorado, and the Grand Utes made their homes along the Colorado River (once known as the Grand River). Those three bands, the Uintah, Yampa, and Grand Utes, were called the Northern Utes.

Three other bands—the Mouache, Weeminuche, and Capote Utes—were referred to as the Southern Utes. The Capote Utes lived in Colorado's San Luis Valley and in north-central New Mexico. The Mouache Utes also claimed the San Luis Valley and the eastern plains of Colorado as their territory, although they occasionally camped as far south as Santa Fe. The Weeminuche Utes dominated southeastern Utah and also ranged along the San Juan, Animas, Mancos, and La Plata River valleys in southwestern Colorado. The seventh band, the Tabeguache Utes, lived and roamed in the Uncompahgre Valley area. They were sometimes called the Uncompahgre Utes.

The Utes raided lands surrounding their territories, skirmishing at times with other tribes, but for the most part they had few conflicts with outsiders until 1854. That year, the eastern bands took part in a raid on a new settlement at Pueblo (see Pueblo in part 2). In 1862 representatives of several Ute bands went to Denver with Indian agent Lafayette

Head to meet with territorial governor John Evans. They assured Evans they would live in harmony with the newly arriving settlers as long as they could retain their own lands in Colorado and Utah. The following spring, a Ute contingent met with President Abraham Lincoln in Washington, D.C., to discuss a treaty. At that meeting, the Tabeguache leader Ouray emerged as one of the principal Ute chiefs.

In October 1863, near Conejos, Territorial Governor Evans made an offer to representatives from the Weeminuche, Capote, and Tabeguache bands. The Mouaches refused to attend the treaty council. Chief Ouray agreed to the terms of the treaty for the Tabeguache band. The Tabeguaches were promised a reservation of 5,785 million acres on the Western Slope, $20,000 in trade goods, and annual provisions for ten years, as well as farm implements and breeding stock for their horse, cattle, and sheep herds. In return, they had to allow mining and the construction of railroads and military posts on their land.

Ouray, a prominent leader among the Tabeguache Utes
—Courtesty National Archives (111-SC-82602, Indians 112)

At the treaty conference, the Capote and Weeminuche Utes were persuaded to accept an agency in southwestern Colorado, and Ouray was asked to urge the Mouaches to join with his band. The U.S. Senate ratified the Treaty of 1863 the next year, though with reduced annual annuities. In spite of the agreement about the new reservation, the Tabeguaches remained near Conejos for another five years, and Lafayette Head served as Indian agent.

In 1868 another new treaty led to establishment of a reservation encompassing nearly one-third of Colorado Territory, with agencies on the White River near present Meeker and on Los Pinos Creek on the west side of Cochetopa Pass. The Indian Agency at Conejos was to be closed. But before the ink was dry on the Treaty of 1868, Colorado territorial leaders began protesting its terms. Territorial governor Edward McCook summed up the sentiments of most when he said, "[I cannot] comprehend the reasons which induced Colorado officials and the general Government to enter into a treaty setting apart one third of the whole area of Colorado for the exclusive use and occupation of the Ute nation. . . . I do not believe in donating to these indolent savages the best portion of my Territory."

The Treaty of 1868 remained in effect for only five years. As mining activity increased in the San Juan Mountains, so did the whites' desire for the Indians to be removed to smaller reservations. Thus the Brunot Treaty of 1873 was adopted, opening additional Indian lands to mining and settlement. The Brunot Treaty further concentrated the Utes in western Colorado by closing the Los Pinos Agency near Saguache and opening a new agency, known as Los Pinos II or the Uncompahgre Agency, near today's Montrose. On October 4, 1873, *Frank Leslie's Illustrated Weekly* reported, "The Utes, of Colorado, have agreed to give up the San Juan mining region, about which there has long been contention between miners and Indians."

The Uncompahgre Valley remained part of the Ute Reservation until 1881, when the residents were relocated to a reservation in Utah. This removal came in response to the 1879 Ute uprising at the White River Agency that became known as the Meeker Massacre (see Meeker in part 6). The Southern Ute bands remained on their reservation in far southwestern Colorado.

Roads of Southwestern Colorado

The primary north-south highway on the east side of this region is US 550, although we will also explore a few roads farther to the east. US 160 takes us through much of the southern part of the region, and various state highways meander through the rest. The trips in this section go from south to north and from west to east.

The area through which most of these roads pass is known as the Western Slope of the Rocky Mountains. The Western Slope has more highway mountain passes than anywhere else in the nation—Lizard Head, Red Mountain, North, Cochetopa, Monarch, and others—many exceeding 10,000 feet. Back-road passes also abound, many with colorful names like Slumgullion and Cinnamon. Along the roads you can get a good view of many of Colorado's Fourteeners—peaks that are at least 14,000 feet high. These mountains give Colorado the distinction of being the highest-elevation state in the nation, thus its nickname "Top of the Rockies."

US 666
New Mexico Border—Dove Creek
61 MILES

TOWAOC

Towaoc is the headquarters for the Ute Mountain Ute tribe, whose members have lived at the foot of Sleeping Ute Mountain for centuries, raising stock and crops. The government formed Ute Mountain Indian Reservation in 1895 for the Weeminuche band of Utes. Today tribal members engage in economic enterprises ranging from providing tours of the region to operating the tribe's casino to making pottery, which is distinctively decorated with the traditional black-on-white designs.

Southeast of Towaoc is the Ute Mountain Ute Mancos Canyon Historic District and the 125,000-acre Ute Mountain Tribal Park, a private park containing thousands of cliff dwellings and pueblo ruins. Though not as well known as nearby Mesa Verde National Park, the Ute Mountain park has some of the best-preserved remains of Ancestral Puebloan culture in this region.

CORTEZ

American Indians have lived in the Cortez area for centuries. The great sage plain was a good area for growing crops and hunting. The earliest dwellings were pit houses, built around AD 1300. There are literally tens of thousands of archaeological sites scattered across the sage plain and in the canyons of this region of Colorado, some of them among the best known in the country: Mesa Verde, Canyons of the Ancients, and Hovenweep, which extends into Utah. Ongoing projects continue to

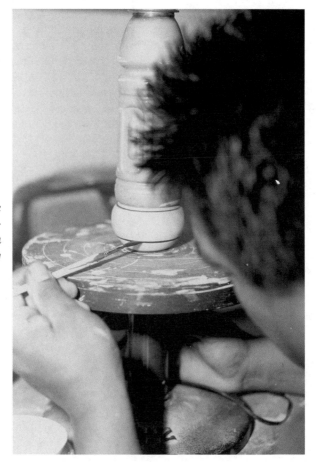

A member of the Southern Ute nation working on a piece of pottery

uncover and explore evidence of early habitation in the area, and Cortez has become a magnet for those interested in archaeological sites.

The largest Colorado community in the Four Corners region, Cortez developed as a trading center for sheep and cattle ranchers. The town was founded in 1886, when settlers first moved into Montezuma Valley. The American Indian presence remains strong due to the nearby Ute Mountain Indian Reservation.

CANYONS OF THE ANCIENTS NATIONAL MONUMENT

On June 9, 2000, President Bill Clinton signed the proclamation that created Canyons of the Ancients National Monument, west of Cortez. The 164,000-acre monument contains the highest known density of archaeological features anywhere in the United States, with at least 20,000 recognized sites. Among them are villages, field houses, check dams, reservoirs, great kivas, cliff dwellings, shrines, sacred springs, agricultural fields, petroglyphs, and sweat lodges. Occupation of the area began more than 10,000 years ago, and the first farmers were active between AD 450 and 1300. They established year-round villages that progressed from simple collections of small pit houses to elaborate, multistory cliff pueblos.

DOVE CREEK

From the time of the earliest native habitation to the present, the region around Dove Creek has been agricultural. One local crop is Anasazi beans, a type of pinto bean that became familiar to American soldiers during World War II as part of the GI ration kit. Dove Creek pinto beans became more than just a staple food for GIs; local marketers also developed such products as pinto bean ice cream and pinto bean cookies. By the 1990s, regional farmers were growing and marketing "heirloom" beans germinated from seeds reportedly recovered at various archaeological sites and dating back more than a thousand years to the original farmers.

Zane Grey lived in Dove Creek when he wrote the classic western novel *Riders of the Purple Sage*. In an article for *Roundup Magazine*, Stephen May described the challenges Grey faced in publishing this popular book:

> *Originally sketched out in a remote cabin in Southwestern Colorado, Riders had a difficult birth. Harper's editors felt the treatment of Mormons too severe, so they recommended major changes. Grey took the manuscript to his buddy Eltinge Warner, editor of* Field and Stream, *who liked it enough to serialize the novel in the magazine beginning January 1912. Only after its serial run in* Field and Stream *did Harper's feel confident enough to publish it in book form. When they did, it became one of the blockbuster novels of the year.*

Grey followed *Riders* with *Desert Gold, The Rainbow Trail, The Lone Star Ranger, The Border Legion, Wildfire, The Desert of Wheat, The U.P. Trail*, and others. Not only did his books make it to best-seller lists, many of them were made into movies for the silent screen. As May put it, "By 1920 he was arguably the most popular writer in America, and perhaps the world. His name had become synonymous with the Western novel." Many of Grey's novels are still in print, including some editions restoring original material that had once been edited out.

CO 141
Dove Creek—US 50 at Whitewater
156 MILES

Driving CO 141 from Dove Creek to Naturita, in Montrose County, can reveal a glimpse of Colorado's past because it goes through largely undeveloped grazing lands. The northern part of CO 141 is known as the Unaweep-Tabeguache Scenic Byway. Near Naturita you can see the remains of a thirteen-mile-long canal and flume that delivered water from the San Miguel River to the Montrose Placer Mining Company's Lone Tree Mine. Constructed in 1889–90, the flume was four feet deep and about five feet wide, capable of carrying some 23,640 gallons of water a day. About five miles of the flume hung above the canyons of both the Dolores and San Miguel Rivers. Now considered an engineering marvel, the hanging flume was abandoned when the mining company ceased operations after only three years.

Throughout Montrose County are sites important in American Indian cultural history. The Shavano Valley Rock Art Site near Montrose has numerous rock art panels, dating from 1000 BC through approximately

Remnants of the hanging water flume that was built above the San Miguel River during the mining era

Adobe ruins along CO 141, the Unaweep-Tabeguache Scenic Byway

1881. Sites near Nucla include Cottonwood Cave, a large rock shelter occupied as early as 270 BC; Tabeguache Cave, which also served as a rock shelter; and Tabeguache Pueblo, the remains of a single dwelling built about AD 1100.

Dolores Cave, near Uravan, was occupied for around 2,000 years, from 600 BC to AD 1400. Archaeologists found a corncob at the site that they were able to date at AD 1500, which shows that corn was grown even after the decline of the Ancestral Pueblo culture, around AD 1300. A second cave in the Uravan area, known as Tabeguache Cave II, was occupied during the same general period as Dolores Cave. Here archaeologists found brownware ceramics, showing another aspect of the Puebloans' cultural evolution.

GATEWAY

For years, people had noticed a canary yellow powder in the canyons near Gateway, and eventually someone realized it was carnotite, a mineral containing radium, vanadium, and uranium. The first mining operations started in 1914 with production of radium. During World Wars I and II, mining operations also included production of vanadium, which is used to harden steel. Uranium mining began in 1947 to supply nuclear weapons and nuclear energy. The Atomic Energy Commission compound in Grand Junction produced uranium from resources throughout the Colorado Plateau. Vanadium production in Gateway continued until the 1970s, by which time uranium mining had superseded it. But a downturn in the price of uranium during the late twentieth century caused those operations to fail as well, and by 1990 mining near Gateway had ceased altogether.

CO 145 and CO 62
Cortez—Ridgway
107 MILES

CO 145 follows the Dolores River from Dolores to a few miles north of Rico. Northwest of Telluride, the highway follows the winding San Miguel River. This trip turns onto CO 62 at Placerville and heads northeast across the Dallas Divide to Ridgway, passing through some of the Western Slope's most beautiful ranch country.

Cattle grazing on lush pastureland along CO 62 between Telluride and Ridgway

At the Anasazi Heritage Center, visitors may view the crumbling walls of the pueblo that the 1776 Domínguez-Escalante party probably found. In the background is Sleeping Ute Mountain.

DOMÍNGUEZ AND ESCALANTE RUINS

The ancient settlement Silvestre Vélez de Escalante observed in 1776 may have been the ruins now known as the Domínguez and Escalante Pueblos, preserved by the Anasazi Heritage Center near Dolores. The center and the ruins are just north of CO 145 on CO 184, on the west side of the McPhee Reservoir.

Escalante Pueblo was built around AD 1120 atop a hill that provides a commanding view of the great sage plain, Sleeping Ute Mountain, and the Dolores River drainage. Down the hillside, but still with a view of Sleeping Ute Mountain, is the smaller Domínguez Pueblo, the remains of what once was a small, semicircular collection of dwellings with garden plots. Between the two sites stands the Anasazi Heritage Center, which houses artifacts salvaged from nearby archaeological sites before they were destroyed by the construction of the McPhee Reservoir.

MCPHEE RESERVOIR

Prior to construction of the McPhee Reservoir, the second-largest reservoir in Colorado, the Dolores Project was undertaken to assess and preserve American Indian cultural resources. It was the largest contract archaeology project in the United States at the time. Because the building of the dam and subsequent flooding of the Dolores River canyon would affect thousands of cultural sites, 1 percent of the construction budget was set aside for mitigation, as part of the Reservoir Salvage Act, in 1968. The money funded the Dolores Project, undertaken jointly by the University of Colorado and Washington State University.

More than 400 archaeologists recorded 1,600 sites and excavated 125 of them. Their work uncovered 1.5 million objects, all of which are now housed at the Anasazi Heritage Center and displayed in rotating exhibits. In 1978 the local water board obtained additional federal funds to build the center, which serves as a repository for the artifacts, keeping them in the region where they originated. The McPhee Dam was completed in 1985.

DOLORES

You know you are in Dolores when you see the Galloping Goose Engine No. 5, a gasoline-powered narrow-gauge railroad vehicle that was first used in 1933 on the Rio Grande & Southern Railroad. The Goose, which operated between Dolores and Telluride, saved the railroad money because it was more fuel efficient than steam-powered locomotives. The gasoline engine was under the hood of a 1928 Pace Arrow touring car converted to run on rails. In 1946 the Goose added a passenger section fashioned from a school bus, and a large rear section with a wood frame covered with galvanized tin served as a luggage compartment. The Galloping Goose allowed the railroad to continue operating in the San Juan Mountains until 1952; without it the line would have shut down much earlier.

Two towns near Dolores, Big Bend and McPhee, no longer exist. In 1870 around a hundred people lived in Big Bend, named for its location at a bend of the Dolores River. The town had two general-merchandise stores, a saloon, a sawmill, a hotel, and a blacksmith shop. In 1891, when the Denver & Rio Grande Railroad bypassed Big Bend and built to nearby Dolores, Big Bend was doomed. Most Big Bend residents abandoned their town and moved to Dolores.

In 1924 the New Mexico Lumber Company established McPhee on the Dolores River about three miles downstream from the abandoned Big Bend. As headquarters for the highest-producing lumber mill in Colorado, McPhee soon became the largest town in Montezuma County. By 1927 it had around 1,400 residents, and some forty miles of narrow-gauge railroad lines provided access to area logging camps and to Dolores.

McPhee, a company town, had different types of housing for Mexican and white workers. The Hispanic employees lived in three-room houses without running water or electricity. Rented for two dollars per month, they were three-quarters of a mile from the mill site. Anglo housing, costing ten dollars per month, was closer to the mill. The white families had running water and electricity in each five-room house, but no indoor bathroom. The company provided all workers with firewood and with ice from an icehouse near the mill pond.

The Great Depression had a significant impact on the lumber industry around McPhee, and by 1930 the mill had closed. Though it reopened in 1935, fires swept through the town in 1941 and 1942, bringing further financial stress. Finally, a big fire at the mill in 1948, causing $100,000 in damage, sealed McPhee's fate. The post office closed that year, and the mill buildings were sold or dismantled.

RICO

Traveling CO 145 between Rico and Telluride takes you into the Pioneer Mining District, along the route of the Rio Grande & Southern Railroad, and over Lizard Head Pass (10,222 feet). It also provides a view of three of Colorado's Fourteeners—Wilson Peak (14,017 feet), El Diente Peak (14,159 feet), and Mount Wilson (14,246 feet)—where the highway skirts the mountainous lands designated as the Wilson Primitive Area in 1932 and renamed the Lizard Head Wilderness in 1980.

This ore cart represents the Rico area's mining days.

Congressional designation of the 41,309-acre area as a wilderness permanently protects it from development and motorized vehicle use.

By 1832 Antoine Robidoux and other fur trappers had pushed into the country around present Rico in search of beaver living in the cold mountain streams, but none of the trappers established a permanent residence. Prospectors came to the area looking for gold and silver in the 1860s. In places, Spanish prospectors had already found and processed some precious metals and taken them back to Santa Fe.

Around 1879, after the discovery of silver deposits, R. C. Darling started the Atlantic Cable Mine, and a 320-acre town site was platted. At the time, Ute Indians controlled the area, making access to the nearby Pioneer Mining District difficult. But by the 1880s, miners had displaced the Utes and freight began moving into the area over the Scotch Creek Toll Road.

In 1891 the Rio Grande Southern Railroad arrived in Rico, on a route that connected Durango with Ridgway, and by the following year the town had nearly 5,000 residents. Supported by the railroad and mining, Rico had two newspapers, a boardinghouse, a bank, a theater, a mercantile, and a county courthouse, plus twenty-three saloons and a three-block red-light district, with two churches to counter their effects. The crash of silver prices and the downturn in the national economy in

Rico's brick courthouse still stands regally in its imposing mountain surroundings.

1893 led to the end of Rico's boom, but the town survived as a smaller, less boisterous version of itself in its heyday.

OPHIR

The mining industry gave rise to Ophir, now a ghost town. In 1945 Lucien L. Nunn, the manager of the Gold King Mill, sought a way to reduce the cost of power for the ore-processing mill, which had been running on coal. Nunn switched to AC electricity and had workers string copper wire one and a half miles from the mill to the Ames hydroelectric power plant (built in 1891 on the Lake Fork of the San Miguel River). The conversion to AC power saved some $2,000 per month and marked one of the first commercial uses of electricity in the United States.

TELLURIDE

Hollywood stars like Tom Cruise, who has a multimillion-dollar home in the area, come to Telluride for the skiing. Tucked into a tiny valley, this small town boasts a spectacular setting. As of 2005, Telluride had about 1,600 permanent residents, plus people with seasonal homes. That is less than half the population of Telluride's mining days.

John Fallon made the area's first mineral claim in 1875, when he registered the Sheridan Mine with the county clerk's office in Silverton. The claim was rich with deposits of gold, silver, copper, iron, lead, and zinc. Within five years a mining camp known as Columbia had formed. The town might have remained Columbia, but there was already a Columbia, California, in the postal system, so the Colorado town became Telluride. How it got that name remains uncertain. Although it is likely a derivation of tellurium, a nonmetallic element often found near gold deposits, some claim it came from a salutation given to San Juan Railroad passengers: "To hell you ride!"

By 1890 Telluride had some 5,000 residents, mostly miners from places including Sweden, Ireland, England, Italy, Finland, Germany, China, and France. They dug more than 350 miles of underground tunnels in their quest for minerals. Telluride became quite a wealthy community, attracting the attention of Robert LeRoy Parker and some of his friends, who in 1889 robbed the Telluride Bank and launched their careers as outlaws. Parker is better known as Butch Cassidy, and the men who rode with him came to be called the Wild Bunch.

Telluride was the site of a bloody labor dispute in 1901, when striking miners took up arms against strikebreaking workers, resulting in three deaths and many injuries. This incident was one of several confrontations between Colorado mine owners and the Western Federation of Miners. (See also Ludlow and Trinidad in part 3.)

Following the national financial slump of 1893, silver mining declined as precipitously as the mountainsides surrounding Telluride, but the discovery of gold brought new prosperity in the early twentieth century. However, this comeback also faded, and by the 1960s the town was barely holding on. Then, in the 1970s, Billy Mahoney Sr. and other local residents realized that the mountains had a gold mine of a different sort—snow—just waiting for development. So began Telluride's ski industry. Soon summer activities attracted tourists and recreationists as well, and today Telluride is a year-round destination. It is also a town of festivals, the cornerstone being its internationally known film festival, but music festivals held throughout the season also bring in lovers of bluegrass, blues, chamber music, and jazz.

Not only does the region attract people who want a home in the Rockies, but it is also a popular backdrop for television commercials and print ads. Budweiser, Marlboro, and Jeep are among the companies that have filmed TV spots around Telluride, and print ads have been shot here for such companies as BFGoodrich, Arizona Jeans, Ford, and Chevrolet.

RIDGWAY

This small community was named for A. G. Ridgway, who along with General William Jackson Palmer helped build the Denver & Rio Grande Western Railroad. D. C. Hartwell founded the town on land he bought from ranchers in 1890. Along with other members of the Ridgway Townsite Company, Hartwell graded, seeded, and fenced some land for a community park. Two years later, residents planted a hundred trees in Hartwell Park to recognize Arbor Day, many of which are still standing. Owned and maintained by the town of Ridgway since 1898, the park was listed on the Colorado State Historic Register in 1991.

Ridgway was a supply center for miners who worked in the nearby San Juan Mountains, and later it became a hub for cattle ranches in the valley, some of which are still in operation. At one time, outlaws, including Butch Cassidy and the Wild Bunch, came through here via a route known as the "Horsethief Trail," used to move stolen horses and cattle between Colorado and Utah. The region's cowboy heritage was brought to life on the big screen when John Wayne filmed *True Grit* in this area in the late 1960s.

US 160
Cortez—Del Norte
163 MILES

Between Cortez and Durango, US 160 follows the Río de los Mancos (River of the Cripples). A mesa to the south rises some 2,000 feet and slopes back about fifteen miles toward New Mexico. Split with rugged canyons, the mesa has been a home for people for thousands of years. The first inhabitants established farms and towns, developed their culture and traditions, and advanced their technology. Remnants of those early settlements are preserved in Mesa Verde National Park.

MESA VERDE NATIONAL PARK

There are no written accounts of the early Coloradans now called Ancestral or Northern Puebloans but popularly known as the Anasazi (a Navajo word meaning "ancient ones" or "ancient foreigners"). There is, however, an impressive record of their culture preserved in remnants of their dwellings, pottery, and tools, which have been studied

Visitors are often amazed by the enormity of the Ancestral Puebloan dwellings in Mesa Verde National Park.

by archaeologists and anthropologists since the early 1900s. Visitors can still see many examples of their work in Mesa Verde National Park, where artifacts and some of the largest and best-known structures are carefully preserved.

It is certain that these early residents, who flourished between 700 and 1,200 years ago, had well-developed social and political structures and that they were heavily involved in both trade and agriculture. They shaped bones, stones, and wood into weapons for hunting and tools for digging and cutting. They made fine baskets from split willows, rabbitbrush, and skunkbrush; later they made pottery of clay and other malleable substances.

Because they worked cooperatively and used their materials and time effectively, the Ancestral Puebloans created more goods than they needed and traded with people from other areas. They bartered woven goods, pottery, baskets, sandals, and arrowheads in exchange for seashells from tribes living along the Pacific coast, and for cotton, turquoise, and pottery from people living farther south. Their trade routes were the first "roads" in America.

The earliest known residents of this area are known as the Basket Makers, so called for their skill at weaving baskets. These nomadic hunter-gatherers lived around AD 300 to 750. For hunting they used a spear-throwing device called an atlatl. They made their clothing from animal skins and fur and wove yucca into sandals. Around AD 450 to 750, they began making pottery and developed the bow and arrow. They also built crude structures known as pit houses, which were dug into the earth, with walls made of timber and roofs covered with an adobelike plaster of clay mixed with grasses or straw. The pit houses were often built on high mesas.

Between about AD 750 and 1100, the natives again improved their standard of living, building multistory houses, now called pueblos, on top of the mesas. The next 200 years saw even more advances. From 1100 to 1300, the Puebloans perfected their building methods, using carefully cut masonry blocks. During this period the people moved from the mesa to the canyons and built sturdy cliff dwellings. Archaeologists speculate that hostile tribes forced the Ancestral Puebloans' retreat to the canyons and the building of their fortresslike structures. The villages they established were complex—true wonders of early architecture.

According to the National Park Service, most of the cliff dwellings were built from the late 1190s to the late 1270s. Some were a single room, while others had more than 200 rooms stacked several stories high. Because they were tucked into natural openings in the cliff walls, the buildings had no standard layout. Most of the walls were single blocks of roughly cut stone held together with adobe mud. Often the interior walls were plastered with mud and decorated with designs painted directly on the wall; in some areas you can still see those designs.

Almost all of the major structures had ceremonial rooms, known as kivas. Generally round and dug into the ground, people entered through a hole in the top and descended a ladder to the kiva floor. Rock or dirt benches stood against the walls around a fire pit. Each kiva had a *sipapu*, symbolizing the entrance to the underworld through which the first of their people had ascended into this world.

The cliff houses were in use for only about a hundred years, or until around 1300, then they were abandoned. It is not entirely clear why the people left their canyon homes, but archaeological information shows that the region experienced a major drought, which may have forced them out. What became of the Ancestral Puebloans is also uncertain, although there is strong evidence suggesting that they simply evolved into today's Pueblo people in the Rio Grande Valley.

History of the Park

Lt. James Simpson of New Jersey was with an 1849–50 U.S. Corps of Topographical Engineers expedition when he first noted the cliff dwellings that are now encompassed by Mesa Verde National Park. In the early 1860s, a U.S. Geological Survey team surveyed a portion of the area, and the first scientific investigation of the ruins began in 1874 as part of an exploratory trip photographed by William Henry Jackson. But Jackson's group missed many of the larger dwellings. Cliff Palace, for example, was first reported by cowboys Charlie Mason and Richard and Al Wetherill, who spied it while looking for stray animals in 1888.

It didn't take long for "pot hunters" to descend upon the area and begin hauling away artifacts. Some were simply souvenir seekers, others scientists. In 1891 Swedish archaeologist Gustaf Nordenskiöld came to the area to study the ruins, leaving with hundreds of artifacts—many of them now housed in the National Museum in Helsinki, Finland. Local residents angered by the removal of artifacts formed the Colorado Cliff Dwellers Association and started lobbying for federal protection. In 1906 Congress established Mesa Verde National Park.

In the early days, Knife Edge Road provided the main access to the park. The narrow one-way road along a steep bluff attracted only the most intrepid adventurers. Today this road is part of the Knife Edge Trail, where you can explore the flora and fauna of the park on foot. The majority of visitors to Mesa Verde today visit the Far View area, which interprets the farming culture of the early Indians. Among the several excavated sites are Far View House, Pipe Shrine House, Far View Tower, Coyote Village, and Mummy Lake. Other popular spots include Cedar Tree Tower and Kiva, both along Chapin Mesa, and the spectacular ruins of Cliff Palace, Spruce Tree House, and Balcony House. The

Some members of the 1874 U.S. Geological Survey stopped for a photo at Mesa Verde, taken by the official photographer, William Henry Jackson.
—Courtesy National Archives (57-HS-359)

Mesa Top Loop passes ruins of pit houses and viewpoints for Sun Point Pueblo, Oak Tree House, and Sun Temple.

Fewer people visit Wetherill Mesa, not because the ruins are less interesting, but because its high elevation makes it inaccessible during much of the year. A 1958 archaeological survey of Wetherill Mesa documented around 900 sites, ranging from pit houses dated AD 450 to 750 to cliff houses dated from AD 1200 to 1300. The cliff dwellings likely housed around 1,000 to 2,000 people. Evidence of extensive farming operations includes complex irrigation systems with check dams and a series of reservoirs. The largest dwelling is Cliff Palace, which had 217 rooms and 23 kivas and sheltered about 250 residents. Long House, on Wetherill Mesa, is the second-largest cliff dwelling in the park, with 150 rooms, 21 kivas, and a large central plaza.

Wetherill Mesa produced most of the artifacts Nordenskiöld took back to Europe after the Benjamin Wetherill family hosted his visit. No major scientific study was conducted in the area until the 1958 survey, when the National Park Service undertook a partial excavation of the mesa in cooperation with the National Geographic Society. Additional studies were conducted in 2001.

HESPERUS

Just south of US 160 on CO 140, about eleven miles west of Durango, is Hesperus. The Domínguez-Escalante expedition passed through here in 1776, and in 1880 it became the site of the relocated Fort Lewis.

Camp Lewis was first established on October 15, 1878, near Pagosa Springs. It later became a fortified post (Fort Lewis) to provide protection for both the Southern Utes and the settlers and prospectors moving into the area. The fort was named for Lt. Col. William H. Lewis, Nineteenth U.S. Infantry, who died in a battle with Northern Cheyennes at Punished Woman's Fork in Kansas on September 28, 1878. In 1880 Lt. Gen. Phil Sheridan, who had gained fame in the Shenandoah Valley during the Civil War, ordered the fort moved to a new site some two miles south of Parrott City (near present Durango), on the banks of the La Plata River.

The new, more centrally located site would serve the Utes as well as the settlers, railroad construction workers, and miners to whom the territory was opened after the 1873 Brunot Treaty. The 6,318-acre Fort Lewis Military Reservation was approved by the U.S. War Department on August 30, 1880. Lt. Col. Robert Crofton, a decorated Civil War veteran, and four companies of the Thirteenth U.S. Infantry began the construction of their new headquarters. The Pagosa Springs site was abandoned in 1882.

While under construction, the post was known as Cantonment on La Plata, but it had been called Fort Lewis at Pagosa Springs, and the new site took that name permanently after it was completed. The new Fort Lewis near Hesperus operated until May 28, 1891, when the federal government closed it and returned the land to the Interior Department. In 1892 an Indian school was established at the former fort, and it operated until 1910. The property was then deeded to the state of Colorado in January 1911, and Governor John Shafroth established an agricultural high school there.

Beginning in 1924, the school offered teacher training in addition to agricultural studies, and a college was added in September 1927. Fort Lewis had both high school and college classes until 1933, when the high school curriculum was dropped. It became a junior college in 1948, and in 1956 the school moved from the old fort grounds in Hesperus to Durango. The old campus became an agricultural experiment station. The new Fort Lewis School began offering four-year college degrees in 1962, and its name was changed to Fort Lewis College the following year.

In the early 1970s, Fort Lewis College, located near the Southern Ute and Ute Mountain Indian Reservations, allowed Indian students to take classes for free. A 1971 law limited such waivers, but it was overturned in 1973, once again letting Indian students attend Fort Lewis College tuition free.

DURANGO

The first town in this area was Animas City, named for the Río de las Animas Perdidas (River of Lost Souls). It was established by farmers and ranchers who supplied hay, grain, produce, and meat to prospectors and miners pushing their way into the San Juan Mining District in the early 1870s. By 1876, when Animas City incorporated, it had several businesses, a school, and around thirty houses. During the winter the town became a refuge from the harsh climate of the mountain ranges to the north.

A few years later, when Denver & Rio Grande Railroad officials decided to build a line to link Denver with the San Juan Mining District, they figured that the logical place to install the headquarters would be Animas City. But Animas City leaders did not cooperate, so the railroad simply built a new town, Durango, just to the south. Charles M. Perin drove the first stake for the new community on September 13, 1880; by the following January, around a thousand people lived in Durango.

With a headquarters established, the Denver & Rio Grande began expansion plans to build north toward the rich San Juan mining country around Silverton. This forty-five-mile narrow-gauge rail line would cross rugged mountains and follow a treacherous river course. Beginning in August 1881, the D&RG graded and laid track for seventeen miles to Rockwood before it hit the difficult stretch known as the Highline. There, crews of mostly Irish and Scottish immigrants had to blast a shelf into hard granite. Some reports estimate that the cost of that portion of the road was $1,000 per foot.

In July 1882, the first train from Durango steamed into Silverton, forever changing both towns. Previously isolated Silverton residents now had ready access to Durango and beyond, and ore could be shipped out easily. Durango in turn prospered from its link to the mines. Silverton's smelter moved its operations to Durango, a loss for Silverton and a gain for Durango. The Durango & Silverton Narrow Gauge Railroad lasted not only through the San Juan mining boom of the late 1800s, but throughout the twentieth century, and it is still going strong today, transporting tourists instead of ore and freight.

Russian Jewish immigrant Otto Mears built additional rail lines in the San Juan mining area. His Rio Grande Southern connected Durango with the D&RG line at Ridgway via Dolores, Rico, Ophir, and Telluride. That line is known for the Galloping Goose, a hybrid engine that had the power to chug through steep canyons and passes. Mears

A Durango & Silverton Narrow Gauge Railroad train on the Highline, where the building crews had to blast a shelf out of the hard granite. The railroad continues to operate as a scenic passenger train.

also built many roads, including some that would become part of the famous Million Dollar Highway.

Coincident with construction of the rail line to Silverton, Durango built a smelter where ore from the region could be reduced to bullion for shipment. The town saw additional economic development with the discovery of coal deposits in the San Juans. Durango's future was assured when it supplanted Parrott City as county seat. By 1885 Durango had 2,254 residents, Animas City had only 83, and Parrott City was virtually a ghost town. A fire swept through Durango on July 1, 1889, destroying seven blocks of the town, including businesses and residences, but it was quickly rebuilt of brick and stone, rather than wood. Durango was here to stay.

More than a hundred years later, following one of the driest winters and springs on record, the largest forest fire in the recorded history of southwestern Colorado broke out June 9, 2002, near Missionary Ridge, north of Durango. In tinder-dry forest and range, the fire spread to 70,485 acres and destroyed numerous homes before firefighters finally controlled the blaze on August 7. The total cost of fighting the fire was $40.8 million.

PAGOSA SPRINGS

A dispute between the Navajos and the Utes over the cluster of hot mineral springs in the Pagosa area was settled when Albert Pfeiffer, Indian scout and aide to Kit Carson, fought a Navajo on behalf of the Utes, using a bowie knife. He won the contest and the springs became the undisputed holding of the Utes. The first known written description of the springs was recorded in 1859 by an expedition of the U.S. Corps of Topographical Engineers. Fort Lewis was originally built near Pagosa Springs in 1878, but in 1880 it was moved west to near Hesperus. That same year, the Pagosa Springs town site was platted.

For thousands of little boys (and a few little girls), the most important thing to come out of Pagosa Springs is the Daisy Red Ryder BB rifle. The Red Ryder BB gun was named after the cartoon creation of local cowboy artist Fred Harman. After spending time near Kansas City, where he worked with Walt Disney, Harman moved back to Pagosa Springs in 1933. Harman had developed a cartoon character called Bronc Peeler. He added a sidekick, an Indian boy called Little Beaver, and changed Bronc Peeler's name to Red Ryder. The comic strip *Red Ryder and Little Beaver* launched Harman's career as a cartoonist. After the Newspaper Enterprise Association began syndicating the strip in 1938, the cartoon appeared in 750 publications each week, and an estimated 40 million people read about the two boys' adventures. Soon there were spin-offs, including books, a national radio show, and thirty-eight movies.

Soon after his success, Harman approached the Daisy Air Rifle Company to manufacture a gun like the Colt single-action pistol Red Ryder carried, but the design didn't work out. Instead, Daisy created a BB rifle modeled after Red Ryder's Winchester lever-action carbine. The gun was a hit, and Daisy sold millions of them in the 1940s, 1950s, and beyond.

DEL NORTE

In 1872 Cary French and his newly created town company filed a plat for what would become Del Norte. The company promised free lots to anyone who would build in the town by May of that year. French had come to the region from Kansas with a group of prospectors, but his mining plans were derailed when he shot himself in the leg. After he recovered, he decided to start a new town. He chose the site of Del Norte anticipating that it would be a gateway to the escalating mining operations in the San Juan Mountains.

The post office at Loma de San José, which had been in operation since 1867, soon moved to Del Norte. A hardware store operated by future Colorado governor Alva Adams helped establish the community further, and when the U.S. Land Office opened in Del Norte in 1875, the town's future was secured.

Del Norte became the seat of Rio Grande County in 1874, but the town had higher aspirations and began lobbying to become the state capital. Throughout the debate over Colorado statehood, residents of the southern part of the territory, including Colorado Springs, wanted to create a separate state, the state of San Juan. Del Norte residents became vocal proponents of the idea and promoted their town as a good candidate for the capital city. A major booster of the campaign was attorney Thomas M. Bowen, an Iowan who had moved to Del Norte in 1875. Bowen had served a stint as governor of Idaho Territory before coming to Del Norte and was looking for a similar opportunity in his new home. But the proposal for a separate state withered, and Congress admitted Colorado as a state in 1876. It wasn't the end for Bowen, however. He became a state senator and was subsequently elected to the U.S. Senate in 1883.

In 1891 the toll road between Del Norte and Antelope Park, known as Antelope Park Road, was extended to Lake City. There was already a tollgate at Antelope Park, but when the road was expanded, an entrepreneur started charging an additional toll near Creede, irritating the local miners. Antelope Park Road remained the primary access road into the San Juans until 1916, when it was replaced by a new highway across Wolf Creek Pass, US 160, also known as the Wolf Creek Highway.

US 550
Durango—Montrose
103 MILES

One of the major north-south routes in southwestern Colorado is US 550, which links up with US 50 at Montrose; US 50 then continues north to I-70. From the New Mexico line, US 550 crosses the Southern Ute Reservation, then heads into the San Juans along part of the route of the Durango & Silverton Narrow Gauge Railroad before continuing north to Montrose. The section between Durango and Ouray is called the Million Dollar Highway, which is part of the San Juan Skyway, a National Scenic and Historic Byway.

The first portion of this scenic route north of Durango parallels the Animas River, with Missionary Ridge to the east and later the Hermosa Cliffs to the west. The highway crosses three major passes: Coal Bank Pass and Molas Pass, between Durango and Silverton, and Red

Mountain Pass, between Silverton and Ouray. Wilderness areas line the highway on both the east and west, where you can catch views of some of Colorado's Fourteeners. Mount Eolus (14,083 feet), Sunlight Peak (14,059 feet), and Windom Peak (14,082 feet), all part of the Needle Mountains, lie on the east. The closest major mountains are Twilight Peak (13,158 feet) and Snowdon Peak (13,077 feet), both in the West Needle Range. West of the highway, near Ouray, is Mount Sneffles (14,150 feet), which can be obscured by Mount Ridgway (13,468 feet).

Early travelers into this region went on foot or on horseback or mule-back over this route. Eventually, stage roads were developed, although the steep country made it a treacherous way to travel. As George Darley, a pioneer preacher in the region, described it, "Traveling in the San Juans, during the years of staging, was not considered a great pleasure by many. In addition to corduroy, holes, stones, stumps, steep grades, and 'muding,' many of the roads were 'sidling' and the curves very sharp, so that four horses were all that could be handled by a stage driver." Dave Day, editor of the *Solid Muldoon* newspaper in Ouray, noted in 1883 that the road was "dangerous even to pedestrians . . . the grade is four parts vertical and one part perpendicular."

Automobiles could not travel between Durango and Ouray until at least 1918. The road known as the Durango-Silverton-Ouray Highway, or the D.S.O. Highway, came about after the 1916 "Good Road Bill"

Sometimes Colorado's roads are difficult to negotiate, as this driver, circa 1925, found out. —Courtesy Fort Sedgwick Historical Archives

established the Colorado Highway Department in 1917. For years there-
after, work on this road through the mountains was almost constantly
under way. Referring to both the high cost of its construction and its
spectacular views, the thoroughfare was dubbed the Million Dollar
Highway.

Even today, the highway is somewhat treacherous in places, definitely
not a road for timid drivers during winter storms. Avalanches sometimes
cascade down the mountainsides, and there have been instances in
which cars and snowplows have literally been swept off the road. The
final descent around hairpin turns from Red Mountain Pass to Ouray is
thrilling even on dry roads, not only for the twists of the highway, but
also for the outstanding scenery, making it clear why Ouray has been
called "Little Switzerland."

Otto Mears, known for his railroad construction, also built several
freight roads in this area, and a portion of the Million Dollar Highway
was built over one of his original routes. Since its construction in the
1920s, the Million Dollar Highway has brought tourists into this former
mining area, revitalizing its sagging economy.

SILVERTON

The presence of precious minerals in the San Juan Mountains was known
as early as 1776, when Spanish priests Domínguez and Escalante made
their way through the southern part of the region. In their journal, the
priests noted that a Spanish explorer had found mineral-bearing rocks in
the San Juan region years before. The opinion at the time was that the
metal in the rocks was silver. A century later, American miners pushed
into the rugged San Juan region seeking gold and silver.

The San Juan Mountains were Ute territory, and the Indians strenu-
ously objected to mining encroachment, but the big gold and silver
strikes in other parts of Colorado fueled the miners' determination to
start digging in the San Juans. The U.S. government, always eager to help
industry, negotiated treaties to let the miners in and push the natives
out. The first small mining camps in the San Juans sprang up around
Bakers Park, northwest of Silverton. The Little Giant mine opened at
the head of Arrastra Gulch, the site of the area's first really promising
gold strike in 1870. By 1874 Howardsville had been established at the
mouth of Cunningham Gulch and Stony Pass. Then, a couple of miles
down the valley, Silverton got its start. Although Howardsville was
the first seat for newly created San Juan County, Silverton eventually
claimed that title after entrepreneurs established both a sawmill and a
smelter in the town.

Silverton's status was cemented when the Denver & Rio Grande
Railroad completed the line linking it with Durango in 1882. Although

the town lost its smelter to Durango, which had better access to coal and other supplies, Silverton prospered from the railroad's presence. It had a stable business district and an active community, complete with a baseball team. Like most mining towns, Silverton had its prosperous citizens who built schools and churches, as well as its rowdies who spent time in the town's brothels and nineteen saloons. Over the next few years, three more D&RG narrow-gauge lines came into town: the Silverton Railroad; the Silverton, Gladstone & Northerly Railroad; and the Silverton Northern Railroad. All were linked to Durango.

Railroads aside, Silverton's prosperity during the nineteenth century hinged on mineral production. The San Juan mines were a very tough place to make a living. Miners had to live and work in harsh weather and isolated locations at high elevations. The high cost of freighting—whether by burro, mule train, wagon, or railroad—drained profits. A

Silverton City Hall, built in 1908, is a reminder of the town's mining heyday.

slump in silver prices during the late 1890s brought a period of gloom, but the mines bounced back with steady production in the early twentieth century. The greatest output in the Silverton area occurred prior to America's entry into World War I. For eleven years in a row, production topped a million dollars, peaking in 1917.

Sadly, the prosperity of those years was soon overshadowed—the influenza epidemic that swept the world in 1918 took a devastating toll on Silverton. Around 150 people in the town, representing 10 percent of the population, died of the Spanish flu and its complications, such as pneumonia. The town did everything it could to halt the spread of the virulent disease. It established quarantines, banned public meetings, and closed schools. Nevertheless, people died, and many of them were interred in a mass grave. "Space and time will not permit us to give but very little notice of the many sad deaths that have occurred in this community since our last issue," the *Silverton Weekly Miner* reported on November 1, 1918. "There has scarcely been a household that has not been touched by sickness or death of a loved one or friend."

The mining industry slowed after World War I, but operations in the Silverton area continued, thanks in part to the tenacity of Charles Chase, who owned the nearby Mayflower Mill. From 1925 until 1953, Chase almost single-handedly kept mining alive in the area. Even during the Great Depression, Chase kept men on the job and actually added improvements to some of his operations. Later he benefited from Franklin D. Roosevelt's New Deal programs, which caused the price of gold to increase from twenty to thirty-five dollars per ounce.

Chase also tackled the issue of pollutants from mining operations being released into streams and rivers. Many residents in the region expressed concern over discharge from tailings ponds seeping into Animas Valley waterways. Into the early 1950s, Chase worked to clean up the streams, even though other mines also contributed to the problem.

By the early 1950s, time was running out for Silverton mining operations. In 1952 local mines produced $2.8 million in ore, but in 1954 they generated only $123,000. The population of Silverton dropped from 1,375 in 1950 to around 890 by 1957.

What saved the town from extinction was tourism. The Million Dollar Highway, US 550, linking Durango, Silverton, and Ouray with Montrose, attracted visitors to the area's spectacular mountain setting. One popular tourist activity is riding the Durango & Silverton Narrow Gauge Railroad, now operated as a scenic excursion train. The train serves hundreds of visitors each year, although there's not much business during the winter, when the train cannot reach Silverton from Durango. As one local merchant put it in *Silverton: A Quick History*, "All they have to do is put a tombstone at the end of town and say we bury this town until the first of May."

OURAY

Ouray was born as Uncompahgre City during the mineral explorations of the 1870s. D. W. Brunton surveyed the town site, which had been laid out in August 1875 by a group of prospectors and hunters, some of whom had already staked mining claims nearby. The first big strike was a lode of silver. The lively little mining camp that sprung up also served as a supply center for the Uncompahgre (or Tabeguache) Ute Indians, who had an agency to the north. On October 28, 1875, a post office was established under the name Ouray, after the Ute chief.

The mail contractor for the new town was railroad man and road builder Otto Mears, who seemed to have his hand in every possible venture in the San Juan area. Carrying the mail to such an isolated place was extremely difficult, especially in the winter, when there was potential for—indeed, a guarantee of—heavy snow. The first winter, Mears sometimes used a sled and dog teams to cover the route, and sometimes he used snowshoes, but for several weeks in the early spring, he didn't make it through at all.

Ouray was officially incorporated on October 2, 1876. Within a year the town was well on its way to permanence, with a school, two hotels, a sawmill, two blacksmith shops, an ore-sampling works, four general-merchandise stores, seven saloons, a few brothels and gambling dens, and some 214 cabins and tents for the 400 or so residents. As of September 5, 1879, it also had a newspaper, the *Solid Muldoon*. Its editor was a thirty-two-year-old Civil War veteran named David F. Day.

After his service in the Civil War, the illiterate Day had settled in Missouri, where he learned to read and write. He became a storekeeper, married, and had a family, then lost everything. He headed west to Ouray, where he began publishing the *Solid Muldoon*. According to some accounts, the name came from Day's chance finding of a log in the San Juan woods with the name "Muldoon" carved into the bark. Solid Muldoon was the nickname of William Muldoon, a popular Irish American fighter of the day. The paper's masthead had the name spelled out in logs. Three years after its first issue appeared, the *Solid Muldoon* became a daily.

Day crusaded against Republicans and dishonest mining promotions and scarcely slowed his pen to answer libel accusations. John Monnett and Michael McCarty describe Day's fiery approach in *Colorado Profiles*:

> [Day] faced as many as forty-two libel suits at one time and even edited his paper for ten days from a jail cell. In a double column advertisement he clearly stated his policy: "The Solid Muldoon is the boss, the only Fearless, Wide awake Red-hot Newspaper published in San Juan—Democratic in Politics; Independent in Development; and no religious convictions worth speaking of." . . . Some people saw the Muldoon as an irresponsible,

provincial, small-town muckraker, the personification of yellow journalism. But to others it was a beacon in a dark night.

Day edited the paper in Ouray for several years before moving himself and the *Solid Muldoon* to Durango.

One of the major mines in Red Mountain District near Ouray was the Mineral Farm Mine, whose owners, A. W. Begole and John Eckles, sold it to the Norfolk & Ouray Mining Company for $75,000 in October 1878. The mine eventually produced gold, copper, silver, and lead valued at more than $1 million. But the biggest mine in the district was undeniably the Yankee Girl, opened on August 19, 1882. It produced $8 million to $12 million in ores in its first ten years.

Ouray's silver-mining operations eventually slowed and had nearly ceased by the mid-1890s, but the town got a new lease on life when miners found gold veins in the region in 1896. Among the discoveries was the Camp Bird Mine, established by Thomas Walsh. Walsh had 103 mining claims in the region, and he eventually employed more than 400 miners at the Camp Bird. The housing Walsh provided his workers had such amenities as electric lights, steam heat, and hot and cold running water. The communal area had pool tables and reading rooms with magazines and newspapers. Walsh also built a boardinghouse that doubled as a restaurant and hotel for travelers. In 1902 Walsh sold the Camp Bird to a British syndicate for $5.2 million; it remained in operation under various owners for about ninety years, producing some $50 million in ore.

Ouray's story is like Silverton's. Once mining activity began to dwindle, the population declined by nearly half. Then the Million Dollar Highway was built, bringing in tourists and keeping the town alive.

MONTROSE

Founded in 1882, Montrose is in the fertile Uncompahgre River valley, and thanks to irrigation projects, its fields and orchards are highly productive. Just south of Montrose on US 550 is the site of the Uncompahgre Cantonment, a military post established in July 1880. It was renamed Fort Crawford in 1886 for Capt. Emmett Crawford, who died in a conflict with Geronimo's band of Apaches. The fort was deactivated in 1890, at which time the buildings were sold at auction and the land was opened to settlement.

At the southern edge of Montrose, the Ute Indian Museum stands on what was once the farm of the Ute chief Ouray.

Chief Ouray

Chief Ouray, leader of the Tabeguache band of Ute Indians, was a true diplomat. Born either in Colorado or near Taos, New Mexico, around

Tabeguache Ute leader Ouray and his wife Chipeta
—Courtesy Wyoming State Archives, Indian Collection

1820, Ouray was the son of a Ute father and a Jicarilla Apache mother. Raised as a Ute, he became one of the most prominent members of the tribe, following in his father's footsteps. His leadership abilities were supplemented by his knowledge. Ouray spoke fluent Spanish and English, which enabled him to negotiate skillfully on behalf of his people.

Although they had an agency in the San Juans at Los Pinos (west of Saguache), the Utes under Ouray settled around a new agency, known as Los Pinos II or the Uncompahgre Agency, near Montrose. Some historians believe Ouray could have averted the Meeker Massacre of 1879 (see Meeker in part 6), but he was away from the agency when it took place. According to some accounts, when, upon his return, Ouray heard of the attack and the capture of the white women and children, he demanded the cessation of hostilities. Whether because of Ouray's supposed order or for their own reasons, the Utes involved in the Meeker incident withdrew.

For his efforts in treaty negotiations and other matters, Ouray received a special annuity of $1,000 per year from the federal government.

Although that compensation allowed Ouray and his second wife, Chipeta, to have a comfortable life on a farm in present Montrose, it created some animosity among the Utes.

Thirteen acres of the original farm are now owned by the state of Colorado and operated as the Ute Indian Museum. Chipeta is buried there, and Ouray's remains, which were initially interred in a cave south of Ignacio on the Southern Ute Reservation, were later moved to the museum site.

Lodges have been erected on the grounds of the Ute Museum near Montrose, on land once farmed by Ute chief Ouray and his wife Chipeta, who are both buried here.

US 50
Grand Junction—Gunnison
127 MILES

GRAND JUNCTION

On September 26, 1881, George A. Crawford and some associates claimed a 640-acre tract for the town site that became Grand Junction. The town was incorporated in 1882, about the same time the Denver & Rio Grande Railroad arrived. The surrounding area is well known for its fruit, particularly the juicy Colorado peach known as the Grand Junction peach. Fruit lovers from Colorado and surrounding states swarm the town in late August to buy peaches at fruit stands or pick their own at area orchards.

In 1909 Walter B. Cross established the Cross Land & Fruit Company, growing apples and pears. The next year he added a barn that served as a large-scale fruit-processing plant. Cross lost the property in the 1920s due to financial difficulties, but the city purchased it, and the Museum of Western Colorado now operates it as Cross Orchards Historic Farm, a living history museum.

During the 1930s, the Civilian Conservation Corps (CCC), a New Deal program for young men seventeen to twenty-three years old, began operations in Colorado. The headquarters for its western division were at Grand Junction. The office managed some twenty-five CCC camps. The CCC men worked on a number of projects, including improvements to the 20,534-acre Colorado National Monument, established in 1911, southwest of Grand Junction.

It was not until later in the twentieth century that another industry unfolded in the Grand Junction area. Mountains with layers of oil-bearing shale stretch across northern Mesa County. Although early extraction efforts took place in the early 1900s, full-scale energy production did not begin until the late 1970s and early 1980s. Construction of billion-dollar facilities in adjacent Garfield County caused a boom in Grand Junction, which had become a regional commercial center. The city's population grew to more than 20,000 in the 1970s, but a period of slow growth followed.

By the 1990s, however, the national economy had rebounded, and Colorado and other western states were enjoying an upsurge in population. By 2000, Grand Junction had 41,986 residents, a stunning 44 percent increase over the 1990 census figures. Part of the growth was a result of mineral production, but another factor was the influx of retirees departing larger cities for the rural atmosphere of Colorado's Western Slope. Agriculture remains a mainstay of the region's economy, and local wineries have recently blossomed, bringing a further boost to the area.

DELTA

The Ute Council Tree, a massive cottonwood in Delta, was a routine gathering place for Ute Indians. The tree still stands on the north side of town. The earliest non-Indian semipermanent residents here were trappers and traders; settlement came long after the beaver trade died out.

Delta displays its history in a collection of murals on downtown buildings, and the community has many structures listed on both the state and national historical registers. One of them is the Egyptian Theater, which started a "Bank Night" promotion to bolster attendance during the Great Depression. The first Bank Night was held in March 1933, and cash prizes were awarded to theater patrons. Within four years, the concept of giving prizes to moviegoers had spread across the nation. The building has been restored to its 1928 look.

Delta is a hub for travelers on the scenic drive to Grand Junction, a seventy-five-mile route that crosses Grand Mesa, called the "world's largest flat-topped mountain." The Grand Mesa Scenic and Historic Byway passes through Cedaredge, a commercial center for the valley, which started in the 1890s as the Bar I Ranch headquarters. The route crosses through the Grand Mesa National Forest between Cedaredge and Mesa.

Fort Uncompahgre

Antoine Robidoux, a well-known St. Louis fur trader and mountain man, entered the Gunnison River region as early as 1824, and four years later he built Fort Uncompahgre, a log fort on the river near present Delta. Although the original fort no longer exists, the city of Delta re-created it and operates it as a living history site.

In 1824 Antoine Robidoux and his brother Louis made their way to Santa Fe, where they met with family friends Auguste Chouteau and Etienne Provost. Late that summer, Antoine joined a party of trappers Provost was leading into what would become western Colorado and eastern Utah, looking for prime beaver country. They found some promising areas, but they had conflicts with Indians and returned to Santa Fe in 1825.

At the time, Mexican laws prohibited Americans from moving into the region north and west of Santa Fe. Although of French ancestry, the Robidoux brothers were Americans, shutting them out of trapping and trading along the Western Slope. In 1828 Antoine married Carmel Benevides, the adopted daughter of the Mexican governor. Within weeks of the wedding, Robidoux had an exclusive license to trap and trade in the river valleys he had visited a few years earlier.

With trading license in hand, Antoine followed the trappers' trail from Taos into the San Luis Valley, then took the Indian trail over Cochetopa Pass, dropping into the Gunnison River country before making his way into the Uncompahgre River valley. The route he took became known as the Mountain Branch of the Old Spanish Trail. He built the trading post that became known as Fort Uncompahgre two miles below the confluence of the Uncompahgre and Gunnison Rivers, near the Ute Council Tree, where the Utes often camped.

At one time or another, some fifteen to eighteen employees worked at Fort Uncompahgre, trading such items as tobacco, sugar, coffee, tea, wool and calico, blankets, clothing, cooking pots, and other items to the Indians, primarily for furs. They also occasionally traded with other American fur trappers working, usually without authority from Mexico, in the region. Though illegal as trade items, both the liquor known as

"Taos Lightning" and firearms often found their way from the store into the hands of Utes and other Indians.

Robidoux traded here for many years before he started a new post at the confluence of the Green and Duchesne Rivers in present Utah. Fort Uncompahgre was abandoned, but it was still standing when missionary Marcus Whitman and frontiersman Asa Lovejoy arrived there in 1842. By 1853 the post had fallen into total disrepair, and when Captain Randolph Marcy passed by in 1857, he noted that the old fort structures had been burned.

BLACK CANYON OF THE GUNNISON NATIONAL PARK

Between Montrose and Gunnison on US 50, CO 347 takes you north into Black Canyon of the Gunnison National Park. The area was set aside by President Herbert Hoover as a national monument on March 2, 1933, and it was established as a national park under President Bill Clinton on October 21, 1999.

Most of the spectacular canyons of the West were cut through relatively soft, often colorful rock, but the Gunnison River sculpted Black Canyon out of hard, black granite. Unusually dark and narrow with steep, jagged walls, Black Canyon has an almost spooky appearance at times. The park and adjacent Gunnison Gorge National Conservation Area offer various recreational facilities.

The Gunnison River, Gunnison Gorge, the town of Gunnison, and all the other Gunnisons in this part of Colorado take their name from Capt. John Williams Gunnison, who explored the area in 1853 with the U.S. Corps of Topographical Engineers while looking for a potential rail route. Reared in New Hampshire, Gunnison graduated from West Point in 1837. He served in the Seminole Wars in Florida, assisted in the removal of Cherokees from Georgia, and conducted surveys in Georgia, Florida, and around the Great Salt Lake before being sent on the 1853 expedition to Colorado.

Gunnison's assignment was to survey a route from the headwaters of the Rio Grande, in the San Juan Mountains, through the Rockies and into Utah. After traveling through Kansas and eastern Colorado, Gunnison confronted the Rocky Mountains. Forging ahead, he surveyed several passes, including Sangre de Cristo Pass, Cochetopa Pass, and Poncha (Gunnison) Pass. Along the way, Gunnison engaged Antoine Leroux as a guide. After reaching the Gunnison River, then called the Tomichi, near the present town of Gunnison, the command continued west, but the men were soon forced to turn south to avoid a deep gorge they could not cross, now known as the Black Canyon of the Gunnison. The party crossed into Utah in late October, camping near Lake Sevier.

View of Black Canyon of the Gunnison National Park
—Courtesy National Park Service

The next day, October 26, the group was attacked by Paiutes. The Indians killed eight men, including Gunnison.

GUNNISON TUNNEL

The Gunnison Tunnel, an early project of the U.S. Bureau of Reclamation, was constructed in the early 1900s at a cost of approximately $3 million. The 5.8-mile-long tunnel transfers water from the Gunnison River through Vernal Mesa to the Uncompahgre Valley. At its deepest point, the tunnel lies 2,200 feet below Vernal Mesa. It is nearly square, about eleven by twelve feet, with an arched roof, and in places it was drilled through solid granite. Though it is not really possible to see or visit the tunnel, it runs from Cedar Creek, near the junction of US 50 and CO 347, to the Gunnison River near the East Portal entrance of Black Canyon of the Gunnison National Park.

The tunnel was the brainchild of Montrose farmer F. C. Lauzon. By 1894 Lauzon had enough support and funds for the work, but it was not until 1905, after federal assistance was secured, that drilling started from each end of the tunnel. President William H. Taft formally opened the tunnel on September 23, 1909. It was the first Colorado project implemented under the 1902 Newlands Act, which established the U.S. Bureau of Reclamation and led to major water projects across the arid West. The Gunnison Tunnel enabled agricultural development in the Uncompahgre Valley near Montrose and Delta.

GUNNISON

The first known homesteader in the Gunnison area was Alonzo Hartman, who settled near the confluence of Tomichi Creek and the Gunnison River around 1871. A colony of settlers from Denver, led by Sylvester Richardson, laid out the town of Gunnison in 1874. A few years later, when prospectors struck gold and silver nearby, Gunnison became a major supply and transportation center, serving camps like Gothic, Pitkin, and Tincup. What really set the tone for the town's future, though, was the arrival in the early 1880s of both the Denver & Rio Grande and the Denver, South Park & Pacific Railroads. After the mining camps dwindled, eventually becoming virtual ghost towns, Gunnison survived as a supply center for area ranchers.

A water tank and a Denver & Rio Grande caboose are displayed at the Gunnison Museum.

These days, the Gunnison region is a popular summer getaway. Many acres of public land, including the Gunnison National Forest, offer various recreational opportunities, and the Blue Mesa Reservoir in the Curecanti National Recreation Area, southwest of the town, draws fishing and boating enthusiasts. The Gunnison Museum preserves some of the area's history, including a caboose from the Denver & Rio Grande Railroad.

CO 149 and CO 135
South Fork—Crested Butte
154 MILES

The stretch of CO 149 between South Fork and Lake City is called the Silver Thread Scenic Byway, a reference to the region's mining history. The road crosses both Spring Creek and Slumgullion Passes as it winds through the Rio Grande National Forest. North of Lake City, the highway follows the Lake Fork of the Gunnison River for a while, then continues north to US 50 and Blue Mesa Reservoir. This trip will hop over to Gunnison and pick up CO 135 to Crested Butte.

SOUTH FORK

Originally a stage stop, South Fork became a Denver & Rio Grande Railroad station in 1882, serving the local mining, timber, and agriculture industries. Today the town is a center for recreationists who enjoy the nearby fishing, hiking, golfing, rafting, snowmobiling, and cross-country skiing. In addition to tourism, lumber and farming still help sustain the town's economy.

LA GARITA MOUNTAINS

In the winter of 1848, as they struggled toward the Continental Divide, the expedition of John C. Frémont foundered at two different campsites in the La Garita Mountains, east of today's CO 149. They remained at the first one, Camp Desolation on Wannamaker Creek, for several days. Benjamin Kern described their time there as "days of horror desolation despair & almost continued heavy winds intense cold & snow storm."

With the expedition's mules pulling their equipment on sleds, the party of thirty-six men moved to another campsite at the head of Embargo Creek, dubbing the place Camp Hope. They spent Christmas there, dining on mule-meat pie, elk stew, biscuits, and doughnuts, along with coffee. Snowbound, they remained there for several more days.

John C. Frémont
—Courtesy Wyoming
State Archives

After a few days, Frémont sent a party out toward what the men believed was the closest town: Abiquiú, New Mexico. Eventually the others started trailing south as well, separating into three groups, each traveling at its own pace. Frémont's group made it to the San Luis Valley on January 11 and continued toward the settlement at Rio Colorado. On the way, they came upon "Old Bill" Williams and two other party members. When they arrived at Rio Colorado, Frémont organized a rescue party to return for the men who were still struggling through the snow. The rescuers found the survivors, but ten men had perished, along with all the mules.

CREEDE

In 1889 prospector Nicholas C. Creede struck a mineral vein on the headwaters of the Rio Grande, spawning the Holy Moses Mine. A town bearing his name developed, squeezing itself into the narrow Willow Creek Canyon. Other mines followed, including the Last Chance and the Amethyst, yielding millions. By 1890 Creede was a boomtown.

Production of silver, gold, copper, zinc, and lead at Creede continued for decades, producing some $69.5 million in ore from 1891 to 1966. But the biggest boom came in 1967, when area mines generated $11.5 million in ore, showing that Colorado's mineral resources could continue to provide income for people living in the heart of the San Juans.

Cy Warman, known as "the poet of the Rockies," launched the *Creede Chronicle* in the town's early days. It was there he wrote one of his best-known rhymes:

> *Here's a land where all are equal—*
>
> *Of high or lowly birth—*
>
> *A land where men make millions*
>
> *Dug from the dreary earth.*
>
> *Here the meek and mild-eyed burros*
>
> *On mineral mountains feed—*
>
> *It's day all day in the daytime,*
>
> *And there is no night in Creede.*

Warman was just one of many Colorado poets who gained a national reputation. Others include Eugene Field, Thomas Hornsby Ferril, and Pueblo's Damon Runyon, whose poetry about his service in the Philippines during the Spanish-American War earned him the title "the Kipling of Colorado."

The Denver & Rio Grande Railroad reached Creede in 189. One observer described this scene in January 1892:

> The train when it comes is a sight to behold, the smoking car being an especial marvel. It is jammed. Men sit on one another, and on the arms of the seats, stand in the aisles and hang on the platforms. Pipes, blankets, satchels form the major part of their equipment. . . .
>
> The saloons and dance houses are in full blast and such houses as they are, and such discarded remnants as the old fairies who flaunt around them never were seen before. Along in the morning when the wheezy accordion lets up, the time is occupied by a riot. . . . There are a few bad men in Creede and many who are reckless.

An infamous incident illustrates the recklessness of Creede. Robert (Bob) Ford, one of the legendary characters of the West, met his end in Creede in June 1892 at the hands of a violent-tempered man named Edward "Red" Kelly. Ford had forged his reputation a decade earlier as the killer of outlaw Jesse James. On April 3, 1882, Ford, who was an acquaintance of James, was visiting the outlaw in his home in St. Joseph, Missouri, when he shot him in the back of the head as James was straightening a picture on the wall. Presumably Ford was hoping for a reward, but instead he was arrested and charged with murder. Ford was arrested and charged with murder. Ford was convicted, but he received an immediate pardon from Missouri governor Thomas T. Crittenden. After the episode, Ford moved to Creede, where he ran a saloon.

Ford was in his saloon after an argument with Red Kelly, who was angry that Ford had accused him of stealing his diamond ring. Ford had pitched Kelly from the saloon, but Kelly returned to settle the score and killed Ford with a shotgun. Kelly was quickly apprehended. Convicted of the murder, he was sentenced to prison at Canon City. He served time there until 1902, when he was paroled. He eventually met a violent end himself, killed during an altercation with police in Oklahoma City.

LAKE CITY

Lake City started as a supply center for area mining camps in 1875. Nearby are remains of various mining operations from that period, such as the Golconda Mine, which produced lead, zinc, copper, and some gold and silver. The Capitol City charcoal kilns, another mining-era artifact, were recently placed on the Colorado State Historic Register. Built in 1877, the brick kilns were designed in the typical beehive shape. Also near Lake City, the Empire Chief Mine and Mill operated into the twentieth century, when it had a 150-ton flotation mill in service.

Lake San Cristobal, the second-largest natural lake in the state, lies just south of Lake City and is the reason for the town's name. On CO 149 between the town and the lake, a plaque memorializes the notorious Alfred Packer incident. In February 1874, prospector Alfred Packer and five companions, against all advice, headed into the San Juan Mountains. What happened there became one of the infamous stories of the frontier West.

Departing the camp of Ute chief Ouray, near present Montrose, on February 9, the party included Packer, a harness maker and drifter from Pennsylvania; Shannon Wilson "Red" Bell of Michigan; James Humphrey of Philadelphia; Frank Miller, a butcher from Germany; Israel Swan of Missouri; and seventeen-year-old George "California" Noon of San Francisco. The six intended to make their way to the Los Pinos Indian Agency near Saguache and eventually seek gold in the Breckenridge area.

Although Packer changed his story many times, according to his original account, after the men established a camp, Packer left his five companions to search for food. He returned to find everyone but Bell dead:

> [Bell was] sitting near the fire roasting a piece of meat that he had cut out of the leg of the German butcher. The latter's body was lying the farthest off from the fire down the stream, his scull was crushed in with the hatchet. The other three men were lying near the fire, they were cut in the forehead with the hatchet. . . . I came within a rod of the fire, when the man saw me,

he got up with his hatchet toward me when I shot him sideways through the belly, he fell on his face, the hatchet fell forward. I grabbed it and hit him in the top of the head.

Though he hadn't killed the four men, or so he claimed, Packer did eat the bodies. Alone in the mountains, he "fetched to the camp the piece of meat that was near the fire. And made a new fire near my camp and cooked the piece of meat and ate it." He lived in those snowy mountains for two months, all the while surviving on the flesh of his former companions. Finally he made his way to the Los Pinos Agency, near present Saguache. Later that year, Packer was arrested for murder. He was jailed in Saguache to await trial, but he escaped. He was not apprehended until 1883, nine years later, when someone at Fort Fetterman in Wyoming recognized him.

Packer's first trial, in Lake City in 1883, resulted in a conviction, and he was sentenced to hang. But a couple of years later he was granted a retrial based on a legal technicality. Retried in 1886 in Gunnison, he was again convicted, this time sentenced to forty years in the penitentiary at Canon City. In 1900 *Denver Post* columnist Polly Pry took up Packer's cause. After a series of articles and with the backing of the newspaper, Pry succeeded in getting him a pardon from Governor Charles S. Thomas. Under the terms of his pardon, Packer was required to live in Denver for nearly seven years. In April 1907, not long before he would have been free to leave, he died and was buried in Littleton. Various cafeterias, including one at the University of Colorado in Boulder, are named ironically after Alfred Packer.

CRESTED BUTTE

North of Gunnison on CO 135, Crested Butte operated as a successful company town for Colorado Fuel & Iron until 1952, when its coal mine ceased operation. By then, however, the area was already being eyed as a potential ski resort. In the 1960s, Mount Crested Butte Resort was built at the base of the mountain, ensuring a winter economy for the area.

CO 114
US 50—US 285 at Saguache
61 MILES

CO 114 traverses miles of national public lands, including both the Gunnison and Rio Grande National Forests, and connects to various Forest Service roads and trails. At the Continental Divide, the highway crosses North Pass, and one of the forest roads crosses Cochetopa Pass. This area was part of a proposed transcontinental railroad route in the mid-1800s. Due to the difficulties explorers encountered here, planners ultimately abandoned the route, but the history of the failure is interesting nonetheless.

COCHETOPA PASS

Missouri Senator Thomas Hart Benton enthusiastically led the campaign for a transcontinental railroad route through the center of the country. He introduced his first railroad legislation in 1849, basing the bill on information from fur trapper Antoine Leroux. Leroux had assured Benton that wagons had crossed Colorado's Cochetopa Pass in 1837 and that "there is not much snow in this Pass, and people go through it all the winter." Thus Benton believed Cochetopa Pass would be suitable for trains.

Cochetopa Pass was on a bison migration route, and the Indians called the crossing Buffalo Pass. Benton similarly referred to it as the "Gate of the Buffaloes." Buffalo, Benton believed, were the "best of engineers, whose instincts never commit mistakes." Therefore, he reasoned, humans need only follow the animals' tracks across the West:

> In their migrations for pasture, shelter, and salt, [the bison] never fail to find the lowest levels in the mountains, the shallowest fords in the rivers, the richest grass, the best salt licks, the most permanent water; and always take the shortest and best routes between all these points of attraction. . . . This is enough to show that the Rocky mountains may be passed without crossing a hill—that loaded wagons may cross it at all seasons of the year.

Benton envisioned a railroad that followed a straight line between St. Louis and San Francisco. He was so confident, he predicted there would be "not a tunnel to be made—a mountain to be climbed—a hill to be crossed—a swamp to be seen—or desert, or moveable sand to be encountered in the whole distance . . . this line for a road, the longest and straightest in the world, is also over the smoothest and most equal surface." Obviously, Benton had never been to Colorado.

To test Benton's theory, the government sent Indian agent E. F. Beale and his cousin, artist Gwinn Harris Heap, to follow the proposed route in 1853. As they entered the San Luis Valley over Sangre de Cristo Pass, Heap noted in his journal that "an excellent wagon road might be made over these mountains, by the Sangre de Cristo Pass, and a still better one through Robideau's."

The party reached Cochetopa Pass on June 18. Cochetopa and what Heap called Carnero Pass (which could have been North Pass) were those most frequently used by Indians, leading Heap to suggest that building a military post between the two in Saguache Valley could help

control Indian movements. (The Los Pinos Agency was later established in the area, under terms of the 1868 Ute treaty.) Beale and Heap's
explorations did not provide adequate information to support Benton's
central railroad route, however.

Capt. John W. Gunnison of the U.S. Topographical Engineers led
another expedition in 1853 to survey a route through the Rockies from
the headwaters of the Rio Grande. Gunnison ultimately recommended
the route over Sangre de Cristo Pass as the only possible option for a
railroad. Benton's dream of a central route had run straight into the rugged peaks of the Rockies, stopped in its tracks before a single rail could
be laid. As Ceran St. Vrain noted on October 8, 1853, in the *Santa Fe
Gazette*, "The idea of locating a railroad through the country mentioned
in Leroux's letter to Colonel Benton was ridiculous and absurd."

In 1857, just four years after Gunnison's survey, another army expedition found itself in trouble as it attempted to cross Cochetopa Pass.
During the so-called Mormon War, Col. Albert Sidney Johnston arrived

*Capt. Randolph Marcy,
who struggled through
the Colorado mountains
in 1857, in search of aid
for Col. Albert Sidney
Johnston's troops. Marcy
later became a general in
the Union Army. Photo by
Mathew Brady.* —Courtesy
National Archives (529676)w

at Fort Bridger, Wyoming, to drive the Mormons back toward Salt Lake City. Before they retreated, the Mormons burned both Fort Bridger and another post, Fort Supply. Johnston established Camp Scott and sent Capt. Randolph B. Marcy to Fort Union, New Mexico, for supplies.

Marcy departed Camp Scott on November 27 with forty infantry soldiers and twenty-four mounted men. The trip was estimated to take twenty-five days. Crossing northwestern Colorado, they hit Cochetopa Pass, where they foundered in the deep snow. Marcy described their plight:

> [We] entered the mountains, where we at once encountered snow which increased in depth as we ascended, and upon this was a hard crust that cut the mules' legs severely and greatly augmented the difficulty of traveling. . . .
>
> Finding it impossible for our jaded animals any longer to break the track, I placed forty men in the advance, who waded slowly through it, alternating from front to rear as they became exhausted, and in this manner a path was beaten, over which the pack mules with difficulty passed.

Marcy sent two men to Fort Massachusetts for supplies while the remainder struggled on through the snow, which was four to five feet deep. The captain later said proudly that his men had "hearts of oak." Two weeks later, Marcy and his men met a relief party from Fort Massachusetts. The troops, Marcy noted, "brought me a handful of coffee, and what was of much more value to the men, a large plug of tobacco, which I cut up into forty pieces, and distributed among the soldiers."

Thus fortified, Marcy's men marched ten miles down the valley to meet wagons filled with beef, bread, coffee, sugar, and more. "Captain Bowman had kindly sent me, among other things, a demijohn of brandy, I issued a good dram to the men, and gave them a supply of tobacco."

On his return trip to Camp Scott, Marcy wisely chose not to retrace his steps through Cochetopa Pass, instead traveling north along the Front Range of the Rockies and west on the Cherokee Trail. The following spring, Marcy's guide, William Wing Loring, forged a wagon road over Cochetopa Pass, giving it the temporary name Loring's Trail.

Though the railroad never passed through here, in one sense, Benton's vision had been right. In a December 5, 1854, speech in Baltimore, Benton said that Colorado "will make another great state . . . and will be settled with unexampled rapidity."

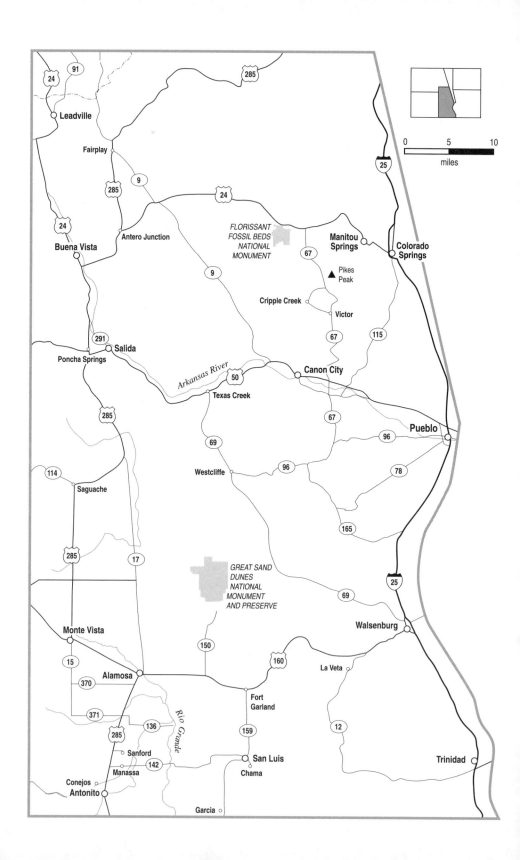

PART TWO

South-central
SAN LUIS VALLEY
AND SOUTH PARK

Two large valleys, with massive mountain ranges looming on three sides, dominate south-central Colorado. In this book, the south-central region is defined as the area bordered on the north by I-70, on the west more or less by US 285, on the south by New Mexico, and on the east by the mountain ranges west of I-25 (including the Sangre de Cristos, the Wet Mountains, and the Rampart Range). Because of the rugged mountains surrounding this part of Colorado, early-day travelers entered the region in much the same way today's motorists do, traversing mountain passes such as North, Poncha, Mosca, La Veta, Tennessee, Independence, Hoosier, Boreas, and Kenosha.

In the southern part of the region, the San Luis Valley, which extends into New Mexico, was once disputed territory of the Ute and Comanche Indians, but the Utes ultimately gained control. The main trail through the San Luis Valley was an old Snake Indian trade route, which early trappers used en route to trade in Santa Fe and Taos. The first settlers in Colorado came to this valley from Mexico in the 1830s and 1840s to start farms, and crops have been grown in the area ever since.

South Park lies in the northern part of the region. This broad basin north of US 24 is some eighty miles long and sixty miles wide and encompasses the headwaters of the South Platte River. Whereas Mexican farming families settled the San Luis Valley, South Park was first developed by miners after the 1859 gold strikes around Idaho Springs.

The first known white explorer to traverse Colorado was Zebulon Pike, whose 1806 expedition paved the way for further exploration and, eventually, American settlement. Most of Pike's explorations were concentrated here in the south-central part of Colorado.

Pike Expedition

In July 1806 Zebulon Pike and his party left St. Louis and traveled on horseback across present-day Kansas and into today's Colorado along

Buildings representing the early days of South Park at the Fairplay Museum

the Arkansas River, seeking its source. Leading a military expedition of twenty-three men on a mission to explore the southern portion of the Louisiana Purchase, he began his journey as a lieutenant and was promoted to captain while in Colorado.

The party reached today's Pueblo on November 23, there constructing a log breastwork that is recognized as the first structure ever built by Americans in Colorado. Pike noted the lovely surroundings in his diary entry for Thursday, November 27:

> *Arose hungry, dray [sic], and extremely sore, from the inequality of the rocks, on which we had lain all night, but were amply compensated for toil by the sublimity of the prospects below. The unbounded prairie was overhung with clouds, which appeared like the ocean in a storm; wave piled on wave and foaming, whilst the sky was perfectly clear where we were.*

After deciding against climbing the peak that today bears his name, Pike took his men west, passing the Royal Gorge of the Arkansas River. It was December and winter was bearing down, but the men had nothing more than cotton overalls to wear. Pike wrote, "I had not calculated on being out in this inclement season of the year." Nevertheless, the expedition pushed on, traveling north of today's Canon City and into South Park. Like many a lost wanderer, however, Pike unwittingly made a circle and a month later ended up where he started.

Heading south, Pike crossed the Sangre de Cristo Mountains, so named by early Spanish missionaries who saw the mountains bathed in the red glow of the late-afternoon sun and envisioned the "blood of Christ." Pike must have seen them in a different light and probably covered with snow, as he called them the White Mountains.

In February 1807, at a camp near today's Sanford, then in Spanish territory, Pike was confronted by the Spanish army. He and his men were held in Mexico for a time but were eventually released. Although it was not to become known for many years, Pike was actually spying for Louisiana Territory's governor, James Wilkinson, determining troop strength in the western lands then under Spanish control.

Pike not only failed to scale the mountain later named for him, but he failed to reach one of his main objectives—to find the headwaters of the Arkansas River. Pike's expedition did, however, succeed in drawing a map that correctly located the South Platte River, the Arkansas River, and the Rio Grande.

Mexican Land Grants

The first known non-Indian settlement in Colorado was in the San Luis Valley, established as Mexican home seekers moved in from the south. In the 1830s and early 1840s, the Mexican government offered land grants to citizens wishing to settle the area, which was still part of Mexico. The valley's Mexican heritage is still evident today. When George Frederick Ruxton traveled through in 1846 and 1847, he noted the harsh living conditions of the valley's Hispanic settlers: "Growing a bare sufficiency for their own support, they hold the little land they cultivate, and their wretched hovels, on sufferance from the barbarous Yutas, who actually tolerate their presence in their country for the sole purpose of having at their command a stock of grain and a herd of mules and horses."

The first land grants in present Colorado were established in 1833, when Mexican officials authorized the Maxwell Grant and the Conejos, or Tierra Amarilla, Grant. These and later grants all had similar terms, requiring that the land "shall be cultivated and never abandoned." The agreements often emphasized self-protection as well. The Conejos Grant, for example, stated that "the grantees must keep themselves equipped with firearms and bows and arrows in which they must pass review as well at the time of their settlement there as at anytime the Alcalde [Mayor] or Justice of the Peace in authority over them may deem proper to examine them. . . . The towns they may build shall be well walled around and fortified."

The fifty families involved in the first Conejos Grant were expected to cultivate the acreage. The settlers did herd sheep in 1840 and 1841, but the Navajos hindered their success by attacking them and forcing them from their farms. In 1843 the governor of New Mexico authorized additional Mexican land grants, including the Sangre de Cristo Grant, which included more than 1 million acres, and the Vigil and St. Vrain

Workers harvesting potatoes ca. 1930s in the San Luis Valley, using a horse-drawn wagon to haul the produce. Many farmers in the area are of Mexican descent. —Courtesy Bob Lovato Collection

Grant, also known as the Las Animas Grant, whose 4 million acres were entirely within present Colorado. The grants may have been given to stave off the Texan influence. Upon winning independence in 1836, Texas claimed land as far west as the Rio Grande. Had those claims been officially recognized, Santa Fe and Taos would have fallen under Texan control, as would the lands in Colorado between the Rio Grande and the upper Arkansas River.

But the land-grant programs became mired in bureaucracy, a problem compounded by the 1848 Treaty of Guadalupe Hidalgo, which transferred the land from Mexican to American control following the Mexican-American War. The original Conejos Grant was declared void, but arguments over ownership continued for decades. One of the largest grants, the Sangre de Cristo—which extended from the Rio Grande on the west to the Culebra Range on the east, and from Sierra Blanca in the north to the south end of San Pedro Mesa—was subdivided in various ways and changed ownership many times over the decades. In 1854 William Pelham, surveyor general for New Mexico, began a review of both the Sangre de Cristo and the Conejos Grants, and Congress confirmed the Sangre de Cristo Grant in 1860. But afterward, through various slick maneuvers, former Colorado territorial governor William Gilpin gained control of the entire Sangre de Cristo Grant and launched plans to sell the land to various companies.

The quagmire regarding the Sangre de Cristo Grant holdings continued. Some grantees were told they would receive deeds to the land they and their forebears had developed, but without water, grazing, or timber rights. Over the years, various oral agreements allowed residents to use water from company irrigation systems, but those agreements constantly changed, leading to unstable relations in the region. Eventually the issue ended up in court. The residents won the first round, but the U.S. Circuit Court reversed the lower court's ruling and cut the residents' water rights in half.

In the meantime, the lands from the Conejos Grant, whose boundaries were not surveyed until 1867, were being treated as public domain. A number of settlers—generally squatters—were holding 160-acre tracts without consent of the grant owners. The confusion over land ownership led the United States to establish courts of land claims. In the 1890s, the son of one of the original grantees filed a petition asking that squatters either be evicted or made to pay for the land. The court dismissed the petition in 1900, saying there was no evidence that the 1833 grant even existed. The declaration cleared title to lands that had been under a cloud for years, and the original grantees and their heirs lost their claims.

To this day, these issues still haven't been fully resolved. On May 16, 1994, *High Country News* reported that the Colorado Supreme Court, in a hotly debated four-to-three decision, ruled in favor of Costilla County residents in a dispute over wood gathering, grazing, hunting, and fishing on Sangre de Cristo Grant lands. The article noted, "Many more years of litigation may be necessary before the courts settle the question of communal rights on the Sangre de Cristo Land Grant."

Because the settlement of south-central Colorado started in the San Luis Valley with the Mexican land grants, we will begin there, traveling from south to north and from west to east.

US 285
New Mexico Border—Alamosa
28 MILES

ANTONITO

Antonito, a mile south of Conejos, obtained its first post office under the name San Antonio in 1880, but within two months it was shortened to Antonito. A lava-stone railroad depot, a bunkhouse, a sawmill, a hotel, several stores, three churches (serving the Catholic, Methodist, and Presbyterian population), and many gambling houses and saloons (to serve the same population) made up the community's collection of buildings.

The Denver & Rio Grande Railroad, which gave rise to Antonito, had other stations at Tres Piedras and Taos Junction, to the south. Nicknamed the "Chili Line," the railroad carried livestock, wool, and lumber, but few passengers. Eventually the D&RG provided a link with Chama, New Mexico, and the line traveled along what became the state border between Colorado and New Mexico, carrying people as well as freight. Regular passenger service ceased in 1951, but plans to pull the line were stopped in their tracks by local railroad buffs. Now in operation as the Cumbres & Toltec Scenic Railroad, the railway carries tourists through the region each summer and fall.

CONEJOS

Conejos was the site of the first church in Colorado, Our Lady of Guadalupe Parish, built in 1858. It was established by settlers who came here from New Mexico.

Under their first treaty with the U.S. government, in 1863, the Utes were given an agency near Conejos. At a second treaty session held later that year, Colorado territorial governor John Evans persuaded representatives from the Weeminuche and Capote Ute bands to accept an agency in southwestern Colorado, which was called the Uncompahgre, or Los Pinos II, Agency. The Tabeguaches, however, remained near Conejos for another five years, with Lafayette Head as their agent. Several subsequent treaties, each with different terms, forced the Tabeguache Utes from place to place until they were eventually settled in Utah. (See also introduction to part 1.)

MANASSA

Manassa is about three miles east of Romeo on CO 142. The Mormon Church, which encouraged colonization in parts of the San Luis Valley, purchased two ranches in this area in 1889: the Zapata Ranch, which had been part of a Mexican land grant, and the Medano Ranch, once part of the Springs of the Medano Land Grant. Together, the ranch holdings were the Blanca Branch of the Manassa Ward of the Church of Jesus Christ of Latter-day Saints. Some also called it the Uracca Mormon Church. The Mormons tried to eke out a living on the two ranch holdings, cutting timber and selling the firewood in Alamosa, but the entire operation ended in bankruptcy, and the land was sold in 1900.

The downfall of the Uracca Mormon operation didn't mean the end of Mormons in the San Luis Valley, however. Other members of the LDS Church had begun farming near Manassa, raising peas, oats, alfalfa, and Sonora spring wheat. While their crops prospered, their relations with their neighbors did not. Some Hispanic neighbors dammed the Conejos

River to restrict irrigation water flowing to Mormon farms; the Mormons retaliated by destroying the dams. Other conflicts also occurred, but eventually both sides settled down and the dispute faded.

Just as they did in other communities throughout the West, the Mormons built a school and a church in Manassa, along with a cooperative store and flour mill. Among the residents of Manassa was the family of Hiram Dempsey. The ninth of eleven children, William Harrison Dempsey (called Harry by his family) was born in Manassa in 1895. He grew up to earn the world heavyweight boxing championship title under the name Jack Dempsey, "the Manassa Mauler." Today Manassa has a museum dedicated to the prizefighter.

SANFORD AND PIKE'S STOCKADE

Along with Manassa, other Mormon towns were established in this vicinity in the late 1800s, including Sanford, five miles east of US 285 on CO 136. A few miles east of Sanford is the site of Pike's Stockade, a small fort built by the Pike expedition in 1807 and reconstructed in the 1950s.

During their expedition, Pike's men camped five miles from present Sanford on the Conejos River, where they built a 36-by-36-foot square fort with twelve-foot walls of sharpened picket stakes. The fort became known as Pike's Stockade. Although Pike claimed he believed he was on the Red River at the time, he had in fact crossed into Spanish territory, and he probably knew it. In his journal Pike noted the presence of a Spanish road near the camp, but he ran up an American flag anyway, the first one known to have flown in what is now Colorado. It was learned years later that Pike was actually spying for the governor of Louisiana Territory, James Wilkinson.

The following February, fifty-nine Spanish dragoons arrived at the fort and requested that Pike return with them to Santa Fe, telling him, "Sir, the governor of New Mexico, being informed you had missed your route, ordered me to offer you in his name mules, horses, money, or whatever you may stand in need of to conduct you to the head of the Red River." Pike and his men were eventually taken to Mexico for questioning and detained there for a few months before being allowed to return to the United States.

ALAMOSA

Alamosa, initially known as Rio Brava, started as a shipping point on the Denver & Rio Grande Railroad. In May of 1878, just two months after the first residents put up their tents and shacks, Alexander Cameron Hunt, president of the Denver & Rio Grande Construction Company, platted the community as the Alamosa Town Company, lending it a new

Potato harvest in the San Luis Valley, ca. 1930s —Courtesy Bob Lovato Collection

name. Even before the rail expansion, the Barlow-Sanderson Overland Stage, Mail & Express Company had a station here. The stage route ran roughly along today's US 160 between La Veta and Alamosa, with stations about a dozen miles apart. Eventually the line extended to Del Norte and Lake City. When the railroad was built, it followed the same general route.

As the Denver & Rio Grande was expanding its operations, the Atchison, Topeka & Santa Fe Railroad hurried to make claims on routes over Raton Pass to the southeast and along the Arkansas River through the Royal Gorge. Forced into turf wars to the southeast and the north, D&RG officials delayed their plans in the Alamosa area. Finally, though, in 1880, the railroad connected Alamosa with communities to both the north and the south. Once the railroad arrived, it didn't take long for development to begin. Banks opened and other businesses followed suit. In its early days the town had two newspapers, the *Independent Journal* and the *Alamosa News*.

By the early 1880s, Alamosa had several churches and a school and was on its way to becoming the largest community in the San Luis Valley. But in December 1891, a fire destroyed much of the city. An explosion at a boardinghouse called the Perry House, caused by a woman trying to light a stove with kerosene, began a blaze that spread quickly to nearby structures. Alamosans soon rebuilt, however, and by 1900 the population had grown to more than 1,000 people.

As the railroad promoters had envisioned, the land of the San Luis Valley supported extensive agriculture. Over the decades, irrigation systems ranging from ditches and canals to dams and reservoirs were built. Early farmers raised wheat for the Blanca and Four Aces flour companies; today they grow malt barley for the Coors Brewing Company. Other important crops include potatoes and lettuce.

US 160
Monte Vista—La Veta
74 MILES

MONTE VISTA

One early settler in the Monte Vista area was a red-headed woman named Lillian Taylor. She drew attention when she rode the train to her stop, which was little more than a rail siding with a water tank. Lariat Siding, or simply Lariat, was known as a cattle shipping point. Taylor arrived in 1881 and built a small cabin near the water tank, using the structure as both home and store. Her mother assisted her in the store, and when a post office opened in Lariat, the two women ran it. Lillian later married rancher Charles Fassett and renamed the business the L. L. Fassett Store.

By 1884 the Empire Farm Company and the Empire Canal Company had begun developing holdings in the area and platted the town of Lariat, soon renamed Henry for Empire Farm Company official T. C. Henry of Denver. The community was obviously intended to be a place for families, as Henry allowed no saloons.

Under the name Del Norte Land & Canal Company, Henry built four canals, totaling 140 miles, to eventually irrigate 500,000 acres. He controlled properties called North Farm and South Farm, then bought the Alamosa, Excelsior, and Empire Farms, which were partially financed by Alamosa businessmen. But by 1885, Henry had overextended himself and the Traveler's Insurance Company took control of most of the property. Henry retained the Alamosa, Excelsior, and Empire Farms, but the community he'd helped build changed its name to Monte Vista in 1886. The Fassetts relocated their store to the new town, which by then had a school.

Thanks to its location, Monte Vista became the gateway to the San Juan Mining District. It also remained a major agricultural area. Potatoes were a primary crop, and the "Peavine" railroad spur, an independent line built between Monte Vista and Center in 1913, hauled other produce from the valley as well, including lettuce and sugar beets. A sugar beet processing plant opened in 1915, and additional irrigation canals were built to allow even greater amounts of land to be used for crops.

LA VETA

Located on CO 12 at La Veta Pass, a few miles south of US 160, the town of La Veta has become known in recent years as an artist's colony, but the area is still big ranch country. Some of the ranches were originally part of the 1843 Sangre de Cristo Grant (see Mexican Land Grants, earlier in this section).

As settlers moved into the valley, Fort Francisco, built here in 1862, became a commercial center for the area as well as a protective presence. In 1876 a narrow-gauge railroad was built through La Veta. The original train depot was moved into town not long ago and refurbished, and it is now listed on the National Register of Historic Places.

From La Veta, CO 12, a Scenic and Historic Byway called the Scenic Highway of Legends, runs south and east to Trinidad, traversing an ecologically diverse area of canyons, lakes, and forests. Following her Indian captivity in 1838, Rachel Plummer may have been describing this area when she wrote this passage:

> The country north of the trace leading from Missouri to Santa Fee [the Santa Fe Trail] is rocky mountaineous, abounding with such variety of animals that pages could not describe them. The natural face of the country is romantic, and to get on top of one of the high mountains you can see one mountain beyond the other, until they are lost in the misty air. You will see the valleys covered with numerous herds of wild Horses, Buffaloes, Elks, and various other animals.

CO 159 and CO 150
New Mexico Border—Great Sand Dunes National Park and Preserve
62 MILES

GARCIA

The earliest Colorado settlement on the Sangre de Cristo Mexican land grant was on Costilla Creek in present Garcia. Settlers built crude homes there in 1849. The community originally went by the name Plaza de los Manzanares, for two early residents, brothers Manuel and Pedro Manzanares. When the Garcia brothers obtained permission for a post office here, the town changed its name to Garcia.

SAN LUIS

The first four settlers on Culebra Creek arrived in 1850, building homes at San Pedro, less than a mile from San Luis, with permission from Sangre de Cristo Grant owner Carlos Beaubien. Indians quickly drove the newcomers out, but they returned the next year along with other men. More attacks caused another withdrawal, followed by another return in the spring of 1852, at which time the Mexicans settled in both the San Pedro and San Luis areas. The intrepid immigrants dug an irrigation ditch for growing corn, beans, wheat, and vegetable gardens. Under the land grants, water was held in common, but on April 10, 1852, the settlers recorded a water right for the San Luis People's Ditch. It was the first water right claimed in Colorado. The San Pedro Ditch, recorded shortly afterward, was the second, and several more followed.

The challenges of living in the isolated valley became somewhat easier in 1857 when Dario Gallegos opened a store in San Luis (originally known as Culebra), where he stocked cornmeal, salt, dried fruit, tobacco, green coffee, sugar, chocolate, matches, yard goods, and other items. So in demand were Gallegos's goods that he found it hard to keep enough merchandise on the shelves of his twenty-by-forty-foot building. The original adobe store burned in 1895, but Gallegos rebuilt it. After Gallegos's death, his daughter and her husband, Antonio Salazar, ran the store, keeping it in operation through the twentieth century.

María Jaquez built the first flour mill in the San Luis Valley in 1856, on the south side of the Conejos River a couple miles east of Guadalupe, using lava stones for the grinding operation. Within a few years, H. E. Easterday, recognizing the potential customer base from a growing number of prospectors looking for minerals in the nearby mountains, had built his American Flour Mill in San Luis. Farmers hauling their grain to the mill significantly increased the traffic on the north-south road between Costilla, New Mexico Territory, and San Luis. The added business helped establish San Luis as the major town in this part of the valley.

In addition to the mill, Easterday and his partner, well-known Taos trader Ceran St. Vrain, opened a store. In his request for goods to stock the store, Easterday also asked St. Vrain to "buy us a good strong negro woman that can do all kinds of house work, and bring or send her with the wagons." Prior to the Civil War, slavery was allowed in Colorado, and Taos had long been a slave-trade center where both Indian and Negro people were routinely bought and sold.

CHAMA

Religious leaders—primarily Catholics—organized churches throughout the San Luis Valley during the 1800s. In Chama, an unusual organization of Catholic laymen, the Los Hermanos Penitentes, settled and spread their beliefs. The Penitentes were known for self-mortification practices, including a reenactment of the crucifixion at Easter. This religious fraternity had its roots in northern New Mexico, then moved north. They were most active in Colorado from 1850 to 1890.

Penitente meeting houses, called *moradas*, were built in towns throughout the region, including present Alamosa, Conejos, Costilla, and Saguache Counties. The Penitentes, who were known for their charitable work, also practiced self-flagellation and other forms of physical penance such as standing on cactuses, walking with stones in their shoes, and binding themselves to crosses. The Catholic Church issued bans against the Penitentes, which drove the brotherhood underground. Although the Catholic Church has long frowned on Penitentes, they continue practicing today.

FORT GARLAND

The town of Fort Garland began as a military post, constructed in 1858 after the abandonment of Fort Massachusetts, six miles to the north. The fort was named after Brig. Gen. John Garland, recognized for meritorious service and gallantry during the Mexican-American War battles of Contreras and Churubusco. It had nine long adobe structures used for barracks and officer's quarters, plus a hospital, laundry, commissary, stables, bakery, and trading post, all built of adobe.

During the Civil War, concern grew about engagements in the West, particularly in New Mexico. Early in the war, the Confederate movement in Texas and New Mexico posed a possible risk to the Union should Southern troops march north into the newly settled region of Colorado. Although Colorado was predominantly sympathetic to the Union, supporters of the Confederacy lived there as well. Organized at Camp Weld, near Denver, in 1861, the Colorado First Regiment Infantry was later stationed at various posts, including Fort Garland. Other army troops were also garrisoned there, and the fort became one of the staging points for organizing volunteer troops in Colorado. McLane's (also spelled McLaine's) Independent Battery Light Artillery used Fort Garland very briefly as a scouting base in October 1863.

Among Fort Garland's commanders, the most famous was Christopher "Kit" Carson, who took on the role in 1866. Carson had spent 1833 in Colorado with mountain man John Gantt before trapping with Jim Bridger in Wyoming. He also traded, trapped, and guided expeditions in Colorado and elsewhere, including John C. Frémont's trips of 1842

Kit Carson spent much time in Colorado, including a stint as commander at Fort Garland.
—Courtesy Colorado Historical Society

and 1843–44. After the Civil War, during which he was made brigadier general, he was assigned to Fort Garland, but he resigned from the army only a year later. The following year, in April 1868, his last wife, Josepha, died after childbirth, and Carson died just a month later, at Fort Lyons near present-day La Junta, from a burst aneurysm.

In 1875 journalist William Rideing visited Fort Garland with the U.S. Geographical Survey. He described the buildings as "flat-roofed, squat, and altogether dispiriting in their unmitigated ugliness. . . . [The] buildings are increasingly dilapidated." Nevertheless, Rideing noted, on the inside the camp was downright cozy:

> *Officers contrive to crowd many significant little evidences of refinement into their incommodious quarters, notwithstanding the difficulty of obtaining anything except the necessaries of life. The rooms are in some instances carpeted with buffalo-robes and bearskins, while the walls are adorned with guns and relics of the chase. To the members of our expedition coming out of the field, this revelation of domesticity and comfort provided a grateful change from the hardships of an American explorers' camp.*

Indian-rights crusader Helen Hunt Jackson saw Fort Garland in 1878, also remarking on its ramshackle appearance. "It is not a fort which could resist a siege—not even an attack from a few mounted Indians," she noted in her book *Bits of Travel at Home.*

*Fort Garland's buildings have been restored
and are now preserved as a museum.*

Fort Garland remained in operation only a few years longer. It was abandoned in 1883, and the troops were transferred to Fort Lewis, near Durango. Private ranchers bought the fort and used it as a headquarters until 1928, when a San Luis Valley organization called the Fort Garland Historical Fair Association bought the property to preserve it. In 1945 the association gave the fort to the Colorado State Historical Society, which still owns Fort Garland and operates it as a museum.

Fort Massachusetts

Although no roads lead to the site of Fort Massachusetts, and nothing remains of it anyway, it was once a significant place. Established in 1852, it was the first U.S. Army post in Colorado. The fort, situated on Ute Creek at the base of Blanca Peak, one of Colorado's Fourteeners (14,345 feet), was far away from primary roads and trails. Being the only outpost in a remote area, it served as an important way-station for explorers in early Colorado, most of whom arrived tired, sore, hungry, and bedraggled. Capt. Randolph Marcy found relief here for his struggling troops in 1857, after completing a harrowing mountain crossing on the way to obtain supplies for Camp Scott, in present Wyoming (see Cochetopa Pass in part 1).

In Gwinn Harris Heap's *Central Route to the Pacific*, about his experiences as a member of an 1853 expedition to explore potential rail routes, the author described Fort Massachusetts as it appeared then:

> *This post . . . is a quadrangular stockade of pine log pickets, inclosing comfortable quarters for one hundred and fifty men, cavalry and infantry. Lofty and precipitous mountains surround it on three sides; and although the situation may be suitable for a grazing farm on account of the pasturage, and the abundance of good timber may render this a convenient point for a military station, it is too removed from the general track of Indians to be of much service in protecting the settlements in San Luis valley.*
>
> *The cavalry at Fort Massachusetts numbered seventy-five men, of whom forty-five were mounted. Though their horses were excellently groomed and stabled, and kept in high condition on corn, at six dollars a bushel, they would soon break down in pursuit of Indians mounted on horses fed on grass. Of this fact the officers at the fort were perfectly sensible.*

Heap replenished his provisions at the sutler's store, had some additional food prepared, had his mules reshod, and bought some supplies. "Everything was put in order for resuming our journey."

Fort Massachusetts was abandoned in 1858, and the troops were moved to the newly built Fort Garland.

GREAT SAND DUNES NATIONAL PARK AND PRESERVE

Great Sand Dunes National Park and Preserve was established as a national monument by President Herbert Hoover in 1932. Encompassing the tallest dunes in North America, some of them 750 feet high, the park also preserves habitat for diverse animal and plant life.

The Sangre de Cristo Mountains border the east side of the park. Hiking trails now traverse two passes over which mountain men and explorers once made their way through the Sangre de Cristos. Mosca Pass (as well as the town of Mosca, in the valley to the west) is named after the Spanish word for mosquitoes or flies. This pass was also called Robidoux Pass for mountain man Antoine Robidoux, originally from St. Louis, who operated trading posts on the Gunnison River in western Colorado and elsewhere.

The other pass, Medano Pass, has also been called Sand Hill Pass or Williams Pass, the latter name for mountain man William Sherley Williams. "Old Bill" Williams trapped and roamed the West with Jedediah

View of Great Sand Dunes National Park and Preserve —Courtesy National Park Service

Two mountain explorers lead their fully laden pack horses (date unknown).
—Courtesy Wyoming State Archives

Smith in the early nineteenth century. He was sixty-one years old in 1848 when Lt. John C. Frémont hired him as a guide through the Colorado mountains on his fourth expedition to find a viable transcontinental railroad route. But Williams actually knew little about the Sangre de Cristos, so the Frémont party missed a better pass over the mountains and descended into the San Luis Valley north of the sand dunes, probably over Medano Pass. When the expedition entered the La Garita Mountains, bad weather hit and they became stranded (see La Garita Mountains in part 1).

In a nearby range is Broken Hand Peak, named after another famed mountain man. Thomas "Broken Hand" Fitzpatrick earned his nickname after accidentally shooting himself in the hand, losing two fingers. After traversing Colorado as a guide for Stephen Watts Kearny's Army of the West in 1846, Fitzpatrick became the Indian agent for the first Cheyenne agency in 1848. Later he negotiated the 1851 Fort Laramie Treaty and another treaty at Fort St. Vrain in 1853. After that, Fitzpatrick left the mountains for St. Louis and never returned. (See also Fort Lupton in part 4.)

US 285
Monte Vista—Fairplay
132 MILES

SAGUACHE

A site some twenty miles west of the present town of Saguache was a popular Ute camping spot known to the Indians as Saguguachipa (Blue Water), for the spring that runs through the place. White traders had trouble pronouncing the Indian name, so they shortened it to Saguache (SUH-watch). Founded around 1866 by Germans mustered out of military service at Fort Garland, the town of Saguache had a street named Sauerkraut Avenue. Early settlers in the area raised wheat, which they harvested with hand sickles.

One early settler, John Lawrence, eventually wrote the bill that led to establishment of Saguache County, earning the title the "Father of Saguache," according to Virginia McConnell Simmons in *The San Luis Valley*. One of Saguache's first developers was Russian entrepreneur Otto Mears. Mears had come to America as a boy and a few years later joined the Union Army. He served with Kit Carson in the Navajo campaigns of the 1860s, and after his 1864 discharge he clerked in a Santa Fe store. He became a partner in retail stores in both Santa Fe and Guadalupe,

New Mexico, before joining with Lafayette Head to build a gristmill and a sawmill in Conejos. Mears moved to Saguache around 1867 to open a new retail store and promote wheat farming. He brought the first threshing machine, mower, and reaper into the Saguache area.

After winning a contract to provide flour to the Ute Indians at the nearby Los Pinos agency, Mears soon developed a friendly relationship with the Tabeguache chief Ouray. But as the government price for flour declined, Mears realized he needed to develop other markets, namely the mining camps. Because the camps were difficult to reach through the mountains, Mears launched the enterprise for which he is best known: road building. He built toll roads over Poncha Pass and Cochetopa Pass and extended routes from Lake City to Silverton and Ouray. Mears became known as the "Pathfinder of the San Juans" and eventually ventured into railroad construction.

FAIRPLAY

Fairplay, a small community at the north end of South Park, started as a mining camp. During the 1859 gold rush, some prospectors grumbled that Tarryall Creek should be called "Grab All" Creek. When those miners found gold farther west, they named their camp Fairplay to reflect their more equitable attitude.

A train engine and depot, water tower, and wagons are among the items and buildings on display at the South Park City Museum in Fairplay.

In 1865, several years after the town's settlement as a gold camp, William H. Stevens, who considered himself a mining engineer, traveled to the area to evaluate its potential for the Pioneer Mining Company. His report was quite favorable:

> Coal is found in great abundance and of a fair quality. Salt is now produced to supply the demand of the Territory. Sulphurate of Soda, a useful mineral as flux to manipulate the ores, is in great abundance. The agricultural privileges are well suited to supply the demands of a dense population. The [South Fork of the] Platte River and its tributaries head near the summit of the great mountain range, and receive a constant supply of pure water.

Now largely a hub for visitors to Pike National Forest, Fairplay is the home of the South Park City Museum, which has a replica of a mining boomtown at its historical museum. Traveling north on CO 9 from Fairplay takes you to I-70 through Alma, over Hoosier Pass (11,541 feet), and down switchbacks to Breckenridge, which started as a gold camp but is now an upscale ski town that attracts thousands of people from around the world each winter.

US 285 and US 24
Poncha Springs—I-70
91 MILES

Few places in Colorado have views as grand as those in the Arkansas River valley between Poncha Springs and Leadville. Several of the state's Fourteeners lie to the west. From south to north, they are Mount Shavano (14,229 feet), Tabeguache Peak (14,155 feet), and Mount Antero (14,269 feet), followed by the Collegiate Peaks—Mount Princeton (14,197 feet), Mount Yale (14,196 feet), Mount Columbia (14,073 feet), Mount Harvard (14,420 feet), and Mount Oxford (14,153 feet)—with other peaks farther west.

Near Leadville, the western skyline is dominated by Mount Elbert (14,433 feet), Colorado's highest peak, but nearby Mount Massive (14,421 feet) is a close second. A bit father north is the famous Mount of the Holy Cross, itself a Fouteener at 14,005. Although the big mountains are to the west, the view to the east has striking peaks of its own, including Cameron Mountain, Green Mountain, and Marmot Peak, all between 10,000 and 12,000 feet tall.

Because of its location in a high mountain valley, this region has always attracted people willing to give up some conveniences in exchange for having recreational opportunities and abundant wildlife right outside their doors. The area is busy year-round, with snow sports in the mountains and rafting on the fast waters of the upper Arkansas River drainage in the summer.

William Henry Jackson's 1873 photograph of the Mount of the Holy Cross —Courtesy National Archives

PONCHA SPRINGS

The name Poncha Springs comes from the area's abundant springs and the Spanish word *poncho*, meaning "cloak" (i.e., warmth), probably a reference to the water's warmth. The town was incorporated in 1880, but the area was inhabited much earlier. Ute Indians camped around the springs from at least the eighteenth century, and explorers stopped here as well. The first homesteaders arrived in the 1860s, and soon the town became a busy stage stop with a store and a hotel. The railroad brought further growth, and by 1883 Poncha Springs had a library, a school, a church, and seventeen saloons.

Several fires in the late 1800s and early 1900s burned many of the town's original buildings, but the historic Jackson Hotel, which hosted such notables as Jesse James and Baby Doe Tabor, still stands. The city of Salida bought Poncha's hot springs in 1935, cemented them over, and piped the water to its own spa resort.

BUENA VISTA

Buena Vista (which locals pronounce BYOO-na VIS-ta, anglicized from the Spanish for "beautiful view") was settled around 1864. The first county seat was in Granite, just north, but in 1880 voters decided to move it to Buena Vista. When Granite residents refused to release the records, a group of Buena Vistans confiscated a railroad engine and flat car, took it to Granite, and raided the courthouse for the documents. By 1928 Salida had surpassed Buena Vista in population, and a new vote moved the county seat south once again. The Buena Vista courthouse was turned into a school and later became the town museum.

LEADVILLE

Gold mining in the upper Arkansas valley, which began in the early 1860s, produced only limited returns, and by the mid-1870s the region was virtually deserted. But in 1877 prospectors near Leadville struck silver, and the rush was on.

Life in Leadville was challenging. The camp sat near the Continental Divide at an elevation of more than 10,000 feet, so residents faced bitter temperatures and strong winds. Furthermore, the riotous town teemed with people and animals, and the confusion was compounded by the

National Mining Hall of Fame in Leadville, honoring the region's mining era

jumble of goods coming into Leadville every day. One account from an unidentified source in *A Colorado History* noted, "Hundreds of freighters arrived daily, their cargoes dumped in confused heaps within twenty enormous warehouses, without attempt at sorting, classifying, or indexing. Merchants with waiting storerooms and clamoring customers were frenzied by their inability to secure consignments after arrival."

Supplies had to be hauled over mountain passes to the high-country camp. Railheads at Canon City, Colorado Springs, and Denver were more than seventy-five miles from Leadville, and the terrain was steep, rocky, and rugged. Thus freighting was expensive, which was one reason that prices in the town were very high. Whiskey could command hundreds of dollars per barrel, and hay cost up to $200 per ton in the winter. Another reason for the exorbitant prices was the fact that people in the boomtown were wealthy enough to pay them. The building of a wagon road over Loveland Pass lowered freighting costs somewhat, but only a rail line could truly ease the problem. Railroad companies vied to build in the area, but the competition became brutal and progress was stymied. The railroad conflict became known as the Royal Gorge War (see Royal Gorge, later in this section).

The Tabor Opera House still stands in downtown Leadville.

By 1879, Leadville boasted 31 restaurants, 51 grocery stores, 17 barbershops, 4 banks, an astonishing 120 saloons, and reportedly the best red-light district in the country. In November, H.A.W. Tabor opened the Tabor Opera House to provide some culture in the rowdy boomtown. Residents of the many smaller mining camps in the Leadville area—including Kokomo, Robinson, and the Eagle River and Holy Cross Districts—also took advantage of the larger town's amenities. From 1882 to 1887, the famous Doc Holliday spent time in Leadville, working at Hyman's Saloon, adjacent to the Tabor Opera House.

Leadville had three daily newspapers. One of them, the *Chronicle*, was edited by Carlyle Channing Davis, who moved to Colorado in 1876 for his health and became an editorial writer for the *Rocky Mountain News*. Lured by tales of Leadville's opportunities, Davis headed there and with Col. John Adkins and printer James M. Burnell formed the Chronicle Publishing Company. But before they could get their printing outfit together, two other editors hit Leadville and started newspapers, one the *Reveille* and the other the *Sentinel*. Both morning dailies were already in operation when the *Chronicle* began publication on January 29, 1879. Within a year, Davis had become sole owner of the *Chronicle*. Writing news columns and cryptic editorials, he often kept his two pistols in plain sight of anyone who might differ with his views.

Over Leadville's first decade, the population skyrocketed from about 500 people to more than 24,000. Among the newer residents were James Joseph Brown and his wife Margaret. He worked as a mine superintendent, eventually making a fortune as others had done. After striking it rich, the Browns moved to Denver. They later had marital difficulties and separated. Margaret "Molly" Brown became a famous survivor of the *Titanic* disaster in 1912 (see Denver in part 5).

To turn Leadville's silver ore into bullion, fourteen smelters were operating by 1881, generating refined silver along with clouds of smoke. The smelting took a toll not only on the air quality, but also on the landscape; thousands of trees were cut down to be used as fuel for the smelter boilers. The smelters were operated mostly by immigrants from Italy, Austria, Croatia, Serbia, and Slovenia. These workers were not getting rich, but others certainly were. Perhaps the most notable of these lucky men was Horace Tabor.

Rags to Riches to Rags

Horace Austin Warner Tabor, who had prospected and run stores in several South Park gold camps, including Oro City and Buckskin Joe, moved his store to the new camp at Leadville in 1877. There he helped organize the municipal government, became the first mayor, and worked as a tireless promoter. The move would lead him into a life of incredible wealth and influence.

One day, two shoemakers-turned-prospectors came into Tabor's store complaining that they had run out of funds. Tabor grubstaked them, meaning he provided them with supplies in exchange for a share of any discoveries they might make. Soon the two struck the great lode of the Little Pittsburg Mine. Within a year the Little Pittsburg Mining Company holdings were valued at $20 million, and Tabor held the controlling interest. Meanwhile he also purchased other claims.

A few years later, while serving as lieutenant governor, Tabor became involved with a much younger woman, Elizabeth McCourt, better known as Baby Doe. When he divorced his wife, Augusta, and married his mistress, it was a social scandal of the first order. Although tolerated by Leadville residents because of his mines' tremendous profits, Horace and Baby Doe were ostracized in Denver society.

Even so, everything Tabor touched seemed to turn to silver. Some $2 million in silver was extracted from the Leadville district in 1878, and more than $9 million the following year. Over the 1880s, some $82 million in silver was shipped from Leadville. But Tabor's luck did not last forever. After serving a short term as a U.S. senator from Colorado, he eventually lost his fortune and returned to hard-rock mining. He died in Denver in April 1899.

Labor Disputes

On May 26, 1880, the Miners' Co-operative Union, a Knights of Labor local assembly, went on strike at the Chrysolite Mine in Leadville. In addition to stagnant wages and long hours, the miners' complaints included prohibitions against smoking and talking socially during working hours. Hundreds of miners walked off the job. "The Stranglers," a citizens' executive committee, was formed to keep order. When that measure failed, Governor Frederick W. Pitkin called out the Colorado State Militia. The strike continued until June 17, when the miners returned to work, mostly at their previous wages. Some of the union leaders were forced out of their jobs.

Mining operations continued at full speed until 1893, when a crash in silver prices led to cutbacks at many mines. On September 4, 1893, miners agreed to wages of $2.50 per day as long as the price of silver was less than 83 1/2 cents per ounce and if prices remained high for supplies and transportation. By 1896, the agreement was tacitly abandoned.

When miners in Leadville, now with the Western Federation of Miners, went on strike again in June 1896, mine managers secretly organized and hired scab workers from Missouri. Tensions erupted, and a mob destroyed the Coronado Mine on September 21, leading to deployment of the Colorado National Guard. The militia remained in Leadville until the following March and finally broke the strike. The miners returned to work under terms dictated by their employers.

Other strikes occurred elsewhere in Colorado during this period. Miners in Cripple Creek walked out in 1894 and again in 1903. In 1899 unmarried Italian miners in Lake City refused to stay at the company boardinghouses, leading to a strike. In 1903, in addition to the Cripple Creek strike, miners walked out in Colorado City and Idaho Springs.

CAMP HALE

The route along US 24 between Leadville and I-70 crosses Tennessee Pass and goes past the site of Camp Hale, where the U.S. Army's Tenth Mountain Division trained for fighting in the mountains of Italy during World War II. Camp Hale, in the Eagle River valley, was the only U.S. military installation ever established solely to train troops for winter and mountain warfare.

When Russia invaded Finland in November 1939, the Finnish soldiers on skis proved to be effective fighters. This led Charles Minot (Minnie) Dole, president of the National Ski Patrol, to begin working to establish alpine troops for the U.S. Army. The first unit of the Eighty-seventh Infantry Mountain Regiment was activated on December 8, 1941, just one day after the bombing of Pearl Harbor. Early training took place on Mount Rainier in Washington, and the National Ski Patrol became the recruiter for the Eighty-seventh Mountain Infantry. Some of those troops participated in the Kiska Campaign in the Aleutian Islands near Alaska.

Soon, however, the rugged landscape of the Colorado Rockies was recognized as a better training ground, and on July 13, 1843, the Tenth Mountain Division was organized at Camp Hale as the Tenth Light Division (Alpine). Combat power was provided by the Eighty-fifth, Eighty-sixth, and Eighty-seventh Infantry Regiments. Camp Hale, at 9,200 feet, had more than 1,000 temporary structures, including barracks, administrative buildings, stables, a veterinary center, a hospital, and a field house. The location gave soldiers a taste of the brutal weather and mountain conditions they might encounter in Europe.

The U.S. Ski Patrol recruited 2,500 men for the Tenth Mountain Division, including Olympic skiers, forest rangers, college students, and even Europeans. The men learned to build and live in snow caves and igloos, scale cliffs, travel cross-country on skis or snowshoes, and make their way over canyons on cables. After a year of training, the men of the Tenth Mountain Division were deployed to Italy, where their decisive victories helped end World War II.

After the war, some veterans of the Tenth Mountain Division returned to the Colorado Rockies to live and play. They helped popularize skiing in Colorado, building ski areas and lodges, improving equipment, and opening ski schools in places like Vail and Aspen.

Although the Tenth Mountain Division was deactivated after World War II, the army used Camp Hale periodically until it was dismantled in 1965. But on February 13, 1985, the Tenth Mountain Division was officially reactivated at Fort Drum, New York. Since that time, infantry troops from the division have had a role in many military engagements, including operations in Kuwait and Iraq in 1990 and 1991; Somalia in 1992–94; Mogadishu, 1993; Haiti, 1994–95; Bosnia, 1997; Afghanistan, 2001–03; and Iraq, beginning in 2003.

US 50
Salida—Pueblo
97 MILES

The route along the Arkansas River between Salida and Pueblo, now US 50, has been traveled for centuries. Before it became a modern road, it was a trade route at least from the time of the Pike expedition in 1806, and American Indians used it long before that. The most prominent natural feature along the route is the Royal Gorge of the Arkansas River, a deep canyon carved over time by the power of the river.

The Arkansas River provided water for early residents of this region. Today, the city of Pueblo has enhanced this area along the Arkansas as the Pueblo Riverwalk.

SALIDA

First known as South Arkansas, Salida, north of the San Luis Valley, was established in early 1880 after the Denver & Rio Grande Railroad successfully built through the Royal Gorge. After a new rail line made Salida a division point for the route to Leadville, D&RG board member and former Colorado territorial governor Alexander C. Hunt prepared the town's plat. The D&RG built a hospital, the Monte Cristo Hotel, a roundhouse, and some shops. In the early days the town's fortunes were tied to the railroad, but Salida also became a trading spot for miners from throughout the mountain country and for ranchers and farmers in the Arkansas River valley.

Like many other western towns built of wood, Salida had fires. Major blazes swept through the downtown business district in 1886 and 1888, leading city officials to create "fire blocks," where all buildings had to be brick. Those blocks ran from Front Street (now Sackett Street) to Fourth Street between C and H Streets. As a result, most of the buildings erected in downtown Salida between 1888 and 1905 are still standing and in use.

Salida's relationship with the D&RG remained healthy until the 1950s, when the railroad moved its division point out of town; most of the railroad facilities in town were subsequently demolished. The

Along the Denver & Rio Grande line in 1905, near Cripple Creek. Along the route are gravel piles from mining operations. —Courtesy Wyoming State Archives

railroad's decision was a substantial economic blow to the community, but Salida rebounded, diversifying its economy by developing tourism, regional trade, homes for retirees, and agriculture.

ROYAL GORGE

In the late 1870s, as fortune seekers rushed to the upper Arkansas valley in search of lead and silver, it quickly became clear that profitable mining operations required fast transportation—namely, a railroad. The Denver & Rio Grande and the Santa Fe Railroads had both already laid tracks in the area, the former around Canon City and the latter around Pueblo. But a big obstacle stood before each of them: the granite walls of the Royal Gorge.

On April 19, 1878, the Santa Fe Railroad sent a hastily assembled construction crew from Pueblo to begin grading at the mouth of the gorge. The D&RG also sent graders to the gorge, but the Santa Fe workers blocked them, winning the first round in the two-year fight that became known as the Royal Gorge War.

When the D&RG attempted to gain a right-of-way in the Royal Gorge, the Santa Fe obtained a court injunction against them. The D&RG filed an appeal. In the meantime, the work crews at the site were becoming violent. The D&RG men constructed stone forts above the roadbed and harassed the Santa Fe crews, throwing rocks down on their

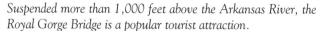

Suspended more than 1,000 feet above the Arkansas River, the Royal Gorge Bridge is a popular tourist attraction.

heads. They threw their rivals' tools in the river and sabotaged their work. Eventually, the D&RG prevailed when the U.S. Supreme Court granted it the primary building right through the gorge.

Today, the Royal Gorge Route Railroad is the only passenger train that travels through the steep granite walls of the Royal Gorge. From both open-air and closed cars, riders can see the remains of some of the D&RG workers' stone forts. The only thing as impressive as looking up from the train at the stark canyon walls is standing on the Royal Gorge Bridge, the world's highest suspension bridge, and gazing down 1,053 feet to the rushing waters of the Arkansas River. Many people drive over the bridge, but to get the full impact of this engineering marvel, you have to walk on its worn wooden planks, feeling them buck and shake from the movement of the traffic.

BUCKSKIN JOE

On the northern edge of Royal Gorge Park is the re-created mining town of Buckskin Joe. The original town, built in 1859, was northwest of Fairplay, near present Alma. Named for miner Joseph Higgenbottom, whose attire earned him the nickname "Buckskin Joe," the little mining

The H.A.W. Tabor general store is the only building in Buckskin Joe that came from the original mining camp.

camp quickly grew into a significant town. Within two years, Buckskin Joe had about 5,000 residents, a newspaper, two banks, a post office, several dance halls and saloons, and other businesses. It even served as the county seat from 1862 to 1866. Famous entrepreneur H.A.W. Tabor opened a general store here in 1861 (see also Leadville, earlier in this section). The store is the only building in the new Buckskin Joe that came from the original mining camp.

The old West town was re-created at its present site in the 1950s. It has served as a location for more than twenty films, including *Cat Ballou* and *True Grit*. When it isn't being used as a backdrop for movies or commercials, Buckskin Joe hosts gunfights, hangings, a medicine show, and other events for tourists. Visitors may also enjoy horse-drawn trolley rides, horseback riding, gold panning, and tours of the Isabell Mine. Scenic excursion trains to the Royal Gorge leave regularly from town.

CANON CITY

Two institutions dominate the history of Canon City: the Santa Fe Railroad and the Colorado State Penitentiary. Trains have been loading passengers at the town's Santa Fe depot for more than a century, and the prison has been housing convicted felons even longer. Reflecting the latter's role in its history, Canon City recently opened the Museum of Colorado Prisons.

In 1869 Canon City had the choice between the state penitentiary and the state university; it chose the penitentiary. The prison attracted national attention on October 9, 1929, when a group of prisoners, led by Danny Daniels, took several guards hostage in one of the worst prison riots in Colorado history. Taking control of one of the cell houses, Daniels threatened to kill the captive guards unless he and his friends were allowed to go free. When prison officials refused his demand, Daniels made good on his threat and shot the guards one by one. During the nightlong standoff, Daniels killed eight guards as well as four fellow prisoners before finally killing himself.

PUEBLO

Spaniards came to what is now Pueblo sometime between 1664 and 1680 in pursuit of Pueblo Indians who had fled their homes in present New Mexico to escape Spanish rule. Juan de Archuleta lead the search and found the fleeing Indians in a place known as El Quartelejo. The location of El Quartelejo is uncertain.

The fleeing Indians were brought back to New Mexico, but in 1680 the Pueblo leaders staged a revolt that forced the Spaniards out. In 1692 the Spaniards regrouped and, led by Diego de Vargas, marched north from El Paso to again establish supremacy over the Puebloans. Four years later, however, the Picuris Pueblo people fled to El Quartelejo once again. In 1706 Juan de Uribarri crossed Colorado to recover the Picuris, marching through today's Trinidad and Pueblo. Near present Haswell, he captured sixty-two runaway Indians and returned them to Santa Fe. While in the area, Uribarri laid claim to the region for Spain, then ruled by Philip V.

By 1719 increasing reports that the French had ventured into the region had the Spanish government deeply concerned. After a Spanish Council of War was held in January 1720, then-governor Valverde ordered Pedro de Villasur into the field. On the Platte River in Nebraska, Frenchmen attacked Villasur's troops, killing Villasur and many of his men. Further Spanish probes into Colorado, Nebraska, and Kansas were also foiled by the French. Eventually, however, during a war with the British in 1762, France ceded all lands west of the Mississippi River to Spain, which controlled the region for the next forty years. During that time, Spain sent several exploratory expeditions into Colorado, including those of Juan Maria Rivera in 1765 and Fathers Francisco Domínguez and Silvestre Vélez de Escalante in 1776.

American Settlement

In 1806 Zebulon Pike camped at present-day Pueblo, and just west of there he built the first American structure in Colorado. Sixteen years later, mountain man Jacob Fowler built a log house and horse pen near Pueblo, but he soon left to pursue trapping opportunities elsewhere. The next development was the establishment of Fort Cass (also called Gantt's Fort), a trading post built in 1832 by Virginian John Gantt, a former army captain turned trader. The post was used for only two years, but soon more traders came into the region. In 1842 mountain man Jim Beckwourth established a settlement called El Pueblo, or Fort Pueblo, at the confluence of Fountain Creek and the Arkansas River. He described the town's genesis in his autobiography, *The Life and Adventures of James P. Beckwourth*:

> In the fall I returned to the Indian country, taking my wife with me. We reached the Arkansas about the first of October, 1842, where I erected a trading-post, and operated a successful business. In a very short time I was joined by from fifteen to twenty free trappers, with their families. We all united our labors, and constructed an adobe fort sixty yards square. By the following spring we had grown into quite a little settlement, and we gave it the name of Pueblo.

Francis Parkman visited Fort Pueblo in 1846 and described it as "nothing more than a large square enclosure, surrounded by a wall of mud, miserably cracked and dilapidated," but he added that the surroundings were beautiful. "Tall woods lined the river, with green

Re-creation of Fort Pueblo at El Pueblo History Museum

meadows on either hand; the high bluffs, quietly basking in the sunlight, flanked the narrow valley."

Mormon soldiers who were unable to serve with the Mormon Battalion during the Mexican-American War spent the winter of 1846–47
in a camp near Fort Pueblo, a replica of which now stands in downtown
Pueblo. "Mormon Town" had one long street with about fifty houses
and a large tabernacle for prayer meetings and dances. During their time
there, the men learned how to make adobe bricks. But they had no desire to settle permanently in the area, and in the spring they traveled
north along the Trappers Trail to Fort Laramie, where they met their
families, then continued on to Deseret (Utah). There they helped construct a fort using adobe bricks.

By the time the Mormons left, two villages, called Punble and Hardscrabble, had developed near Pueblo. Both were protected by twelve-
foot-high adobe walls. In his 1847 report to the commissioner of Indian
Affairs, Indian agent Thomas Fitzpatrick wrote, "Those villages are becoming the resort of all idlers and loafers. They are also becoming depots
for the smugglers of liquor from New Mexico into this country; therefore
they must be watched."

The twin settlements, Fitzpatrick noted, were composed mostly of
American, French, Canadian, and Mexican former trappers and their
Indian wives, but two families were Mormon. In spite of the "idlers and

Interior of store at El Pueblo History Museum

loafers," the villages were not transient camps. "They have a tolerable supply of cattle, horses, mules &c.; and I am informed that this year they have raised a good crop of wheat, corn, beans, pumpkins, and other vegetables. They number about 150 souls, and of this number there are about 60 men, nearly all having wives, and some have two."

On Christmas Day in 1854, the settlement at Pueblo suffered an Indian attack. Mouache Utes raided several ranches, killed fifteen men, and captured a woman and two boys. The military immediately sent troops from Fort Union, in present New Mexico, under Gen. John Garland. The Indians withdrew from Pueblo and crossed into the San Luis Valley, where they raided more ranches. The military pursued the Utes throughout the winter and spring, eventually forcing them to surrender.

A few years later, the settlers around Fort Pueblo were joined by miners. In July 1860, following gold discoveries in the nearby mountains, the present city of Pueblo was established. In 1990 Fort Pueblo was reconstructed near its original site and is operated as the El Pueblo History Museum.

Charles Goodnight Ranch

A few miles west of Pueblo, on the south side of the Arkansas River, pioneer Texas cattleman Charles Goodnight and his wife, Mary Ann Dyer Goodnight, established a ranch in 1869. Goodnight's partner, Oliver

Loving, had driven the first cattle into Colorado in 1866, pioneering a cattle trail from Fort Belknap, Texas, to Denver. On his first trip, Loving took "Uncle Dick" Wootton's toll road over Raton Pass. But Goodnight, refusing to pay the toll of twenty-five cents per man and five cents per head of cattle, forged a new trail farther east, passing through Trinchera, east of Trinidad. Thus the famous Goodnight-Loving Trail was created.

The next year Goodnight and Loving took another herd north over the trail, but on that journey Comanche Indians wounded Loving, who later died near Fort Sumner. Goodnight took the herd through to Denver, then retrieved his partner's body and took it back to Texas. More than a century later, author Larry McMurtry immortalized the story in his famous novel *Lonesome Dove*.

Goodnight raised cattle at his Pueblo ranch, which he called Rock Canyon Ranch, until 1876. He started with Texas longhorns but eventually imported shorthorn bulls to upgrade his herds. He raised corn for feed and planted a large apple orchard on the ranch. While living in the area, Charles and Mary Goodnight helped establish the Methodist Episcopal Church.

In 1873 Goodnight and some partners organized the Stock Growers Bank in Pueblo, but after the bank lent money to fellow ranchers at low rates, the Panic of 1873 struck. The crash, Goodnight later said, "wiped me off the face of the earth." This was an exaggeration, however. Goodnight returned to Texas, where he and the Irish-born John Adair started the JA Ranch, which eventually ran about 100,000 head of cattle in the Palo Duro Canyon area. The stone barn Goodnight built near Pueblo is now listed on the National Register of Historic Places.

CO 69 and CO 96
US 50 at Texas Creek—Pueblo
81 MILES

From US 50, which runs along the Arkansas River, CO 69 heads south through the beautiful Wet Mountain valley to Westcliffe. From there, CO 96, part of the Frontier Pathways Scenic and Historic Byway, passes through the historic mining town of Silver Cliff, past a few ghost towns and an old stage stop, and through the San Isabel National Forest before continuing east to Pueblo.

WESTCLIFFE

Westcliffe, in the Wet Mountain valley east of the Sangre de Cristos and west of the DeWeese Plateau, began as one of the first agricultural colonization projects in Colorado. In 1869 Carl Wulsten, president of the newly organized German Colonization Society in Chicago, sent a committee to Colorado Territory to select a site for their colony. They decided on a spot in the Wet Mountain valley and appealed to Congress for a 40,000-acre land grant. The request was denied, so the society organized some 300 settlers to go there and claim individual homesteads.

Arriving by train at Fort Wallace in western Kansas, the colonists, led by Wulsten, prevailed upon the army to give them some wagons and provide a military escort to their homesteads. By March 1870, the German colonists were building homes and plowing fields in the Wet Mountain valley. They named their settlement Colfax, in honor of U.S. Vice President Schuyler Colfax, and agreed to pool their resources and revenues.

Almost immediately, however, dissension arose. Wulsten was described as "hot-headed, arbitrary, and impracticable." Eventually James Judd replaced Wulsten as president, but the tensions remained. The final blow came when the federal government seized the colony's lumber and shingles, claiming that they failed to pay fees for the timber. Before long, most of the settlers had left the valley. Many of them found individual success on their own, but the colony itself was a complete failure. A decade later, the town of Westcliffe was established near the site of Colfax by Dr. William A. Bell.

CO 67 (PHANTOM CANYON ROAD)
US 50—Cripple Creek
28 MILES

Near Florence, east of Canon City, CO 67 becomes a backcountry road heading north to the gold-mining country of the Pikes Peak District. The original wagon road, built in 1894 and called the Florence and Cripple Creek Free Road, was soon replaced by the Florence & Cripple Creek Railroad, known as the Gold Belt Line. Today's Phantom Canyon Road follows the old narrow-gauge railroad bed to Cripple Creek. This rugged mountain road is unpaved and has one-lane sections where it is often necessary for vehicles to pull over to allow oncoming cars to pass. Only drivers who want a taste of old-time travel should take this rough gravel road.

VICTOR

With Pikes Peak overlooking it like a sentinel, Victor was once a good-sized city but is now a very small town. The hill just above Victor had the richest mines in the Pikes Peak district, and even the ground on which the town was built was laced with gold. Workers digging building foundations sometimes found gold, and some of the gravel covering the streets had ore in it. In 1936 the town mined ore right in front of the post office, raising $5,000.

Victor was involved in the violent mining strikes of 1903. The state militia was sent in to restore order, but after the troops withdrew the situation deteriorated again. On June 6, a riot broke out in Victor, leading to many injuries and at least two deaths. The militia was once again dispatched to stop the fighting. In the end, the mine owners set up a system that successfully broke the union's strength.

CRIPPLE CREEK

Cripple Creek sits in the heart of what was known as the Bowl of Gold, one of the most important gold-production areas in Colorado. The Hayden Survey first discovered gold in the area in 1874, but the ore did not appear to be plentiful enough for profitable mining. Ranchers took over the region while miners looked elsewhere. A decade later, a

Mining relics dot the hillsides around Victor.

View of Cripple Creek around 1903 —Courtesy Wyoming State Archives

prospector reported scooping up gold nuggets by the handful, causing a brief rush to the area. Again, the finds were disappointing.

Finally, in 1891, intriguing reports of gold from cowboy Bob Womack prompted serious explorations in the high rocky country. Soon Cripple Creek, with its legendary Independence and Washington Mines, was on its way to becoming the richest gold town in Colorado. Mining continues here today, and more than $800 million in gold has come out of the region to date.

Like other mining towns, Cripple Creek was originally built of wood, and fires soon destroyed most of the town's first incarnation. The first blaze broke out in a parlor house and quickly spread. Residents dynamited some buildings in an effort to stop the conflagration, to little avail. Nearly a third of the business district was destroyed. Five days later, another fire roared through town, torching most of what was left and killing a dozen people. Cripple Creek was almost immediately rebuilt, this time using brick and stone. Many of those buildings remain as cornerstones of the town.

By 1900 the new Cripple Creek boasted 139 saloons, 3 hospitals, 34 churches, 14 newspapers, 41 assay offices, and dozens of doctors, dentists, and lawyers. By 1903 Cripple Creek was linked to Victor by electric trolley lines, and railroads such as the Florence & Cripple Creek and the Colorado & Midland also served the community, whose population had ballooned to around 35,000.

Labor Strikes

In 1894 miners balked at their employers' demand that the workday be extended from eight to ten hours a day with no increase in pay. When the mine owners refused to negotiate, the miners went on strike. Skirmishes erupted between miners and scabs, and soon the situation became so contentious that the sheriff called in state troops. In the end, the workers won the dispute, but at a cost. Thirty-seven miners were eventually brought up on charges including dynamiting a mine and instigating riots. During a trial in Colorado Springs, animosity ran so strongly against the miners that one of their attorneys was abducted from his room at the Alamo Hotel by fifteen masked men, who then stripped him, applied a coat of tar and feathers, and left him to walk the five miles back to town.

Various other labor strikes occurred in Colorado over the next several years, such as those in Leadville and Idaho Springs. Some of them became violent; most were unsuccessful. In 1903, after the demands of ore-mill workers in Colorado City failed, union organizers again headed to the mines around Cripple Creek. Another slew of strikes and violence followed, and again the state militia came in to restore order. This time, the union was crushed. The Western Federation of Miners, however, would regroup as the United Mine Workers of America and try again, leading to further bloody conflicts (see Trinidad and Ludlow in part 3).

US 24 and PIKES PEAK HIGHWAY
US 285 at Antero Junction— Manitou Springs
71 MILES

US 24 runs through the heart of the area known as South Park, first developed as a mining region in the 1860s. In August 1859, miners struck pay dirt on Tarryall Creek. Denver's *Rocky Mountain News* reported: "Five days ago the rush began for South Park; ever since, a continual stream of miners have passed through our streets. Wagons, carts, pack animals and footmen—all heading one way; all bound for the same destination—the head waters of the Platte."

South Park included the mining camps of Tarryall, Fairplay, Buckskin Joe, and several others. Many of these camps were abandoned when the gold ran out. Today, a wealth of recreational opportunities brings visitors to South Park year-round.

Near Cascade, US 24 connects to the Pikes Peak Highway, which leads to the summit of Pikes Peak. This is the second-highest-elevation automobile road in the state, exceeded only by Trail Ridge Road in Rocky Mountain National Park. The first people to ascend Pikes Peak, which is about ten miles west of Colorado Springs as the crow flies, made the steep, rocky climb on foot or muleback, but eventually a carriage road and a cog railway made the trip easier. The current highway follows the winding route of the old carriage road, and the cog railway still operates. The first automobile ascended Pikes Peak on August 12, 1901, driven by W. B. Felker.

The Pikes Peak Highway was built as a toll road in 1915. It became a free highway for a time, but due to high maintenance costs, it became a toll road again in 1948. Once popular for automobile races, the partially paved road, no longer a toll road, now serves mostly tourists and recreationists.

Some mules, circa 1900, follow the rails of the cog railway that served traffic from Colorado Springs to Pikes Peak. —Courtesy Wyoming State Archives

The view from the rocky summit of the peak is stunning. Foothills and plains lie to the east, and the massive peaks of the Rocky Mountains surround the north, south, and west. As testiment to its inspiring vista, Katharine Lee Bates wrote the classic song "America the Beautiful" after her visit to the peak.

PIKES PEAK

In his journal entry for November 15, 1806, Zebulon Pike described the moment he first saw the Rocky Mountains and the peak that now carries his name: "At two o'clock in the afternoon I thought I could distinguish a mountain to our right, which appeared like a small blue cloud. . . . When our small party arrived on the hill they with one accord gave three cheers to the Mexican mountains."

Pike himself never ascended his mountain namesake, which he called the Grand Peak. Other early maps labeled it simply Highest Peak. While camped at today's Pueblo, Pike explained his decision not to attempt the summit:

> The summit of the Grand peak, which was entirely bare of vegetation and covered with snow, now appeared at the distance of fifteen or sixteen mile from us, and as high again as what we have ascended, and would have taken a whole day's march to have arrived at its base, when I believe no human being could have ascended to its pinical. This with the condition of my soldiers, who had only light overalls on, and no stockings, and every way ill provided to endure the inclemency of the region; the bad prospect of killing anything to subsist on, with the further detention of two or three days, which it must occasion, determined us to return.

The first man known to have climbed Pikes Peak was Dr. Edwin James, a member of Maj. Stephen Long's expedition, in 1820. Carrying blankets, buffalo meat, and some cornmeal, James and two companions started up the mountain. It took them two days to reach the summit. Along the way James collected specimens of the alpine plants growing there. The Long party called the mountain James Peak in his honor, but in the end it was the earlier name that stuck. In 1835 Col. Henry Dodge officially recorded it as Pikes Peak.

More than half a century after Pike explored this region, others made their way into these rugged mountains intent on striking it rich. In 1858 gold discoveries in the mountains west of Denver led to the frenzy that came to be called the Pikes Peak gold rush, named for the prominent landmark, although gold wasn't found around the peak itself for another two decades.

The first woman known to have scaled the peak was Julia Holmes, who had traveled there with an early group of prospectors in 1858. In her letters, Holmes wrote of watching the stones she dislodged during her climb roll into the "yawning abyss." At the top, she paused to write her mother, "In all probability I am the first woman who has ever stood upon the summit of this mountain, and gazed upon this wondrous scene which my eyes now behold."

MANITOU SPRINGS

During the Pikes Peak gold rush, miners flooded central Colorado seeking fortune. For the ones who found it, Manitou Springs was established to help relieve them of the burden of carrying extra gold in their pockets. Here the wealthy could enjoy fine dining, fine lodging, and fine libations, as well as the mineral springs' naturally carbonated waters. Both drinking from and soaking in the springs, which bubble up from underground limestone aquifers, were thought to be healthful, even curative. The effervescent waters drew health seekers throughout the late nineteenth and early twentieth centuries.

After the fad of "taking the waters" died down, Manitou Springs adapted and became a general summer tourist town, offering hotels, restaurants, and entertainment for travelers passing through the area. Revived interest in the springs in the late twentieth century led to their restoration, and the town remains a popular vacation spot today.

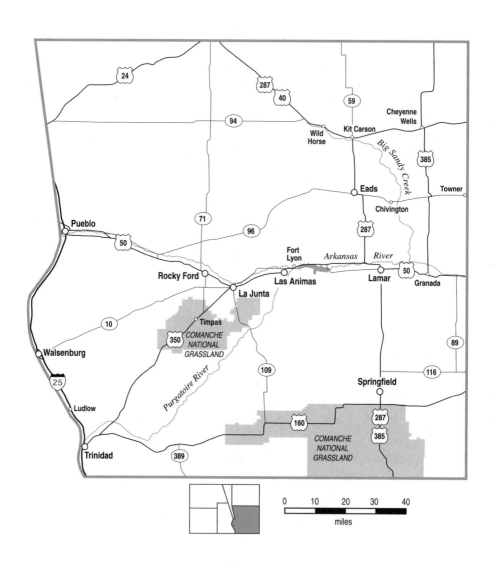

PART THREE

Southeast
SANTA FE TRAIL AND
SMOKY HILL TRAIL COUNTRY

Southeastern Colorado's rolling plains country, with its lush river bottoms, attracted thousands of buffalo up until the mid-1800s. Indians including the Cheyennes, Arapahos, Kiowas, and Comanches took advantage of the herds for food and hides. The area was also a major travel corridor for the first explorers and traders in Colorado. This part of Colorado, as designated in this book, is bordered on the north by I-70, on the west by I-25, on the south by New Mexico and Oklahoma, and on the east by Kansas.

The establishment of the Santa Fe Trail in 1821 and Bent's Fort, near present La Junta, in 1833 spawned early development in this area. After the buffalo were killed off in the early 1870s, ranchers claimed vast sections of these prime grazing lands, where they were soon running tens of thousands of cattle. Homesteaders also claimed land for growing wheat and other crops. Agriculture is still an important part of the economy today, and the land along the Arkansas River near Rocky Ford is particularly known for its cantaloupe. But harsh conditions on the plains, particularly drought, continue to challenge farmers and ranchers. In 2002 residents faced drought conditions that surpassed even those of the 1930s Dust Bowl.

Mining also played a big role in the development of this part of Colorado. In the early 1900s, labor disputes erupted in the mining areas of southern Colorado, including the towns along the southern part of I-25—Trinidad, Ludlow, and Walsenburg. The situation came to a head in a conflict known as the Southern Coal Field War.

In this section, we will travel from south to north and east to west, basically following the pattern of early travel and settlement. We will begin with I-25 and move on to US 350 and US 50, which trace the general path of the Santa Fe Trail through Colorado.

Southeastern Colorado's temperate climate and water from the Arkansas River make this region ideal for agriculture. Fruit stands are a common sight in summer and fall.

I-25
Trinidad—Walsenburg
37 MILES

TRINIDAD

The streets of Trinidad are crooked. That's because they overlie the Mountain Branch of the Santa Fe Trail. Oxen and mules tended to walk in zigzag patterns as they pulled their heavy loads, and the crooked trails they made became crooked roads. William Becknell made his first trip through the area in 1821, forging the trade route known as the Santa Fe Trail, but travelers had passed through the valley long before, and Indians had frequented the region for generations.

One of the first settlers in the Trinidad area was Gabriel Gutiérrez, who in 1859 found range here for his sheep. Prospectors Felipe Baca and Pedro Valdez camped at the site of present Trinidad in 1860, en route to the gold diggings at Cherry Creek (near present Denver). They noted that the land along the Purgatoire River seemed promising for agricultural production, and later that fall, Baca returned to claim land.

When homesteaders Riley Dunton and William Frazier arrived, they decided that the little settlement needed some organization. Joined by brothers Albert and Ebenezer Archibald and Dr. John Whitlock, who had been chief of surgeons with the New Mexico Volunteers, Dunton and Frazier took it upon themselves to lay out some streets. The present intersection at Commercial and Main Streets in Trinidad is where the Santa Fe Trail and the north-south road from Denver came together. In all, five streets made up the original town of Trinidad.

The early residents raised cattle and sheep, and herds still range in the area today. But Trinidad also had rich coal seams, and coal mining soon became an important industry. In 1867 Frank Bloom began what was likely the first commercial coal mine in the area. The coal was removed in wheelbarrows and later in horse-drawn sleds. Eventually, wagons on wooden rails transported coal from Trinidad's mines, known as the Southern Coal Fields. With these industries and its long-standing connection to the Santa Fe Trail, Trinidad quickly became the commercial center for the region.

Trinidad War

In its early years, Trinidad had a diverse population of Mexican farmers, Anglo settlers, and miners from Italy, Greece, Bulgaria, Slovakia, and

This sculpture in downtown Trinidad depicts the area's coal mining heritage.

Japan. Around Christmastime in 1867, an impromptu wrestling match escalated into a full-fledged conflict between Mexican and white residents. Frank Blue, a driver for the Barlow & Sanderson Stage Company, issued an open challenge to anyone willing to wrestle him. Soon Blue found a taker, a stout Mexican. The contest quickly became a division of cultures, with Anglo residents supporting Blue and Mexican residents backing the other man. Blue quickly got the upper hand, slamming the Mexican to the ground and breaking his leg in the process.

The violence touched off the crowd, and the Mexicans came after Blue, who fled into a nearby adobe house. In the melee, Pablo Martínez was shot and killed, further inflaming the irate mob. The Mexicans tore up the roof of the house Blue was in, but Blue remained unharmed. Sheriff Juan N. Gutiérrez arrived, took Blue into custody, and escorted him to a guardhouse. The sheriff left six Anglos and six Mexicans to watch the prisoner.

On New Year's Day, a friend of Blue's arrived on the scene with men he had recruited from out of town. They persuaded Deputy Juan Tafoya to release Blue, then started off for the Colorado Hotel. En route they were confronted by some of Trinidad's Mexican residents, and a shootout ensued. The Anglos retreated into the hotel, where they were held under siege. Cutting portholes in the hotel's walls and constructing a barricade with lumber and sacks of flour, Blue and company transformed the Colorado Hotel into a makeshift fort. At least two Mexicans were killed and several were wounded that day.

Both the Anglo and the Mexican factions in the "Trinidad War" wanted army intervention to quell the conflict, and local authorities sent a request for federal troops to Fort Lyon. The troops arrived on January 5, under the command of Brev. Brig. Gen. William H. Penrose. Troops from Fort Reynolds joined them, and the combined forces quickly established martial law in Trinidad. Eventually Blue and his friend escaped from the hotel, and the other men surrendered their weapons.

W. R. Thomas, a reporter for the *Rocky Mountain News* in Denver, suggested that Blue's supporters had incited the riot, but in the end all charges were dropped and the federal troops departed.

Southern Coal Field War

By the early 1900s, coal mining employed a significant percentage of Colorado's population. The Colorado Fuel & Iron Company and other big mining corporations had immense political power, and they all but owned their employees. Workers, who were largely immigrants and mostly from eastern and southern European countries, were allowed to live only in company housing, to shop only at the company store, and to see only the company doctor. Moreover, working conditions in the mines were unhealthy and unsafe, but this was of little concern to the mining companies.

By 1913 the United Mine Workers of America had already been active in the coal fields north of Denver and near Frederick. A miner's strike up there was still in a stalemate when the union moved in to organize the Southern Coal Fields, the mining region between Trinidad and Walsenburg. On September 16, 1913, the United Mine Workers of America held a special convention in Trinidad. Among other things, their demands included increased wages; recognition of the union; eight-hour work days; enforcement of mining laws; the right to choose where they lived and where they purchased goods; and the right to visit any doctor they chose.

The miners already knew they would not get what they asked for, so union organizers prepared for a strike. They leased some land in the area and put up tents for temporary housing. As expected, soon after the miners walked off the job on September 23, they were forced out of their company homes, so they moved to the tent camps, including one at Ludlow, eighteen miles north of Trinidad.

When the strike began, the Colorado Fuel & Iron Company, which operated the Southern Coal Field mines and many others, was also ready for it. The company had already hired literally hundreds of deputy sheriffs, several from the Baldwin-Felts Detective Agency, to enforce its rules and intimidate union members. The deputies were armed and even had an armored train car, complete with a machine gun. The miners called it the "Death Special."

A show of force against the strikers came almost immediately. On October 15, fifty picketing miners were arrested and marched at gunpoint, with the Death Special rolling down the railroad track behind them, to Trinidad, where they were placed in the Las Animas County Jail. Two days later, the Death Special appeared at the camp in Forbes. One of the men got out of the armored train car and approached the strikers, waving a white handkerchief tied to the end of a stick. In his account of the strikes, *Buried Unsung*, Zeese Papanikolas described what happened next:

> As he came up he asked if they were Union men, and receiving their reply in the affirmative, he threw down the flag, jumped to one side and said, 'Look out for yourselves.' At that the machine gun cut loose on the crowd. One hundred and forty-seven bullets were put through one tent; a boy 15 years old was shot 9 times in the legs; one miner was killed, shot through the forehead.

The conflict between the deputies and the strikers continued through the autumn. Miners were threatened, beaten, and shot at by snipers. An explosion in a mine in New Mexico briefly diverted attention from the Colorado strikes, but even while union organizers were in New Mexico to help with the emergency, the situation in the Southern Coal Fields deteriorated. In Walsenburg, strikers shouted taunts at the wife of a scab worker as she was moving her furniture. The jeering turned to screams of horror when deputies began shooting. Three strikers died.

On November 20, George Belcher, one of the Baldwin-Felts gunmen, stepped out of the Hausman drugstore in Trinidad and was shot in the back of the head. Belcher was widely hated in Trinidad, so few people offered information about the shooter. In apparent retaliation, a number of residents were arrested on varying charges. Finally, five days later, a man admitted he had killed Belcher and implicated two union organizers in the plot. Several union organizers were arrested and held at the Las Animas County Jail, but no charges were ever filed.

In the meantime, the escalation of tensions prompted Governor Elias Ammons to order the Colorado National Guard to the strikers' camps. Although Company owner John D. Rockefeller had several chances over the winter to settle the strike, he failed to take advantage of them, and the standoff continued into 1914. In the spring, most of the Guard soldiers were withdrawn because of financial constraints. Soon afterward, in April 1914, one of the most violent episodes in U.S. union history occurred at the camp in Ludlow (see Ludlow, later in this section).

Retaliations followed the Ludlow incident, but within ten days, federal troops arrived and ended the violence. Eventually the miners called off their strike. Many of them returned to work in the mines; others sought new occupations. It took nearly two more decades for the union finally to establish itself in Colorado.

Mother Jones

It was in Trinidad that the United Mine Workers of America held their 1913 convention. Among the burly miners was a frail-looking woman, her hair neatly coiled into a topknot. She was the "most dangerous woman in America": Mary Harris Jones, aka "Mother Jones." She had come to Trinidad to help the miners organize a strike. Having been involved in coal strikes in West Virginia, she knew what she could be up against. Upon her arrival in Trinidad, she wrote to friends back East, "They have my skull drawn and two cross sticks beneath my jaw to tell me that if I do not quit they are going to get me."

Mother Jones was a tough woman. In West Virginia, she had told company gunmen, "I've sat on a bumper inhaling mule farts and it smelled better than you sons of bitches." In Trinidad, she led marches and made speeches. And at the Ludlow mining camp, north of Trinidad, she organized the women and taught them how to defend their homes and families. She handed out rifles to the strikers, saying, "I hope you use it."

Jones was jailed on January 4, 1914, in Trinidad, but authorities held her for only a few hours, then put her on a train to Denver. On January

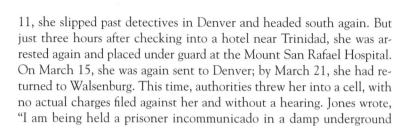

11, she slipped past detectives in Denver and headed south again. But just three hours after checking into a hotel near Trinidad, she was arrested again and placed under guard at the Mount San Rafael Hospital. On March 15, she was again sent to Denver; by March 21, she had returned to Walsenburg. This time, authorities threw her into a cell, with no actual charges filed against her and without a hearing. Jones wrote, "I am being held a prisoner incommunicado in a damp underground cell. . . . [But] not even my incarceration . . . will make me give up the fight in which I am engaged for liberty and for the rights of the working people. . . . I shall stand firm."

Jones remained in Colorado through the trying times at the Ludlow camp until the strike was resolved. Her union activities made her a legendary figure in labor history.

LUDLOW

Early in the twentieth century, Ludlow, about eighteen miles north of Trinidad and just west of I-25, was the site of the infamous "Ludlow Massacre," part of the brutal labor conflict known as the Southern Coal Field War. Today, a monument to the victims stands in a small park just west of I-25, placed there by the United Mine Workers of America. Vandals damaged part of the memorial in 2003.

It was raining when the striking miners and their families moved to their new tent camp in September 1913. Only sixteen tents were in place when they arrived, but the families found a canteen, set up by union organizer John Lawson, where they could get hot coffee and bottles of milk. Some of the miners had only a few of their possessions with them. In Segundo, for example, when miners tried to retrieve their things from their company-owned residences, enforcers turned them back. The Colorado Fuel & Iron Company deputies tried to bar the miners' way into the tent camps as well, but eventually they made it through. In the process, however, they killed company guard Bob Lee. It was the first violent act of the Southern Coal Field strike.

Once completed, Ludlow Camp was the largest of the striker camps, home to some 1,300 people. There was a Greek bakery, a few stores and saloons, and even a post office. The hundreds of tents were set up in orderly rows. Some had underground pits in which to hide women and children should the camp be attacked, as everyone at Ludlow fully expected it would be, having heard reports of violence at other tent camps, such as Forbes and Delugua.

On October 9, during a baseball game, the first shots were fired in Ludlow, aimed at but missing the players. That same day, however, a striking miner working at a nearby ranch was shot and killed. Coupled with the incidents at other camps, the shootings left Ludlow residents in

This monument honors those killed in the attack on the Ludlow miners' camp on April 20, 1914.

a state of near panic. They feared that the company's armored train car, dubbed the "Death Special," would move down the nearby rail tracks, spraying them with machine-gun fire.

The situation was clearly escalating, and soon Governor Ammons ordered the Colorado National Guard to the area. Ludlow residents were told that the soldiers would disarm both the strikers and the company guards, and that scab workers would not be allowed to enter the mines. The Guardsmen of Company K set up their own tents at the camp. Initially things settled down as the soldiers engaged in games and dances with the strikers. But the Guardsmen had been told that if violence erupted, they were to shoot to kill.

The ones to fear, the militia believed, were the Greeks. It was true that some of the Greek miners had refused to surrender their guns. The *Trinidad Chronicle-News* reported on November 4 that "a band of war-like Greeks . . . have been carrying on guerrilla warfare in the hills for weeks and . . . have repeatedly declined to obey the orders of the strike leaders."

By April 1914, most of the National Guardsmen had been with-drawn. The remaining militia was composed mostly of mining-company guards and volunteers. On April 19, Greek Orthodox Easter, the Greek residents of Ludlow celebrated by roasting a lamb and playing some baseball games. During the festivities, four armed militiamen rode up to the camp, and the women traded taunts with them. Before they rode away, the militiamen made some ominous comments, leaving the strik-ers with a feeling of dread. At a dance that night, tensions between the guards and the strikers mounted.

In the morning, four militiamen demanded to talk with union orga-nizer Louis Tikas. They ordered Tikas to surrender one of the men in the camp, but he refused. The residents expected that the guards would soon return in force to search the camp. Instead, they saw two flare bombs explode from the militia camp. It was a signal for reinforcements. Al-most immediately, gunfire broke out. It isn't clear which side fired first. Women and children fled, some seeking refuge in the tent cellars, as the militia sprayed machine-gun fire at the camp.

The shooting continued through the day. That evening, many of the tents caught fire, and the militiamen marched in. Some helped pull women and children from the tent cellars; others just looted. In one of the cellars, two women and ten children suffocated from the smoke. It was later dubbed the "Death Pit."

Eighteen Ludlow residents died that day, eleven of whom were children. Also killed were union organizer Louis Tikas and four other strikers. Charges were brought against two members of the Colorado National Guard, but both men were acquitted.

WALSENBURG

The original settlement at what is now Walsenburg was known as La Plaza de los Leones (the Square of the Lions), after a prominent Spanish family. The city of Walsenburg was laid out in 1873 by Fred Walsen, a German merchant, at which time it was given his name. Walsen also opened the first mine in the area. Today, Walsenburg is the seat of Huer-fano County and the home of the Walsenburg Mining Museum.

US 50 AND US 350
Kansas Border—Trinidad
168 MILES

The famous trade route known as the Santa Fe Trail, which linked western Missouri to Santa Fe (then part of Mexico), developed two branches. The longer northern one, the Mountain Branch, followed the Arkansas River across eastern Colorado, basically parallel to present US 50, then angled south near La Junta, along what is now US 350, toward Raton Pass, south of Trinidad at the New Mexico border. The southern branch, called the Cimarron (or Jornada) Route, followed the Cimarron River and cut through only the far southeastern corner of present Colorado. The Cimarron was the more heavily used route.

Early explorers traveled parts of the Mountain route before it became an established trail. One of the first was Frenchman Pierre Vial, who

Today, sandstone markers commemorate the route of the Santa Fe Trail.

traveled from St. Louis to Santa Fe in 1792. American Zebulon Pike followed the Arkansas River portion of the future trail on his 1806 expedition over the Sangre de Cristo Mountains.

Father of the Santa Fe Trail

William Becknell developed the Santa Fe Trail as a trade route in 1821, shortly after Mexico won its independence from Spain. Mexican independence opened the door to lawful trade relations with the United States. Even before the official word reached St. Louis, Becknell had anticipated the outcome and organized a trading company. He took out an ad in the *Missouri Intelligencer* to recruit partners: "Every man will furnish his equal part of the fitting on for our trade, and receive an equal part of the product. If the company consist of 30 or more men, 10 dollars a man will answer to purchase the quantity of merchandise required to trade on."

But Becknell's party had only three or four men and some pack mules when it left Arrow Rock, Missouri, on September 1, 1821, arriving in Santa Fe in November. The trip was very profitable, however, and upon the traders' return, news of their success caused a frenzy, as Robert Duffus later recalled: "My father saw them unload when they returned, and when their rawhide packages of silver dollars were dumped on the sidewalk one of the men cut the thongs and the money spilled out and clinking on the stone pavement rolled into the gutter. Everyone was excited and the next spring another expedition was sent out."

The next year, Becknell had twenty-one men and three fully laden wagons. This time, they weren't the only ones on the trail. Col. Benjamin Cooper and fifteen men had already left Missouri, and trappers Jacob Fowler and Hugh Glenn and traders Thomas James and John McKnight were hot on Becknell's heels.

Knowing he would never be able to take his heavy, cumbersome wagons through the mountains, Becknell forged a cutoff along the Cimarron River and across northeastern New Mexico. This route was shorter and avoided the mountains, but it was also more dangerous because water was scarce. Taking the new route almost cost Becknell his life and the lives of his men. Crossing the desert, the men ran out of water and resorted to cutting the ears of their mules so they could drink the blood and killing their dogs for the same reason. In spite of its hazards, the southern trail became the preferred route of many travelers over the next several decades.

Expanding Commerce

Trade with Mexico was lucrative: silver, furs, and mules were among the prizes to be had. Recognizing the Santa Fe Trail's importance, Missouri senator Thomas Hart Benton sponsored legislation in 1825 to survey the route. The survey's goal, Benton wrote, was "thoroughness," point-ing out that "it is not a County or State road which they have to mark out but a highway between Nations." President James Monroe signed the legislation, which provided $10,000 for the survey itself and an ad-ditional $20,000 for gifts to offer Indian tribes in exchange for right-of-way across their lands.

Soon traders were hauling massive amounts of goods over the trail in huge Conestoga wagons. From 1826 to 1835, 775 wagons carried $1,365,000 worth of merchandise along the route. Among the goods transported were cotton cloth, sewing notions, ready-made clothing, and hardware such as tools and knives, along with hundreds of other items. At Santa Fe, traders obtained gold and silver coins as well as woolen blankets, beaver pelts, mules, and other things to resell in Missouri.

Traders were not the only ones using the Santa Fe Trail. The military made much use of the route, especially during the Mexican-American War. In 1846 Stephen Watts Kearny led his Army of the West over the trail to Santa Fe, where he claimed the region for the United States. Af-ter the war, the army established several posts along the route to protect freighters and other travelers.

With the increased security, commerce burgeoned. Stagecoach com-panies established mail and passenger lines, and some of the stations eventually grew into towns. Although only limited numbers of emi-grants used the Santa Fe Trail, traffic did pick up during the 1849 gold rush as prospectors and entrepreneurs took the trail to Bent's Fort, where they picked up the Cherokee Trail to Fort Bridger, and from there con-tinued west to California. Miners also used the Santa Fe Trail during the Colorado gold rushes.

Construction of the Atchison, Topeka & Santa Fe Railroad, com-pleted in 1879, reduced the need for freighting over the Santa Fe Trail and ultimately led to its demise as a trade route.

Raton Pass Road

From Becknell's first trip, the Santa Fe Trail's Mountain Route saw gradual improvements, but getting wagons over the steep and rugged Raton Pass remained nearly impossible until trapper Richens Lacy "Uncle Dick" Wootton built a road over the pass in 1866. Originally from Virginia, Wootton worked in the fur trade for years before settling down on the Colorado side of Raton Pass. After taking a stab at farming, Wootton decided to build a toll road to earn his living:

> I had long had in mind the building of a stage road through the 'Raton Pass,'
> and when I made up my mind to quit farming . . . I thought it a good time
> to put through my road project. I had been over the mountains so often . . .
> that I knew almost every available pass in Colorado and New Mexico. . . .
> I knew that the Raton Pass was a natural highway, connecting settlements

*already in existence, and destined to be a thoroughfare for other settlements.
. . . What I proposed to do was go into this winding, rock-ribbed mountain
pass, and hew out a road, which barring grades, should be as good as the
average turnpike.*

Obtaining charters from both the Colorado and New Mexico territorial governments, Wootton built his thoroughfare. He charged 25 cents
per person, $1.50 per wagon, and 5 cents per head of cattle; to Indians,
however, he gave free passage. He operated the toll road until 1878,
when the railroad bought his right-of-way.

GRANADA

The tiny community of Granada, near the Kansas state line, is mostly
known for the nearby site of Camp Amache, a World War II relocation
camp for people of Japanese descent. Established in 1942 as the Granada
Relocation Project, Camp Amache was one of ten such camps built during the war. The compound housed thousands of ethnic Japanese evacuees, nearly two-thirds of whom were American citizens, primarily from
California.

Camp Amache relocation center in Granada, 1940s
—Courtesy National Archives (210-6-E415)

In January 1942 President Franklin D. Roosevelt signed Executive Order 9066, authorizing the relocation of all U.S. residents of Japanese ancestry to guarded internment camps. Both immigrants and native citizens were required to register with the Wartime Civil Control Administration, after which they had one week to put their personal affairs in order and make arrangements to leave their homes, businesses, major belongings, and even their pets. They were allowed to take only whatever clothing, bedding, toilet articles, and kitchen goods they could physically carry. In spite of the government's treatment, many Japanese Americans volunteered to serve in the U.S. military during the war.

A truckload of evacuees bound for Camp Amache
—Courtesy National Archives (210-6-E72)

In all, some 110,000 men, women, and children were ordered to the various camps. Camp Amache housed a total of about 10,000 internees from 1942 to 1945, with a peak population of 7,318. The compound included barracks, stores, schools, a hospital, and other buildings, as well as an adjacent farm.

No buildings remain at Camp Amache, but a few structural foundations and some of the roads are still visible. A monument at the site is dedicated to the camp's internees, especially those who died in U.S. military service during the war.

LAMAR

Travelers on the Santa Fe Trail followed the Arkansas River into Colorado, as did many others before and after. A monument dedicated to women who traveled the wagon trails, the Madonna of the Trail, stands in a park in Lamar. The twelve-foot granite statue of a woman with two children is one of twelve such monuments in the United States.

Lamar was originally established as Blackwell by cattleman A. R. Black, but when the railroad arrived in 1886, the town's name was changed in honor of L.Q.C. Lamar, Secretary of the Interior under President Grover Cleveland. With plenty of water available from the Arkansas River, Lamar began as an agricultural community and remains so today.

FORT LYON

The original Fort Lyon was established in 1860 as Fort Wise, near present Granada. On June 25, 1865, it was renamed Fort Lyon for Nathaniel Lyon, a Civil War general who died in the 1861 Battle of Wilson's Creek in Missouri. The fort was an important staging location for Colorado troops during the Civil War. Three companies of the First Regiment Infantry from Camp Weld, near Denver, were transferred to Fort Wise in late 1861. In March 1862, they marched from Fort Lyon to Fort Union, New Mexico, where they joined other Colorado regiments in the battles at Glorieta Pass. In 1864 several companies from the First Colorado Regiment at Fort Lyon were part of Col. John Chivington's command at the infamous Sand Creek Massacre.

Due to its vulnerability to flooding from the Arkansas River, the original Fort Lyon was abandoned on June 9, 1867. The new post was built about two and a half miles below the mouth of the Purgatoire River, in an area less flood prone. Fort Lyon II remained in service until October 1889. The following January, the military reservation was transferred to the Interior Department. In 1934 the post became a United States Veterans Hospital.

LAS ANIMAS

At Las Animas, US 50 crosses the Purgatoire River, which according to legend was named El Rio de Las Animas Perdidas en Purgatorio (the River of Lost Souls in Purgatory) after Spanish soldiers searching for gold died in the vicinity without receiving last rites. Later, Anglo ranchers and cowboys corrupted the French trappers' Purgatoire into "Picket Wire."

Preceding Las Animas was Las Animas City, built in 1869 as a stopover for Santa Fe Trail travelers. Four years later, the Kansas Pacific

Railroad built another town, West Las Animas, which grew as Las Animas City faded. Today, the Kit Carson Museum celebrates the early days of Las Animas and Bent County.

Situated in the heart of southeastern Colorado cattle country, Las Animas was and still is a trade center for ranchers. Homestead laws of the early twentieth century encouraged expanding agricultural development in this region. Large ranching operations in the Purgatoire River valley included the Eugene Rourke family ranch, which eventually grew from a 160-acre homestead to 73,500 acres, and the huge Prairie Cattle Company.

Brothers James, Peyton, and Stephen Jones organized the J.J. Cattle Company in 1869, expanding it to 2.2 million acres on which they ran some 55,000 head of cattle and 300 horses. In 1881 the brothers sold to Scottish investors, who formed the Prairie Cattle Company. The company had holdings in Colorado, New Mexico, Oklahoma, and Texas. Net profit the first year totaled $50,000 and soared to $125,000 the next year, when the company branded 26,000 calves.

Like other big ranches of the era, the Prairie Cattle Company used land it didn't own. As homesteaders staked legal claims to land along the Purgatoire River, they (and a few squatters) began fencing their land, restricting access to grazing areas and water holes. In addition, a congressional investigation in the late 1800s authorized the removal of the company's unlawful enclosures. Faced with these difficulties, the Prairie Cattle Company voluntarily dissolved in 1915.

BENT'S OLD FORT NATIONAL HISTORIC SITE

Just north of La Junta is a reconstruction of William Bent's original trading post, a significant place in Colorado's early development. Bent, believed to have been the first permanent white settler in Colorado, played a key role in the Centennial State's history. Born in Charleston, Virginia (now West Virginia), in 1809, Bent later moved to St. Louis with his family. His elder brother, Charles, was a fur trader on the Upper Missouri River, and in 1829, William accompanied him on a trading excursion over the Santa Fe Trail.

Over the next two years, William took part in two trapping expeditions, during which he befriended the Cheyenne Indians, who would remain an important part of his life. He eventually married a Cheyenne named Owl Woman. The Cheyennes had moved onto the plains near the Arkansas River in the 1820s after being pushed out of their native Great Lakes homeland. Other tribes also traded in the area, including the Arapahos, the Kiowas, and occasionally the Comanches.

In 1831 Charles and William Bent joined with St. Louis trader Ceran St. Vrain in forming the Bent, St. Vrain Company, a commercial trade business that would last eighteen years and cover thousands of square miles in Colorado, New Mexico, Texas, Oklahoma, Kansas, Nebraska, Wyoming, Utah, and Arizona. The company opened its first store in Taos, and in 1833 William Bent oversaw the construction of an adobe trading post on the Arkansas River. Initially dubbed Fort William, it was eventually called Bent's Fort. After the post was abandoned and Bent's New Fort was built, the original site became known as Bent's Old Fort.

William Bent's ties to the Cheyennes meant that the fort had a ready trade market when it opened, and it took very little time for the Bent, St. Vrain Company to dominate trade in the upper Arkansas River valley. The 142-by-122-foot adobe fort had twenty-six rooms surrounding a small courtyard, with space inside for corrals, a black-smith shop, and wagon sheds, as well as trading areas. The American flag flew over the structure. In 1847 George Frederick Ruxton described the fort in detail:

> The walls are built entirely of adobes—or sun-burned bricks—in the form of a hollow square, at two corners of which are circular flanking towers of the same material. The entrance is by a large gateway into the square, round which are the rooms occupied by traders and employees of the host. They are small in size, with walls coloured by a white-wash made of clay found in the prairie. Their flat roofs are defended along the exterior by parapets of adobe, to serve as a cover to marksmen firing from the top. . . . In the centre of the square is the press for packing the furs; and there are three large rooms, one

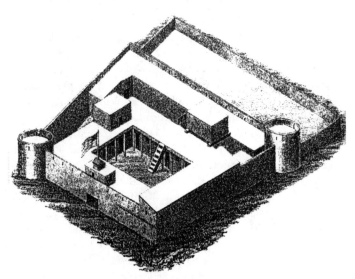

Lt. James W. Abert made this sketch of Bent's Fort in 1845 in his report to Congress.

used as a store and magazine, another as a council-room, where the Indians assemble for their 'talks.' Whilst the third is the common dining-hall, where the traders, trappers, and hunters, and all employes, feast upon the best provender the game-covered country affords.

The year after Bent's Fort opened, the Bent, St. Vrain Company was required to obtain a trading license according to a new law. The two-year license was issued to Charles Bent for three posts: Fort William, Union Point, and an unnamed post on the Colorado River. Trade was allowed "with the Arapahoes, Cheyennes, Kiawas, Snakes, Sioux and Arickaras." Although the licenses specifically prohibited the distribution of liquor, selling whiskey was a common practice in the West. Interestingly, however, by 1847 whiskey trading had become more trouble than it was worth for Bent and other large operators. Indian agent Thomas Fitzpatrick mentioned the issue in a report to the commissioner of Indian Affairs:

The principal traders in the country, have long since ascertained that the traffic in spiritous liquors was becoming very unprofitable, and therefore have, I believe, discontinued it altogether; and, I have no doubt, would willingly assist in putting it down. This laudable change in their business has not emanated from a regard of the law, nor from philanthropic motives, but from the fact of its becoming a great nuisance, and very dangerous to those having large investments in the trade, and whose expenses were heavy, and, not being able to compete successfully with the numerous small traders who infest the country, and whose expenses were comparatively nothing—whose whole stock in trade amounted to only a few trinkets and three or four hundred gallons of liquor, procured on the Missouri frontier, New Mexico, or from the Hudson Bay company.

In 1846 William Bent scouted for Lt. Stephen Watts Kearny on their march to Santa Fe at the start of the Mexican-American War. Kearny took Santa Fe without firing a shot. Charles Bent was named governor of New Mexico, but he served only a short time before he was killed in the 1847 Taos Revolt. The tragedy enraged William, and he immediately made plans to retaliate. But, according to soldier Morse H. Coffin, Bent, supported by hundreds of Cheyenne and Comanche Indians, was "on his way to avenge the death of his brother, when he was met by Kit Carson and persuaded to turn back and relinquish the idea."

Later, Owl Woman died, either in childbirth or perhaps during an intertribal battle. Soon afterward, in 1849, a cholera epidemic devastated the Cheyennes around Bent's Fort, killing nearly half the tribe. The grief-weary Bent abandoned the fort. Legend claims that he burned the fort before he left, but in reality the post served for a time as a stop on the Kansas City, Denver & Santa Fe stagecoach line.

A trader at heart, Bent constructed a new sandstone complex in 1853, near what later became Fort Lyon. Bent's "New" Fort, sometimes referred to as Bent's Trading House, stood on a bluff overlooking the Arkansas River, about eight miles west of today's Lamar. Wagon traveler Luke Tierney wrote of the new post: "It is a strong, massive building, of oblong shape, three hundred feet long and about two hundred feet wide. It presents a beautiful appearance from without. The interior is divided into spacious apartments."

Bent's freighting business and ranching operations had wide-reaching tentacles from the new base. When the Pikes Peak gold rush hit in 1858, Bent was still operating as a trader and working as an Indian agent. The army took over the new fort around 1860. Bent died May 19, 1869.

LA JUNTA

Originally called Otero, for Spanish settler Miguel Otero, La Junta became a trade center and a shipping point for wagons on the Santa Fe Trail. La Junta means "junction" in Spanish, referring to where the Santa Fe Trail split off from the Arkansas River. The Atchison, Topeka & Santa Fe Railroad arrived here in December 1875. Some of the railroad's original buildings still stand, and a local museum is dedicated to La Junta's railroad era.

TIMPAS

Near Timpas, ruts from the Santa Fe Trail are clearly visible from the highway. Just southwest of the present town, Pawnee Indians attacked a Bent, St. Vrain Company trade caravan led by Marcellin St. Vrain in September 1837. One member of the party was killed and three were wounded. The Indians also stole three horses and nine mules carrying more than $3,000 in trade goods. The stolen items included hundreds of dollars' worth of fabrics, twenty-three buffalo robes, three guns, a rifle (taken from the man who was killed), ammunition, some paper and ink, two prayer books worth $20 each, and supplies such as coffee and sugar. The mules and horses, along with their saddles and bridles, were worth over $1,000.

COMANCHE NATIONAL GRASSLAND

Between La Junta and Trinidad, US 350 passes through part of the Comanche National Grassland. Two sections make up this national reserve—the northern part, called the Timpas Unit, is near Timpas and the southern part, the Carrizo Unit, spreads south and west of Springfield. US 350 passes through the Timpas Unit, while the Carrizo Unit is traversed east and west by US 160 and and north and south by US 385.

During the extended drought of the 1930s, known as the Dust Bowl, homesteaders who had claimed lands throughout southeastern Colorado packed their belongings and left. Congress subsequently passed legislation for the government to purchase these failed crop lands, retire them from cultivation, and implement a program to preserve and restore them. By 1938 the Department of Agriculture had acquired 419,095 acres of land, forming the nucleus of what would become the Comanche National Grassland.

The government established a work center south of Springfield and hired citizens to plow the arid land and reseed it with grass. For years, people in the Springfield area called the work center "Little Washington" because of its large number of government employees.

The lands were transferred to the Forest Service in 1954, and in 1960 Congress designated the holdings as a federal preserve, the Comanche National Grassland. In addition to abundant wildlife, these acres of mostly short-grass prairie have numerous archaeological sites, including dinosaur tracks and Indian rock art.

Among the preserved areas is Picture Canyon, in the Carrizo Unit, where prehistoric Indians left petroglyphs on the south canyon walls. Other rock art is visible in the Timpas Unit's Picket Wire Canyonlands, with some sites dating back 4,700 years. Also in the Timpas Unit is a dinosaur trackway with about 1,300 dinosaur footprints preserved in the rocks, representing both adult and juvenile dinosaurs, most of which were sauropods, or plant eaters. Sections of the Santa Fe Trail also passed through this part of the grasslands; the route is marked with signs.

US 50
La Junta—Pueblo
64 MILES

The area east of Pueblo was once cattle country. Where the Huerfano and Arkansas Rivers join, near the present town of Boone, French trader Charles Autobees established a ranch around 1840. Autobees's ranch was a gathering spot for frontiersmen, and from 1861 to 1868, it served as the first seat of Huerfano County, which at that time included nearly all of southeastern Colorado. Today this section of US 50 lies in Pueblo and Crowley Counties, an area that is still mostly rural.

ROCKY FORD

Cantaloupe is the icon of Rocky Ford, Colorado. This popular melon was first planted here by George Swink in 1890, using seeds he ordered from Massachusetts, and it soon became the cash crop of the region.

Cantaloupe is a staple crop in the Arkansas River valley.

As early as 1900, carloads of the fruit were being transported to eastern markets and even shipped to England. Cantaloupe remains a principal crop of this Arkansas River valley community.

FORT REYNOLDS

Capt. William Craig, a West Point graduate from Indiana, established Fort Reynolds on July 3, 1867. Col. Randolph B. Marcy, Inspector General of the U.S. Army, chose the site, on the Arkansas River about two and a half miles above the mouth of the Huerfano River. The fort was named for Gen. John F. Reynolds, who died at the Battle of Gettysburg in 1863.

The post comprised thirty wood and adobe buildings situated around a 400-square-foot parade ground. Facilities included quarters for officers, enlisted men, and laundresses; a three-bed hospital; stables with stalls for eighty-five horses; several kitchens and mess halls; a blacksmith shop; a carpentry shop; and a commissary. The large dining hall was also used for dances that the officers and their wives sometimes hosted for area residents. Fort Reynolds officially closed on July 15, 1872, and the property was transferred to the Interior Department two years later. The land was finally sold to private interests in May 1881.

CO 96
Kansas Border—Eads
41 MILES

TOWNER

In far eastern Colorado, where fierce weather can blow up unexpectedly, more than one tragedy has played out over the years. A particularly sad incident occurred near Towner in March 1931, when a bus full of schoolchildren became stranded during a blizzard.

Bus driver Carl Miller had made it to school without difficulty that Thursday morning, but only a short time later a tremendous plains blizzard struck. School was dismissed and Miller set off to return the children home as quickly as possible. In his urgency Miller took a shortcut, but snow obscured his view and the bus went off the road into a snowbank, whereupon the engine died.

Miller and the twenty children stuck together on the bus during the long frigid night, eating their frozen lunches and burning anything they could—including their schoolbooks—to stay warm. The next day, Miller left the children in the bus and went for help, but the cold was too severe and he died of exposure. The youngsters in the bus did their

Winters can be brutal in this part of Colorado. One snowstorm in 1931 caused a tragic schoolbus accident near Towner. This photo shows the aftermath of another Towner blizzard, in 1949, in which snow nearly buried this house. The children are Bob Lovato, left, and his cousin Pete Barella. —Courtesy Bob Lovato Collection

best to stay warm and alert, exercising and playing games. By the time rescuers found them, the children had been stranded for thirty-three hours. Five of them, including Miller's daughter, Mary, did not survive.

CHIVINGTON

The small town of Chivington takes its name from Col. John M. Chivington, leader of U.S. forces in the most significant Indian-military conflict in Colorado history, the 1864 Sand Creek Massacre. Before this controversial episode, Chivington had a long career as a minister, farmer, freighter, soldier, and officer. During the Civil War, he led Union troops in New Mexico to destroy a Rebel supply train and stop a Confederate advance in the Battle of Glorieta Pass, which became known as the "Gettysburg of the West." In 1863 Chivington was appointed commander of the Military District of Colorado, where he led many missions against the Indians—the last one being the Sand Creek attack—before leaving the army in 1865.

Sand Creek Massacre

The large village of Cheyenne and Arapaho Indians camped on the north side of Sand Creek in November 1864 had been specifically asked to remain in that vicinity, where their people had been promised protection by the army at Fort Lyon. At the camp, Cheyenne chief Black Kettle flew an American flag above his lodge, as the army had advised him to do, as a sign of amity. Yet on the morning of November 29, troops under the command of Col. John M. Chivington attacked the Indian camp in what was described, by nearly all accounts, as a massacre.

Testifying before Congress on March 14, 1865, John S. Smith, an Indian interpreter who witnessed the attack, recalled the early-morning events of November 29, 1864:

> [Just before sunrise] a large number of troops were discovered from three-quarters of a mile to a mile below the village. The Indians who discovered them ran to my camp, called me out, and wanted me to go and see what troops they were, and what they wanted. . . .
>
> I then left my own camp and started for that portion of the troops that was nearest the village, supposing I could go up to them. I did not know but they might be strange troops, and thought my presence and explanations could reconcile matters. Lieutenant Wilson was in command of the detachment to which I tried to make my approach; but they fired several volleys at me, and I returned back to my camp and entered my lodge.

George Bent, the son of trader William Bent and his Cheyenne wife Owl Woman, was with Black Kettle at the time and provided this account:

> When I looked toward the chief's lodge, I saw that Black Kettle had a large American flag up on a long lodge pole as a signal to the troop that the camp

George Bent, son of trader William Bent, with his wife, Magpie. He was present at the Sand Creek Massacre and later wrote of the incident. —Courtesy Wyoming State Archives, Indian Collection

was friendly. Part of the people were rushing about the camp in great fear. All the time Black Kettle kept calling out not to be frightened; that the camp was under protection and there was no danger. Then suddenly the troops opened fire on this mass of men, women, and children, and all began to scatter and run. At the beginning of the attack Black Kettle, with his wife and White Antelope, took their position before Black Kettle's lodge and remained there after all others had left the camp. At last Black Kettle, seeing that it was useless to stay longer, started to run.

Chivington's command of approximately 700 men of the Third and First Colorado Regiments fired upon a camp of about 600 Southern Cheyennes and Arapahos. More than 100 Indians, mostly women and children, were killed in the attack; some estimates were as high as

300. Army casualties were fewer than 10 killed and around 40 wounded. Most of the survivors fled north. After pursuing one band for a while, Chivington arrived back at Fort Lyon around December 10. Some praised Chivington's actions, but critics called for an investigation. Several Congressional hearings were held in the months following the episode, eventually condemning it as a massacre. Chivington, whose military term had expired in January 1865, had to testify but faced no charges.

To understand why the Sand Creek massacre occurred, it is necessary to consider its context. In 1862 a Santee Sioux uprising in Minnesota left many settlers dead, and since then, violence on the plains had been escalating. Many people feared that the Cheyennes and other tribes were poised for their own uprising.

Cheyennes raided throughout the spring and summer of 1864, stealing livestock and supplies, attacking wagons and homes, even kidnapping women. Many settlers and soldiers, including some in Colorado Territory, were killed. A May 30 army report stated, "Some four hundred Cheyennes attacked Lieutenant Clayton on the Smoky Hill. After several hours' fight the Indians fled leaving twenty-eight killed. Our loss was four killed and three wounded. Look out for Cheyennes everywhere."

Among the targets of the Cheyenne raids were several stage stations and homesteads along the South Platte River. A telegram sent from Valley Station (near Sterling) reported, "Women and Children all leaving for Denver. Dead cattle, full of arrows, in all directions. General Indian war anticipated."

In June, a brutal attack on blacksmith Ward Hungate and his family particularly inflamed many Coloradans, including residents of Denver, twenty-five miles to the west. In the June 11 attack, Indians killed and mutilated Ward Hungate, his wife, Ellen, and their two young daughters, Florence and Laura. Local officials put the victims' bodies on public display in Denver. The fear degenerated into near hysteria on July 15, when reports circulated that Indians were camped just nine miles outside Denver. Public outrage had reached a fever pitch, ultimately leading to the retaliation at Sand Creek.

Arapahos had also engaged in hostilities that summer. In one incident, Arapaho raiders stole horses from Charlie Autobees's ranch near Pueblo. In another, they killed two men and captured a white woman near Bent's Fort. On August 14, 1864, Colorado territorial governor John Evans authorized the organization of the Third Colorado Regiment, to serve for 100 days. But for the first three months, these troops saw no major action, and by late November they had become known as the "Bloodless Third." This fact contributed to the events at Sand Creek, as the soldiers sought to prove their mettle.

During the turbulent summer of 1864, Black Kettle, known as a peacemaker, had tried to control the warriors in his band, but the raiding continued. He admitted to government authorities that Cheyennes had attacked and killed settlers in northeastern Colorado, and he acknowledged the coordinated Cheyenne raids at stations and ranches along the Oregon Trail. On September 10, 1864, Black Kettle released four captives to Maj. Edward W. Wynkoop as a show of good faith, but the matter was far from settled.

After his meeting with Wynkoop, Black Kettle appealed to Governor Evans for a peace agreement. But Evans told the chief that only Gen. Samuel Curtis, commander of the Department of Kansas, could grant peace status. Curtis opposed peace with the Cheyennes, writing in a September 28 telegram from Fort Leavenworth, "I shall require the bad Indians delivered up. . . . I want no piece [*sic*] until the Indians suffer more. . . . No peace must be made without my direction."

Black Kettle went to Fort Lyon to surrender his arms, and Wynkoop told the chief that his people would be safe if they stayed near the fort. When General Curtis learned of Wynkoop's actions, he replaced

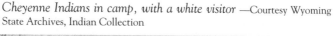

Cheyenne Indians in camp, with a white visitor —Courtesy Wyoming State Archives, Indian Collection

Wynkoop with Maj. Scott Anthony. Anthony, too, assured Black Kettle that "no war would be waged" against the Indians at the Sand Creek camp, but along with Chivington he broke that promise on November 29.

Pvt. Morse H. Coffin, who wrote about Sand Creek in articles in the Greeley *Colorado Sun* in 1878–79, defended the military action as an engagement with hostile Indians who had shot at the soldiers. He admitted, however, that women and children were targeted. "The idea was very general that a war of extermination should be waged; that neither sex nor age should be spared. . . . One often heard the expression that 'nits make lice, make a clean thing of it.'" He explains further in this painful account:

> When we reached the Sand, and in full view of the Indian camp, and distant from it about a half a mile, the command was halted. . . . Colonel Chivington, turning to the command said, 'Boys, I shall not tell you what you are to kill, but remember our slaughtered women and children,' or words similar. . . . A little farther on were two squaws the others had left for dead, but one of these was lying face down, and writhing and groaning in great agony. . . . After thinking it over for a minute or so, and believing it an act of mercy, I drew my revolver and shot her through the head.

The aftermath of the Sand Creek attack was wide-reaching. The Indians, notably the Cheyenne warriors known as Dog Soldiers, retaliated with continued attacks, burning Julesburg, raiding stations along the Overland Stage route for 100 miles, and generally waging war all across the region. The Sioux rose up with their Cheyenne allies to join the fight. As Hunkpapa Sioux chief Sitting Bull put it, "I rose, tomahawk in hand, and I have done all the hurt to the whites that I could." With this escalation of violence, 1865 became known as the "Bloody Year."

In his defense of the Sand Creek attack, Chivington told Congress, "My reason for making the attack on the Indian camp was, that I believed the Indians in the camp were hostile to the whites. That they were of the same tribes who had murdered many persons and destroyed much valuable property." He claimed that the Indians were in a defensive position on Sand Creek, that they had prepared rifle pits, and that no white flag flew over the camp. He also maintained that very few women and children had been killed.

Later, in Denver, Chivington placed the blame for Sand Creek on Major Anthony:

> I was informed that the Indians on Sand Creek were hostile. Major Anthony, commanding the post [at Fort Lyon] . . . informed me, on different occasions, that the Indians were hostile, that he had repeatedly fired upon them; that the Indians had sent him word that if he wanted a fight to come out to Sand Creek and they would give him as big a fight as he wanted; that every man of his command would go gladly, and urged an immediate departure. . . .

> *If Major Anthony, in representing the relations that existed between the troops and the Indians, willfully lied, then Major Anthony is the responsible party.*

Black Kettle survived the attack at Sand Creek. Ever the peacemaker, he signed treaties in 1865 and 1867, moving his people to a reservation in Kansas, then in 1868 to the Washita Valley in Oklahoma. But in a dawn raid on November 27, 1868, troops under Lt. Col. George Armstrong Custer attacked Black Kettle's village, killing dozens of Cheyennes, including Black Kettle and his wife, and taking around fifty women and children captive. Custer also destroyed the village and killed hundreds of Cheyenne horses.

Sand Creek Massacre National Historic Site

Two historical markers memorializing the Sand Creek Massacre were erected in 1950, one on CO 96 near Chivington and the other at what was believed to be the massacre site, on a bluff overlooking the Dawson South Bend of Big Sandy Creek (Sand Creek), about fifteen miles north of Chivington. In November 2000, Congress authorized the establishment of a National Historic Site at and around the Sand Creek battle location.

The Sand Creek Massacre National Historic Site Establishment Act of 2000 was developed with the extensive cooperation of the Kiowa County Commissioners, the Northern Cheyenne Tribe, the Northern Arapaho Tribe, the Cheyenne and Arapaho Tribes of Oklahoma, the state of Colorado, and many property owners in Kiowa County. The legislation recognized about 12,480 acres along Sand Creek in Kiowa County, much of which is on private property, as the potential area of the historic site. As of this writing, archaeological excavations are under way to identify the site and the National Park Service is negotiating to purchase property or obtain access rights from willing owners.

At the Senate subcommittee hearing on the legislation, Colorado senator Ben Nighthorse Campbell, a Northern Cheyenne chief whose ancestors died in the massacre, revealed the discovery of two letters written by soldiers who had been there. The letters, which Campbell called "the Dead Sea Scrolls of Sand Creek," verified oral accounts of the event. "I don't cry often," Campbell testified, "but I had tears in my eyes as I read these letters." He shared some of the details:

> Children were killed while they begged for mercy. Body parts were cut off and used as trophies in a victory parade. One woman actually cut the throats of her own children rather than let the surrounding soldiers torture them. . . .
>
> It may shock some people that, because of a legal loophole, the soldiers who committed these crimes were never tried in civil or military courts. While we can never correct that, we can do something to ensure this nation

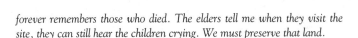

forever remembers those who died. The elders tell me when they visit the site, they can still hear the children crying. We must preserve that land.

EADS

When the railroad arrived in 1887, settlers from Dayton, Colorado, moved their homes and businesses to the new site at Eads to be on the railroad line. Designated the Kiowa County seat in 1901, Eads grew fairly steadily, eventually establishing itself as a supply center for area ranches.

US 40
Kansas Border—I-70
102 MILES

US Highway 40 generally follows the route of the Smoky Hill Trail. It and the Santa Fe Trail were the two major trails across this part of Colorado in the nineteenth century. Named for the Smoky Hills (a low clay ridge between the Smoky Hill and Republican Rivers in present Kansas), the trail offered the quickest way to the Colorado goldfields, but the scarcity of game and water along the route earned it the nickname "Starvation Trail." Broken in by gold seekers in the late 1850s, the trail later served stagecoach lines between the Missouri River and Colorado mining communities.

As news of gold in the Pikes Peak region spread, several Missouri River towns vied for the business generated by the rush, each promoting itself as the best jumping-off place. Leavenworth, Kansas, was the starting point of the Smoky Hill Trail, and Lucien J. Eastin of the *Kansas Weekly Herald* set out to persuade gold seekers that this was the best route to Colorado. In an article published on March 1, 1859, Eastin pointed out that the Leavenworth route made a beeline to Colorado up the Smoky Hill Fork of the Arkansas River. Travelers could shave days off the trip by choosing the Smoky Hill Trail over the well-established northern road (the Oregon-California Trail), which started at Independence, Missouri. It was also more than 100 miles shorter than the Santa Fe Trail.

To back his claims, Eastin published letters from people who had taken the trail, including J. C. Hemingray and F. Hawn, who wrote, "On that route the emigrant can obtain an abundance of wood and water, grass and game; it is about 150 miles shorter than any other. . . .

[Experienced travelers] all concur that the route up the 'Smoky Hill Fork' must become the great thoroughfare to the mines."

But the enthusiasm was premature and misleading. The route had not been fully explored and was in fact dangerous. Eastin's bad advice, combined with a start too early in the year and just plain old bad luck, led to the most horrific tragedy on any trail to Colorado's goldfields.

Tragedy on the Smoky Hill Trail

Three brothers, Alexander, Charles, and Daniel Blue, began their trudge across the plains to the Pikes Peak gold diggings in the early spring of 1859. The next year, Daniel Blue wrote a narrative of the trip entitled *Thrilling Narrative of the Adventures, Sufferings and Starvation of Pike's Peak Gold Seekers on the Plains of the West in the Winter and Spring of 1859.* Blue begins his tragic tale by explaining the impetus for the quest that turned into catastrophe:

> Gold has a magic power upon the human mind. The hope of its possession has infatuated thousands, and the pursuit of it [has] plunged tens of thousands into

With his gold pan tied to the saddle, a miner heads to the mountains (date unknown). —Courtesy Wyoming State Archives

misery and premature graves. . . . No one will either be surprised or blame
me when I state that the object of our undertaking and adventures which
I am about to relate, and which resulted so disastrously to myself and my
companions, was the getting of gold.

Leaving their families in Illinois, the brothers traveled by train to
St. Louis and by steamer down the Missouri River to Kansas City. After
buying a horse in Lawrence, Kansas, to haul their bedding, they proceeded on foot. In Topeka, they added a couple hundred pounds of flour
to the horse's load.

Carrying packs and leading their horse, the brothers started across
Kansas, taking shelter with an Indian during a storm near Manhattan,
then joining John Gibbs and eight other men also headed to the goldfields. The expanded party continued uneventfully to Fort Riley. There,
ten of the men decided to take the Smoky Hill route, hoping to cut
about 100 miles off their trip. But this would prove to be a mistake for at
least two reasons. First, they believed John Gibbs had already traveled
the Smoky Hill Trail and knew its hazards. Second, it was March, and
the potential for ferocious spring blizzards was still very much a threat.

The men had been on the new trail for a few days when a snowstorm
overtook them, during which the brothers' horse was lost. Still hundreds of miles from their destination, they ate the last of their provisions
and discarded whatever supplies they could to lighten their heavy back-
packs. When the party reached the head of the Smoky Hill Fork, Daniel
recalled, they made another fateful decision:

> We then sat down in the peaceful, solemn wilderness, like pilgrims, lonely
> and solitary in a strange country, and talked over our past adventures and
> future prospects. We had nothing to eat, having consumed everything we
> had. The question for us to decide, then, was whether to stop and hunt for
> game before proceeding farther, or to go on and 'trust to luck.' We had been
> informed . . . that the distance from this point to Denver City was only
> about fifty-five miles. This was our great mistake, the actual distance being
> about 170 miles. . . . We determined to go on without stopping to hunt for
> game. Oh! It was a fatal, terrible mistake.

As they trudged on, another blizzard swept over the plains, blasting
them with cold and wind and snow for five days. They became "confused, lost, drenched and blinded, in the general chaos of falling and
driving snow." Here, two of the men took off on their own, leaving eight
behind. The remaining party subsisted on bitter grasses, an occasional
rabbit, and a dog that had followed them. At one point they tried but
failed to kill a wild horse. Daniel described their misery:

> While going down the side of a ravine, Alexander sank down exhausted
> and in severe pain. We wrapped him up in blankets, bathed him with snow
> water, and tearing our shirts into strips, bandaged his feet and head . . . and
> then we all laid down in our blankets on the snow and rested till morning.

> *Oh, for something nourishing to eat! How hunger gnawed in our stom-*
> *achs, parched our lips, and dried up the moisture of our throats and mouths!*
> *It reduced us to very skeletons, and we stalked about, emanciated [sic],*
> *with death's hollow sound in every word we tried to speak, with death's*
> *dull, leaden fixedness in our eyes, and with death's pale look in our sad and*
> *wretched faces.*
>
> *It was here, in the midst of these tribulations, while we were lying on the*
> *ground together . . . that our conversation turned to the subject of eating*
> *each other! . . . The subject having been mentioned, we kept thinking of it,*
> *and subsequently we again spoke of it, and all then agreed that whichever of*
> *us should die first, should be eaten by the rest. We then slept till morning.*

As the next day dawned under clear skies, Daniel spied the snowy peaks of the Rocky Mountains and exclaimed, "The Peak! the peak! I see it afar off there in the westward! Take courage, boys, and let us go on." Their hopes raised, the men resumed their journey. But they did not get far:

> *I carried Alexander a portion of the way, Charles and Soley [George Soleg*
> *of Ohio], though very weak, being still able to walk. Stevenson, Scott and*
> *Campbell bore up wonderfully. But we had not gone over forty rods, when*
> *Alexander fell down exhausted again. . . . I now deemed it improper for my*
> *brothers to try to go on further, and it was then proposed that all of the party*
> *who were able, should go on, and if they found help, should return to the*
> *rescue of the others.*

Stevenson, Scott, and Campbell urged Soleg to come with them, but he declined, and they left. Soleg and the Blue brothers tried to continue, but Soleg soon collapsed. Daniel recalled, "Charles rallied a little during the day, and he walked slowly, while I carried the two helpless men along, first bearing Soley a certain distance, and setting him down; then going back after Alexander; and then again returning for our satchels. . . . We had now been eight entire days without food, except boiled roots and grass and the snow."

Soleg soon died. The brothers respected his corpse for three days before exploiting their "last resort for hope of preservation":

> *Driven by desperation, wild with hunger, and feeling, in its full force, the*
> *truth of the sentiment, that 'self preservation is the first law of nature,' we*
> *took our knives and commenced cutting the flesh from the legs and arms of*
> *our dead companion, and ate it! This was the hardest of our trials—this be-*
> *ing forced to eat human flesh. . . . After having, with eager relish, devoured*
> *part of a leg and part of an arm, the corpse began to mortify and to smell,*
> *and we could eat no more of it.*

The sustenance from Soleg's body was too little too late for Alexander, who soon died. The two surviving brothers held out for two days before "the uncontrolable and maddening cravings of hunger, impelled Charles and I to devour a part of our own brother's corpse!" Then, taking part of the body with them to eat later, they resumed the journey. They traveled across Colorado's eastern plains for several days, reaching a stream Daniel called Beaver Creek (probably Bijou Creek, south of present-day Agate). There Charles collapsed. Daniel fed him prickly pear and tree bark, but to no avail. Charles died. Daniel described his anguish:

> I was left alone in company with my dear brother's corpse—alone in a boundless waste of prairie, weak, helpless and starving. . . . I laid me down in sorrow by the side of my dead brother's body, weeping and moaning over his death. . . . While my brothers were still living, the hope of saving them and yet bringing them to a place of shelter and relief, bore me up, and inspired me with courage, strength and resolution; but now they were dead, and I was alone, having no one but myself to care for. My spirit shrank in despair within me, and I made up my mind to die.

But Daniel's instinct to survive overcame his desire to die, and once again, one brother's body nourished the other. Afterward, Daniel gave in to his exhaustion. There on Bijou Creek, Daniel Blue would have died, and his horrific story with him, had it not been for an Arapaho Indian who found him lying on the prairie. The man carried Daniel to his lodge, where his wife fed the white stranger antelope blood and raw antelope liver, saving his life. Daniel's gratitude was boundless:

> God bless that young Indian brave and his good squaw! They nursed me as carefully and gently, during those days I spent in their rude but hospitable tent, as my own mother would have done—and they saved my life! I could not understand their language, nor they mine; but in this case, on both sides, 'actions spake louder than words'—theirs of kindness, mine of gratitude. Men talk about the humanity of civilization, and the cruelties of barbarism; but I have the best of reasons for knowing and feeling that there is as much humanity 'in the savage breast'—if these Indians are indeed savages—as can be found in the breast of the most perfect civilization that mankind has ever known.

On May 4, 1859, two months after he'd struck out in jaunty step with his brothers for the goldfields, Daniel Blue was deposited on the doorstep of the recently built Station 25 of the Leavenworth & Pike's Peak Express Company on Bijou Creek's east fork. The first stage had just arrived at the station, carrying passenger Libeus Barney, who wrote, "An Indian brought into camp this evening a man he had picked up the day before in an almost dying state." J. Heywood, another man at the station, noted, "The poor sufferer was almost a skeleton. His cheeks sunken and his eyes protruded from their sockets. He looked wild and had almost lost his sight. At times his mind would wander, and he seemed very much affected."

Barney described how Daniel related in great detail his tale of woe. Perhaps not quite believing the saga, the following morning Barney and another man from the station accompanied the Indian to the place he had found Daniel. There they found Charles's ravaged remains. After burying what was left of the body, they "took the poor, bereaved, heart-broken, weak, disconsolate, half-crazed, remaining brother to camp and left him to recruit."

Blue remained at the station for several days under the care of the station manager's wife. Upon regaining his strength, he was given a free ride to Denver, where he arrived on May 11. Only four of the men Blue had traveled with reached Denver; the others perished. Blue later returned to Illinois.

Journalist Henry Villard also wrote of Blue's plight and recounted similar stories from other Smoky Hill travelers. So common was the problem, he reported, that as he traveled west by stage that spring, he found "every one of the western stations of the Express company beset by gangs of half-starved men—mostly of the hand-cart and walking gentry—that had consumed their last [supplies], days ago, and were now driven to appeal to the feelings of compassion of the employes of the Express company. And heartily and humanely was this appeal responded to in most cases."

Hearing these horrendous tales of the Smoky Hill route, miners dubbed it the "Starvation Trail," and Denver's *Rocky Mountain News* called it the "Smoky Hell" route. Almost no one used the trail after the spring of 1859. Instead, miners walked the wandering track of the Leavenworth & Pike's Peak stage line. Some traffic resumed in the fall, although by then the *Rocky Mountain News* blared that those responsible for promoting the trail "stand today, in the sight of Heaven, guilty of manslaughter."

Smoky Hill Expedition

Trying to redeem the Smoky Hill Trail and boost business for its starting point, Leavenworth, Kansas, promoters sent out a survey party in the spring of 1860, hoping to better establish the route. Freighting mogul William Green Russell was paid $3,500 to follow the trail and write a travel guide specifying its water, grass, and fuel resources. Russell, who at that same time was launching the Leavenworth to Pikes Peak stage line following the Platte route, reported favorably on the potential of the Smoky Hill route.

Leaving nothing to chance, Leavenworth promoters then raised $7,500 to build a road along the trail, hiring a crew to improve grades, build fords, and designate campsites. Led by civil engineer O. M. Tennison and surveyor Henry T. Green, the crew, using sod markers, blazed the way from Salina, Kansas, to Big Sandy Creek at present Limon. On September 9, 1860, Green reported on their progress:

We put up a sign-board, with the following inscription: "To Cheyenne Well, 22 miles." For a distance of seven miles the road laid over a fine, level bottom, thence across the divide between the Sandy and Smoky Hill rivers. [At] Cheyenne Well . . . we arranged two troughs at the well in such a manner as would facilitate the emigrant in watering stock. We also erected a signboard, giving the distances to the Sandy, and to Colorado and Denver cities; also, to Leavenworth.

But after all that, buffalo destroyed many of the sod markers, and soon the Civil War effectively shut off regular traffic over the Smoky Hill Trail. Finally, however, in 1865 a regular stage line was established.

Butterfield Overland Despatch

Entrepreneur David Butterfield, recognizing the potential for business between Kansas and Denver, raised $3 million in 1865 to establish a stage and freight line along the Smoky Hill route. Using the maps from Henry T. Green's 1860 expedition, he built stations, each stocked with mules, about every 10 to 20 miles along the route's approximately 600-mile length.

In Colorado, the Smoky Hill Trail had two primary branches, which split at Old Wells (or Indian Wells, near present Cheyenne Wells). The

A small marker indicates the site of Grady Station on the Smoky Hill Trail, on private property west of Wild Horse.

southern branch followed Big Sandy Creek, while the northern route, the one the Butterfield Overland Despatch used, took a slightly shorter cutoff. The two branches merged for a short way between today's Hugo and Limon, then split again. Both routes had their own stations. The North Road, which roughly followed what is now US 40/I-70, passed through many stations, including Big Springs Station (north of present Kit Carson), Cedar Point (still found on maps), Bijou Springs (where Daniel Blue received aid), and Kiowa Station (near today's Bennett), then on to Denver. The South Road approximated the route of CO 86, passing through, among others, Grady Station (west of present Wild Horse), Kiowa Creek Station (today's Kiowa) and Ruthton (near Elizabeth), then angling north to Denver.

The first Butterfield Overland Despatch stagecoach left Atchison, Kansas, on September 11, 1865, and arrived in Denver on September 23. Although the first run was completed without incident, this success was not to last. Butterfield had started his venture at a time when tension in the region between Indians and whites was at an all-time high.

Since the Sand Creek Massacre of November 1864, the Cheyenne and Arapaho Indians were in an all-out war for the survival of their way of life. Not wanting a stage line through the heart of their territory, the Indians launched a series of attacks. Beginning with an assault on Monument Station in present Kansas on October 2, 1865, the Indians continued raiding into December. During the week of November 19 to November 25, they attacked most of the stations in western Kansas, killing eight Butterfield Despatch employees and several government freighters and running off about 300 head of mules and horses.

With no government mail contract to guarantee income, Butterfield was losing money. Wells, Fargo Company, hoping to expand its business to compete with Ben Holladay's Overland Stage Company, made a bid for the Butterfield Despatch. But in March 1866, Holladay cut a deal with Butterfield and acquired the line. Making the Butterfield Despatch his primary service line to Denver, Holladay also continued the Overland Stage in northeastern Colorado and southern Wyoming.

Holladay held on to the operation only a short time, however. The Union Pacific and Central Pacific Railroad Companies were already laying track across the country, so Holladay, likely recognizing that stages would soon be obsolete, sold out to Wells, Fargo on November 1, 1866.

Two monuments to the Smoky Hill Trail stand along the highways in Cheyenne County. One, six miles west of Cheyenne Wells on US 40, was erected in 1939 and is engraved with a man on horseback. The other is north of Kit Carson along CO 59, at the spot where the Smoky Hill Trail crossed the highway; it honors both the Smoky Hill Trail and the old cattle trails from Texas to Montana. Erected in 1954, this massive marker of volcanic flint, concrete, and stone has a wagon wheel on top.

Monument to the Smoky Hill Trail on CO 59 north of Kit Carson

Just a couple of miles west, on private land, is the site of the Big Springs stage station.

CHEYENNE WELLS

The Butterfield Overland Despatch stage station of Cheyenne Wells, also called Old Wells or Indian Wells, was built inside one of several caves beneath a bluff. Journalist Bayard Taylor wrote this description while traveling on Holladay's stage line in June 1866:

> At Cheyenne Wells we found a large and handsome frame stable for the mules, but no dwelling. The people lived in a natural cave extending some thirty feet under the bluff. There was a woman and when we saw her, we

argued good fortunes. Truly enough, under the roof of conglomerate lime-
stone, in the cave's dim twilight, we sat down to antelope steak, tomatoes,
bread, pickles, and potatoes—a royal meal, after two days of detestable
fare. Here we saw the last of the Smoky Hill Fork.

When the Kansas Pacific crossed the plains in 1870, Cheyenne Wells
was moved about five miles south and became a railroad station. Railroad telegrapher Louis N. McLain arrived in the area in 1872 and staked
a homestead nearby. According to one local history, he had a contract
to gather buffalo heads, have them mounted, and ship them to customers all over the world as a way to advertise Colorado. A post office was
established in 1876, and McLain became the postmaster. Eventually, he
also built up a large ranching operation.

Already known as a major stop on the Smoky Hill Trail, the Butterfield Overland Despatch, and finally the railroad, Cheyenne Wells
had industrial potential as well—natural gas was discovered in the area
in 1884. In 1887 McLain and some real estate associates established the
Cheyenne Wells Town & Investment Company, surveyed lots, and held
an auction, selling sixty lots for an estimated $19,000. The town grew
quickly, and by the time it was incorporated in 1890, it was the Cheyenne County seat and a division point for the Union Pacific Railroad.

The Cheyenne County Courthouse dominates this view of Cheyenne
Wells in the early 1900s. —Courtesy Cheyenne County Museum

Display of antique household items at the Cheyenne County Museum

Cheyenne Wells remains a vital town (although the caves are no longer accessible). The county jail has been converted into a museum, displaying relics from the early days in Cheyenne County.

KIT CARSON

The Kansas Pacific Railroad built through eastern Colorado in 1870, leading to the establishment of several towns. One of them was Kit Carson, named for the famous western scout and mountain man. On the line of the nearest railroad serving both southern Colorado and New Mexico, the town quickly became an important supply point and commercial center. Soon it had a couple of good hotels and a steady stream of freight wagons and stagecoaches passing through. From the early days, the grazing lands around Kit Carson—formerly the rangelands of tens of

Buffalo bones scattered on the prairie —Courtesy Wyoming State Archives

thousands of buffalo—attracted cattlemen, who set up ranches all over southeastern Colorado.

Before the demise of the free-ranging buffalo herds, Russian Grand Duke Alexis came to Kit Carson on a buffalo hunt in late January 1872. Among His Highness's entourage were "Buffalo Bill" Cody, "Texas Jack" Omohundro, Gen. Phil Sheridan, and Lt. Col. George Armstrong Custer. The grand duke got five of the approximately fifty-three buffalo killed that day. The meat was given to the Indian guides who had accompanied the hunters. The next day, the grand duke boarded the Kansas Pacific Railroad and began his trip back to Russia.

WILD HORSE

Survey crews established Wild Horse camp in 1869 as they worked on the route of the Kansas Pacific Railroad. A cavalry detachment assigned to protect the surveyors gave the camp its name after seeing several hundred wild horses at a nearby water hole. The camp evolved into a good-sized town with many businesses, including a large lumberyard. A devastating fire in 1917 burned the entire business district to the ground. Wild Horse rebounded but never became the vibrant community it had been before the fire.

A 1910 community gathering in Wild Horse, featuring the town band —Courtesy Curtis and Leona Schrimp Collection

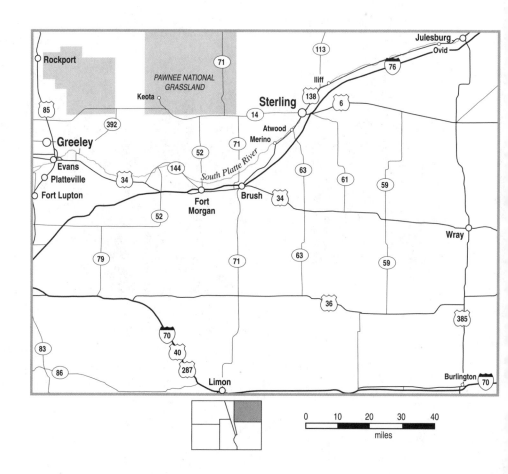

Rockport

PAWNEE NATIONAL
GRASSLAND

Keota

85

392

Greeley

Evans
Platteville

Fort Lupton

34

144

52

79

83

86

70

40

287

Limon

52

Fort
Morgan

Brush

34

71

South Platte River

Atwood

Merino

14

71

Sterling

138

Iliff

113

63

63

36

71

6

61

59

59

Wray

385

Burlington

70

Julesburg

Ovid

76

0   10   20   30   40

miles

PART FOUR

Northeast
OVERLAND TRAIL COUNTRY

The northeastern section of Colorado is plains country. In this book, the borders of the region are Wyoming and Nebraska on the north, US 85 on the west, I-70 on the south, and Nebraska and Kansas on the east. While many early visitors and settlers came to Colorado via the Smoky Hill Trail and other trails to the south, after 1862 a large influx entered via the Overland Trail. The main Oregon-California Trail ran along the North Platte River, north of Colorado, but by the early 1860s, due to increasing tension with Indian tribes, much of the emigrant and stage travel had shifted to the Overland Trail, which veered south near Brule, Nebraska, and followed the South Platte into present Colorado. Unfortunately, it turned out that this route was not much safer. During the mid-1860s soldiers regularly escorted wagon trains to discourage Indian attacks.

The Pike's Peak Express stagecoach company established the Overland Trail route in 1859, and Ben Holladay's Overland Stage Company took it over in 1862. Pony Express riders also used part of this route during their short-lived but long-remembered operations. In Colorado, the Overland Trail followed the South Platte roughly along today's I-76 and US 34 to present Greeley, where it turned south to Denver. From Denver the route went north and west along the Cherokee Trail (see part 5) to Fort Bridger, Wyoming.

Claiming the Land

The earliest inhabitants of this part of the state left behind artifacts, such as stone tools and weapons, from the Clovis culture (8900 to 9200 BC), the Folsom culture (8000 to 8500 BC), and the various prehistoric Plains cultures (AD 650 to 1550). In the eighteenth and early nineteenth centuries, Spanish and French explorers followed the South Platte River into what is now Colorado.

In 1820 Maj. Stephen Long was likely the first American military man to see this region, then inhabited by Arapaho and Cheyenne Indians. As the nineteenth century progressed and white settlement increased, the tribes were forced onto increasingly smaller reserves. With the 1861 Fort

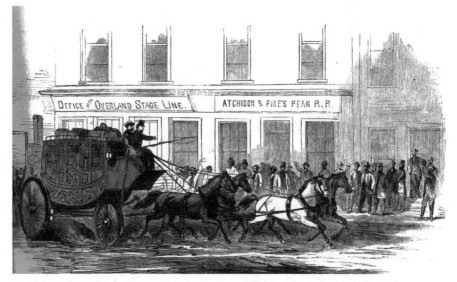

This 1866 drawing by William H. Merrick shows an Overland Stage Company coach leaving Atchison, Kansas, for Denver. The route the company used, known as the Overland Trail, was developed years before by the Pike's Peak Express Company. —From *Harper's Weekly* January 27, 1866

Wise Treaty, negotiated by Indian agent Louis Vasquez, the Cheyennes and Arapahos ceded most of their remaining lands except for a triangular area between Big Sandy Creek (Sand Creek) and the Arkansas River.

Although the terms of the treaty stipulated that whites were not to move into that area, it wasn't long before stage-station operators and early ranchers violated this provision. The 1862 Homestead Act drew more settlers into Colorado, and homesteaders staked claims throughout the region, including the Indians' high plains territory. Eventually the squeezed-out Indians rebelled, staging many violent raids in the mid-1860s before they were finally subdued.

In addition to pushing out the natives, the Homestead Act ushered in dramatic changes in land use. Buffalo that had grazed for centuries on Colorado's eastern plains and along its rivers were driven from their ranges or killed off.

The Homestead Act allowed adult men and single women who were U.S. citizens or immigrants who had applied for citizenship, and who had never fought against the United States, to claim up to 160 acres of

Merchants unload goods from a train car into wagons at Julesburg's Union Pacific rail yard in the early 1900s. —Courtesy Fort Sedgwick Historical Archives

land. To gain title, they had to live on the land at least six months per year for five years and make improvements on the property. Alternatively, people could simply buy a homestead for $1.25 per acre, which was known as preemption. Many eastern Colorado homesteaders raised wheat and sugar beets, two staple commodities still grown in this area.

To further encourage settlement, the government gave land grants to railroads. The railroads in turn ran promotions to entice homesteaders to the plains, knowing that new settlers would need supplies shipped in, meaning business for them. Homesteaders would also grow crops, which would need to be shipped out. As the railroads pushed through, towns sprang up all along the lines. Some of them flourished, some faded away, and some remain quiet farming communities to this day.

Natural Enemies

In the West, weather and the forces of nature have always had profound effects on lives and fortunes. Droughts, blizzards, floods, and winds determined whether or not people prospered. Plains settlers learned to watch the sky for signs of storms. Sometimes, it was not rain clouds that loomed on the horizon, but grasshoppers. Millions upon millions of these green insects flew in swarms and descended upon the

Homesteader Mrs. D. S. Redford, right, in buggy at this cow camp in north-east Colorado, early 1900s. —Courtesy Fort Sedgwick Historical Archives

land, devouring anything and everything in their path. Fields of corn and wheat, clothing, and even leather goods fell prey to the plague of grasshoppers.

On September 7, 1864, the *Miner's Register* of Central City, Colorado Territory, reported on one such invasion:

> *The immense clouds of grasshoppers which passed over the city yesterday were a sight, we believe, has never before been witnessed in the Territory. By looking towards the sun they could be seen in a dense cloud like a swarm of bees. They appeared to be coming from the western slope and going eastward to the plains. They were very high up, probably 2,000 feet, as they were flying entirely above all the mountains about here. A few straggling ones lighted here, but the vast majority of them passed over. We should expect to see everything swept before them wherever they go.*

But worse was yet to come. In the 1870s, 1880s, and 1890s the eastern plains of Colorado suffered severe infestations that ravaged crops and fouled water supplies. Farmers built grasshopper traps, burned sulfur to drive the pests away, and incinerated the straw piles into which the grasshoppers burrowed. More plagues hit in the 1930s and again in the 1950s. The threat occurs anytime there is a serious drought.

Even without grasshoppers, droughts bring disaster to farmers, especially on the already arid eastern Colorado plains. During the late 1920s and early 1930s, seasonal moisture—marginal in this country even in a good year—never came. By summer, the hot, dry winds settlers called "black rollers" began to arrive, blowing dirt into big clouds and pushing it into drifts against fences. The billowing dirt settled on grasslands, too, reducing the productivity of pastures.

In 1934, as part of President Franklin D. Roosevelt's New Deal, the federal government began purchasing drought-ravaged land from farmers who wanted to sell. The program's Division of Land Utilization was authorized to purchase millions of acres and convert the land to its best use, which usually meant reseeding it with grass. Some of the restored land was later resold or leased to farmers, some was transferred to the USDA Agricultural Research Service, and some was retained as federal public land.

Attempting to reduce the loss of topsoil and restore the land to productivity, the government eventually planted some 60,000 acres in crested wheat grass. The Forest Service took over administration of the lands in 1954, and on June 20, 1960, nineteen former land-utilization projects across the nation were designated as national grasslands. (See Comanche National Grassland in part 3 and Pawnee National Grassland later in this section.)

Farming continued throughout the eastern Colorado plains for the rest of the twentieth century, but the cycles of dry years persisted. Articles in the *Denver Post* during one of these droughts, in February 1954, described what it was like:

> *Banks of silt were piled against fences. . . . From Springfield in Baca County, it was reported that what wheat was not ripped out of the ground by terrific winds was covered by sand and silt. . . . Visibility in many places was reduced to zero. Traffic creeped, with lights on. Noon darkness compelled street lights being turned on. Schools closed. . . .*
>
> *"The damage is inconceivable, much greater than in the dust bowl days of the early '30s," said Governor Gordon Allott. "That one storm alone on Washington's birthday did more damage than all of them in the '30s."*

In Colorado in 2002, the worst drought in a century saw a return to near dust-bowl conditions for farmers. Fields that had been plowed and prepared for planting lay unchanged as the spring days passed. Farmers did not plant crops, knowing they would not have adequate water to grow. Despite modern innovations, farming on the plains remains an ongoing struggle, just as it was for the first settlers.

From the beginning, most travelers and settlers came into this region from the east, so we will explore it from east to west as well, and from south to north.

I-70
Burlington—I-25
162 MILES

Interstate 70 is a major travel route across Colorado's eastern plains. As you travel west, the gently rolling fields of wheat, corn, and sunflowers give way to the suburban sprawl of the Denver metro area, which has exploded since the 1990s. The small towns east of Limon—Burlington, Bethune, Stratton, Vona, Seibert, Flagler, Arriba, Bovina, and Genoa—were spawned by early settlers and the construction of railroad lines. Between Limon and Denver, I-70 follows the general path of the Smoky Hill Trail (see part 3) and passes through lands originally claimed by homesteaders.

BURLINGTON

At least a year before the Chicago & Rock Island Railroad reached this area in 1888, freighters had carved a road between Cheyenne Wells and Burlington, but the latter was then little more than a collection of tents surrounded by homesteads. The railroad's arrival brought prosperity and permanence to Burlington, which soon became the seat of Kit Carson County.

The railroad served the area's farmers until it ceased operations in the early 1900s. Even so, agricultural production continued and is still an economic mainstay here. Kit Carson County is the top wheat-producing county in Colorado and a primary grower of beans, sunflowers, corn, and barley. Cattle and hogs are also important commodities, auctioned at the Burlington Livestock Exchange.

Burlington's Old Town Museum complex has numerous historic buildings and reconstructions, ranging from the Bethune Depot (circa 1889), to a farmhouse from Stratton (circa 1900), to a rural schoolhouse from the Cope area (1911), along with various shops and other buildings. Perhaps the most impressive structure is a huge barn brought in from a farm north of Kanorado, Kansas.

LIMON

Like many other communities along I-70, Limon was established when the Chicago & Rock Island Railroad pushed across Colorado in 1888. Rail workers began calling this spot "Limon's Camp," after foreman John Limon, and the name simply stuck.

Today, Limon is known as the "Hub City" for its location at the intersection of several highways: I-70, CO 86 to Castle Rock, US 24 to

Colorado Springs, US 40/287, and CO 71. The latter two roads are part of a primary trucking route between Mexico and Canada.

US 385
Burlington—Julesburg
123 MILES

US 385 cuts north and south through Colorado's eastern plains, and two other highways, US 36 and US 34, cross east and west. US 36 serves the small towns of Idalia, Kirk, Joes, Cope, Anton, Lindon, and Last Chance, hooking up with I-70 at Strasburg; US 34 passes through Laird, Wray, Eckley, Yuma, Otis, and Akron before intersecting with I-76 at Brush. The Arikaree River and its various forks, which cut across this section of Colorado, have provided water for farmers and ranchers from the 1800s into the twenty-first century. When the Cheyenne Indians lived here, this was their prime hunting territory.

BEECHER ISLAND

About fifteen miles south of Wray, signs along US 385 clearly mark the turnoff for Beecher Island, the site of one of Colorado's most important Indian battles. On a county road east of the highway, the well-marked route winds toward the Arikaree River and to the spot where U.S. troops and a large group of Indians, mostly Northern Cheyennes, had an eight-day standoff in September 1868. The battle took place on what was then a river island; now, due to development and lower water levels, the island no longer exists. Trails follow the cottonwood-lined river channel and markers point out sites where the battle played out.

In response to Cheyenne raids in Kansas and eastern Colorado that summer, Col. George A. Forsyth organized fifty experienced scouts to pursue the raiders. On September 16, Forsyth's troops camped beside the Arikaree River in eastern Colorado. The next morning, hundreds of Cheyenne warriors led by Roman Nose swept in to attack the soldiers' camp. Forsyth was wounded twice and twenty-four soldiers—nearly half the company—were killed or injured. The surviving soldiers retreated to an island in the river and set up their defenses. The troops had Spencer seven-shot repeating carbines and Colt six-shot percussion revolvers with 170 rounds of ammunition per man, plus an additional 4,000 rounds in reserve.

The Indians laid their siege north of the river on a long, low ridge now known as Roman Nose Ridge, named for the most prominent

*Monument at
Beecher Island,
where U.S. troops
engaged Cheyenne
Indians in an
eight-day battle in
September 1868*

Indian to die in the battle. On nearby Squaw Hill, the Indian women waited in safety. Within a few days, the soldiers ran out of provisions and had to eat rotting horse meat. On the second night, Colonel Forsyth sent a pair of scouts to Fort Wallace, in western Kansas, with a request for help. The next night, September 19, Forsyth sent out another pair of scouts with a second message, saying he had "eight badly wounded & 10 slightly wounded" men. "Lt. Beecher is dead & Acting Asst. Surgeon Moore probably cannot live the night out. He was hit in the head on Thursday & has spoken but one rational word since. I am wounded in two places, in the right thigh & my left [leg] broken below the knee."

Forsyth estimated that 450 Cheyennes, armed with Spencer and Henry rifles, surrounded the island. All the horses and mules had been killed. "You better start with not less than 75 men & bring all the wagons and ambulances you can spare," Forsyth advised, also requesting a six-pound howitzer and a surgeon. "I can hold out here for 6 days long if absolutely necessary but please lose no time."

Amazingly, Forsyth's troops did indeed hold out until help arrived. At Fort Wallace, Lt. Col. Henry C. Bankhead sent Capt. Louis H. Carpenter and the Tenth Cavalry, a company of all-black soldiers commonly called the Buffalo Soldiers, to Forsyth's aid. This relief party arrived on the eighth day of the siege and forced the Indians to withdraw. Bankhead rode in with more soldiers the next day.

The battle site became known as Beecher Island, for Lt. Frederick H. Beecher of Virginia, who was killed there. The Cheyennes refer to the Battle of Beecher Island as the "Fight Where Roman Nose Was Killed." After his recovery, Forsyth, who was cited for meritorious service, launched a devastating winter campaign against the Indians. His strategy was based on the knowledge that during the winter Indian men were usually in camp or hunting, not out raiding and fighting.

Forsyth's campaign ultimately led to the end of the Indian wars in Colorado. At the November 1868 Battle of the Washita, in present Oklahoma, Southern Cheyenne chief Black Kettle and dozens of his followers were killed. The following July, Tall Bull fell in a raid at Summit Springs, in northeastern Colorado, breaking the back of the Southern Cheyennes. Soon the final bands surrendered and moved to reservations in Oklahoma. Later offensives against the Northern Cheyennes forced that tribe's capitulation as well.

WRAY

Wray sits in a scenic valley along the North Fork of the Republican River, near the border of Colorado, Kansas, and Nebraska. Named for an early settler, Wray became the seat of Yuma County in 1902. Like other towns in this area, Wray was and remains an agricultural community, with an economy based on cattle ranching and crops, primarily corn and potatoes. With a new community center, high school, hospital, and other facilities, Wray was designated an "All-American City" in 1993. The Wray Museum focuses on native cultures and archaeology as well as local history.

JULESBURG

Julesburg has gone through four incarnations. Jules Beni built the first Julesburg, a trading post later referred to as Old Julesburg, in 1859. It served as a station for both the Overland Stage and the Pony Express. In 1865, during a period of intense raiding, Cheyenne and Lakota warriors looted the settlement and burned it to the ground.

Six miles to the east, on the south bank of the South Platte River, a second Julesburg was built, also serving stage traffic. It was abandoned in 1867 after the Union Pacific Railroad laid its tracks north of the river, and Julesburg number three sprang up along the rail line. The third settlement was originally named Weir, for Union Pacific foreman James Weir, but tradition won out and it, too, became known as Julesburg. Accommodations here were limited at first. One train traveler, arriving at the end of the tracks in 1867, noted in a letter to her mother that she "ate meals at the hotel and slept in the [railroad] car at night."

The Union Pacific Railroad gave birth to the third incarnation of Julesburg when it laid tracks through the area in 1867. When the UP moved its line fourteen years later, residents of Julesburg moved their town. This depot was built in 1930. —Courtesy Fort Sedgwick Historical Archives

The third Julesburg became a hell-on-wheels, end-of-the-tracks town, sometimes called the "wickedest city in the West." It was perhaps the most colorful of the four Julesburgs. Henry Stanley, who visited Julesburg in 1867, wrote this vivid description:

> *These women are expensive articles, and come in for a large share of the money wasted. In broad daylight they may be seen gliding through the sandy streets in Black Crook dresses, carrying fancy derringers slung to their waists, with which tools they are dangerously expert. Should they get into a fuss, western chivalry will not allow them to be abused by any man whom they may have robbed.*

In 1881 the Union Pacific completed a new line to Denver from Julesburg, but the junction point was three miles east of town. Although they had already moved twice before, Julesburg residents packed up and did so a third time, to the site that finally became permanent. The last Julesburg was a more stable and subdued community, surrounded by homesteaders' farms and ranches. The Union Pacific depot was moved away from the tracks in the 1990s and now serves as the Fort Sedgwick Historical Society's Depot Museum.

*Woman and little girl on a farm near Julesburg taking their horse out for a ride,
early 1900s* —Courtesy Fort Sedgwick Historical Archives

Fort Sedgwick

Just west of present Julesburg is the site of Fort Sedgwick, which sat
about a mile south of the South Platte River at the mouth of Lodgepole
Creek. Established as Camp Rankin in July 1864, the post was renamed
a year later for Maj. John Sedgwick. The army abandoned the fort in
1871.

After a string of Indian depredations along the South Platte Trail
in the spring and summer of 1864, the army ordered Brig. Gen. Robert B. Mitchell to build a fort to protect the "finest natural highway in
the world." Parties of fewer than fifty people were considered at risk of
attack, and Mitchell advised freighters not to travel in small parties.
Camp Rankin regularly provided army escorts for civilian travelers and
sent troops to defend Union Pacific workers against Indians. For a time
the army presence seemed to deter Indian violence, as Capt. Eugene F.
Ware, stationed nearby, noted in *The Indian War of 1864*:

> *About half of our post was continually on the road, every day escorting stages
> and trains. The trains went in a consolidated manner with many armed
> men, and at night they were corralled and regular picket guards established.*

Replica of Anton Schonborn's painting of Fort Sedgwick as it looked in June 1867
—Courtesy Fort Sedgwick Historical Archives

The burning of Julesburg and siege of Fort Sedgwick, February 2, 1865, sketched by witness T. H. Williams. —Courtesy Fort Sedgwick Historical Archives

THE BURNING OF JULESBURG, FEBRUARY 2, 1865, AND THE SIEGE OF FORT SEDGWICK,
As drawn at the time by T. H. Williams, of Colorado

Indians were seen around at all times, but in small numbers, and nothing of particular event took place except theft and stampedes of loose stock.

But the peace did not last. After a failed raid at Valley Station in January 1865 (see Sterling, later in this section), Indians set up camp on the north bank of the Platte River across from Camp Rankin. When they could not engage the soldiers, the Indians began attacking buildings in nearby Julesburg. Smoke rose from the town's burning structures as the Indians carried away loot from stores and homes. When the raid was over, Julesburg lay in smoldering ruins. While the residents took refuge at the fort, the Indians turned their attention to destroying the telegraph line. Upon hearing that a large party of soldiers was en route to relieve the beleaguered Camp Rankin, the Indians finally withdrew, heading northeast into Nebraska Territory with their plunder.

US 138
Julesburg—I-76 at Brush
90 MILES

If there had been a guest register in this corner of Colorado in the eighteenth and nineteenth centuries, it would include some of the most important names in the history of the American West, such as Maj. Stephen Long, Lt. John C. Frémont, and Kit Carson, as well as Pony Express riders, railroad builders, and assorted explorers and trappers.

US 138 parallels I-76 on the approximate route of the South Platte River Trail, or Overland Trail. Pedro de Villasur followed this route in 1720, trappers used it in the early 1800s, and gold seekers beating a path to Colorado after 1859 often took this trail. It was also the route of the Pike's Peak Express Company and Ben Holladay's Overland Stage, so it is dotted with the sites of former stage stations from Julesburg west.

Spaniard Pedro de Villasur, traveling from Santa Fe in 1720, was the first known explorer to see this corner of Colorado. Villasur was killed on that expedition by Pawnees in present Nebraska. Nearly two decades later, French brothers Paul and Pierre Mallet passed through, headed for the Southwest in 1739. In 1820 Maj. Stephen Long led the first U.S. military expedition to enter this part of Colorado, and Lt. John C. Frémont's 1842 exploring party, guided by Kit Carson, also came through here. By the 1860s, the South Platte River had become a major travel route.

Pike's Peak Express Company

Freighting entrepreneurs William Russell, Alexander Majors, and William Waddell (the partners of Pony Express fame) organized the stage-coach operation known as the Pike's Peak Express Company (also called the Leavenworth & Pike's Peak Company) in 1859 with $500,000 in capital. With a choice of routes between Leavenworth, Kansas, and the goldfields around Denver, the company opted to follow the "Great Military Road" across Kansas and Nebraska along the Platte River, which was also the Oregon-California Trail route. At the confluence of the North and South Platte Rivers, the stage route split from the Oregon-California Trail, which followed the North Platte, and turned southwest along the South Platte into present Colorado, roughly following today's I-76 and US 34 to Greeley, where it dropped south to Denver.

The company's first coach left Leavenworth on April 18, 1859, returning there in early May. The cost of passage, advertised as a trip of just seven days from Leavenworth to Denver City, was $100, with "good meals" available at the stage stations for fifty cents. Through Kansas and Nebraska, the stage line had twenty-one stations, most of them at or near established Oregon-California Trail stops. Past the fork of the Platte were newly built stations in Colorado, including Lillian Springs, Beaver Creek, Fremont's Orchard, and Denver City.

At their peak, Russell, Majors, and Waddell were leaders in freighting and transportation to the West. They employed some 1,500 freighters and owned tens of thousands of oxen and mules and hundreds of freight wagons, hauling both private goods and government supplies. Early in 1860 the partners began formulating plans for the Pony Express, which would use some of the Pike's Peak Express route. Renaming their company the Central Overland California & Pike's Peak Express (COC&PP), the partners launched the Pony Express in April 1860. Its eighteen-month run ended in the partners' financial ruin, by which time the company had been nicknamed "Clean Out of Cash and Poor Pay."

Taking over the COC&PP's interests was Ben Holladay, who began the Overland Stage Company in 1862. The Overland Stage ran three times weekly in the 1860s, while the Western Stage ran once weekly on the Overland Trail between Denver and Omaha. In 1866 Wells, Fargo bought out Holladay and several other stage companies.

There were two types of stage stations: relay (or swing) stations, where drivers changed horses and little else, and home stations, where drivers and passengers could have meals and in some cases stay overnight. Among the stations along the South Platte route, traveling west (upstream), were Julesburg, Antelope Station, Spring Hill, Lillian Springs Ranch, Riverside Ranch, Dennison's Station (near Iliff), Valley Station (near Sterling), Washington or Wisconsin Ranch, Kelley's Station (aka

American Ranch), Beaver Creek, Junction House, Bijou Creek (near Fort Morgan), Fremont's Orchard, Eagle's Nest, and Latham (near Greeley). Later, other paths were forged to Denver, including a cutoff that went due west from Junction Station (near present Fort Morgan).

Eventually, railroads put stage companies out of business. Train travel was not only faster, but also safer and more comfortable. One train traveler was Frances Casement, who visited Colorado in June 1867 with her husband, Union Pacific construction foreman Jack Casement. She gushed in a letter to her mother back in Ohio that her trip had been "a journey of 385 miles and back in two days and three nights. 385 miles from Omaha, almost across the plains, and tell Aunt Lide we *didn't see an Indian, not one.*"

OVID

Beginning in the late 1880s, homesteaders came to this area to claim land along the South Platte. Eventually, foreign immigrants, including Japanese settlers and ethnic Germans from Russia, came to farm in the region from Ovid to Greeley.

In the early twentieth century, a sugar-beet plant was built in Ovid, making the town a center for beet processing. Horse-drawn wagons

Children of Russian farmers near Ovid, 1910 —Courtesy Fort Sedgwick Historical Archives

A horse-drawn wagon taking beets to the Great Western Sugar Company's beet dump next to the train tracks —Courtesy Fort Sedgwick Historical Archives

hauled the vegetables to the beet "dump" on the Union Pacific Railroad right-of-way, just south of Sedgwick, from which the beets were loaded onto train cars. The dump was constructed in 1908 and dismantled in 1935, when automatic loaders were installed.

Thad Sowder

In the early days of rodeo, the bronc-riding champion at Cheyenne Frontier Days automatically became the world champion bronco buster, and the first man to hold that title came from Ovid, Colorado. Reared on a homestead just northeast of town, Martin T. "Thad" Sowder went on to meet President Theodore Roosevelt, to win top awards at rodeos in both Cheyenne and Denver, and even to organize his own Wild West show.

Sowder was born in Kentucky in 1874, the seventh child of Martha and David Sowder. The family moved to Iowa, then to Julesburg, Colorado. Soon afterward, Martha bought a homestead ranch just east of Ovid from her son-in-law, calling it the Lazy D. By the time Thad was a teenager, he had made it his job to ride every horse on the place. One time, he was pitched off an unbroken horse and received a severe concussion.

After competing in the first-ever Cheyenne Frontier Day bronc-riding competition in 1897, Sowder broke horses for Teddy Roosevelt's Rough

Riders during the Spanish-American War. The next year, he rode a horse called Royal Flush at the Cheyenne Frontier Day bronc-riding contest.

While he was working for the Diamond Ranch near Gillette, Wyoming, in 1901, Sowder traveled to the Denver Festival of Mountain and Plain. There, atop horses named Peggy and Steamboat, he won his first title as a champion bronco buster, along with a $500, ruby-studded silver belt buckle. Sowder returned to the Denver festival in 1902 and again won the buckle.

In 1903 the directors of the Denver contest agreed that the buckle would be awarded not at their event, but at the Cheyenne Frontier Days. The *Wyoming Tribune*, published in Cheyenne, noted that "Cheyenne will have in name what she has always had in fact, the only event where the real broncho busting championship can be decided." Sowder, who would have been allowed to keep the buckle permanently had he won three times in a row, lost the prize that year to Wyoming cowboy Guy Holt. Holt kept it for one year, but after that, the buckle was retired. It is now part of the collection of the Colorado History Museum in Denver.

In 1903 Sowder organized his own Wild West show, touring in Nebraska, Iowa, Indiana, Illinois, Ohio, and Pennsylvania. Returning to the Cheyenne competition in 1905, he shook the hand of President Roosevelt after his bronc ride. But Sowder had to give up the tough

Learning to ride bucking horses on his mother's ranch near Ovid, Thad Sowder went on to become a rodeo champion.
—Courtesy Wyoming State Archives

job of conquering bucking horses when he began to suffer from partial paralysis. He died in March 1931 and is buried in the Ovid Cemetery, just a few hundred yards from the family homestead where he learned to ride broncs.

ILIFF

You know you are in Iliff when you see the well in the middle of the intersection by the post office. That well dates back to the days when this was a cattle town.

First called Riverside, the town owes its current name to cattle mogul John Wesley Iliff. In Kansas, Iliff helped found the town of Princeton and was engaged in both farming and the mercantile business. He came to Colorado in 1859 with an ox train of supplies and opened a general store in Denver. Having learned the cattle business from his father, Iliff soon started purchasing cattle, which he grazed in northeastern Colorado. In 1866 he bought 800 head from Oliver Loving and Charles Goodnight, the legendary Texans who forged the famous Goodnight-Loving Trail. Iliff himself extended the Goodnight-Loving Trail into Wyoming as he expanded his herds by the hundreds, then the thousands. He supplied beef to the construction crews on the Union Pacific Railroad, as

Cattle feedlot near Iliff. John Iliff brought some of the earliest cattle into Colorado, eventually establishing a ranch near the town that bore his name.

well as to Indian reservations and the army. He also shipped cattle to eastern markets.

Because Iliff's 15,558 acres were strategically situated along the South Platte River and at other sites with water, he effectively controlled a range many times larger than his deeded property. Cattle wearing his LF brand ranged from Greeley to Julesburg, as well as in Wyoming, Nebraska, Kansas, Oklahoma, and Texas. Buying Texas longhorns for around $10 or $15 a head, fattening them for a year or two on rich plains grasses, and selling them for double or triple the amount he'd paid made Iliff a wealthy man. By the time of his death at age forty-six in 1878, he owned numerous properties in Denver in addition to his ranch holdings.

CEDAR CREEK

Cedar Creek crosses US 138 about midway between Iliff and Sterling. Along this stream is the site of a major fight in an Indian war that raged along the South Platte in 1864 and 1865. The first confrontation took place at Crow Creek, near Kuner, on April 12, 1864 (see Crow Creek, later in this section). The next occurred here at Cedar Creek on May 3. Tensions intensified in January 1865—a period that historian Nell Brown Propst called "Bloody January"—and violence erupted at various stage stations along the Overland Trail.

Following the Crow Creek battle, continuing thefts of livestock from stage companies and settlers in the region had troops pursuing the Cheyennes for weeks with no real success. Finally, Maj. Jacob Downing, commanding Companies C and H of the First Colorado, spied an Indian approaching the stage station known as American Ranch. According to one soldier, the major "summoned about 50 troopers and had them get their horses ready. [He instructed] them to divide into two equal parties in leaving the corral and to ride with all speed for the ravine, deploying right and left. . . . The gates were swung open, and away we went in a cloud of dust."

The troops caught the Indian, identified as Spotted Horse, who told Downing that the Cheyennes were camping on Cedar Creek. Downing attacked the camp, killing and wounding many Indians. A week later, with eighty men and plenty of ammunition, Downing returned to Cedar Creek but found only empty lodges.

Downing subsequently faced court-martial for "inciting a revolt" at Cedar Creek, in part because he had provided some Indians with guns to fight other Indians. The court-martial was never taken seriously, but Gen. Samuel K. Curtis, commander of the District of Kansas, reassigned Downing to southern Colorado. But by removing the military presence along the South Platte, Curtis unwisely set the stage for further difficulties. A series of raids on settlers in the summer of 1864 eventually led to the infamous attack at Sand Creek that November (see Chivington in part 3).

A buggy making its way down a county road near Sterling, circa 1905
—Courtesy Wyoming State Archives, J. E. Stimson Collection

STERLING

Built along the Union Pacific line in 1881, Sterling was named after Sterling, Illinois, the hometown of the town's surveyor. Many of Sterling's first residents came from a nearby farming settlement. Sterling became the Logan County seat in 1887. The discovery of oil in Sterling in the 1950s brought further economic growth to the town.

In downtown Sterling's Columbine Park are some whimsical tree sculptures of local artist Bradford Rhea. In these unusual creations, various creatures, including multiheaded giraffes, are carved into the branches of the cottonwood trees.

Valley Station

Just east of Sterling sat Valley Station, one of the home stations on the Overland Trail. In the fall of 1864, Maj. Samuel M. Logan established an army headquarters here after tensions between area settlers and Indians started heating up. The trail had been closed periodically over the summer, but it was reopened when the army set up some new posts along the route. Some settlers took the opportunity to leave the region. They were wise to do so, because in January 1865, the Indians launched what became known as the "bloody year on the plains."

Valley Station suffered the first attack, on January 7. A telegram from the station operator reported, "9:30 a.m. Coach from east fired on four miles below [downstream] from Valley. No one hurt. 9:00 a.m. Indians attacked train in sight of station here. Two men and two Indians killed. Troops chasing Indians. . . . Large train which has been encamped for winter about five miles below here attacked by about seventy-five Indians who came from South. Burned all wagons, killed twelve men, and report also says killed some emigrants. I am going to take all my things and go down road until things get more quiet."

That same day, Indians also attacked Julesburg and Camp Rankin (see Julesburg, earlier in this section), burning the town of Julesburg and killing fifteen soldiers and a handful of civilians. Perhaps fifty-six Indians died in that fight. Further attacks occurred along the South Platte throughout the month. District commander Gen. Robert B. Mitchell, who had been in the Arkansas River country, returned in late January with an order to burn the prairie so the Indians would not have feed for their stock or access to wild game.

From January 14 through February 2, the Cheyenne and Arapaho raids intensified. They looted wagons, cut telegraph wires, and stole livestock. In a January 28 attack on Washington Ranch, a few miles west of Valley Station, Indians plundered the provisions and wounded Jim Moore, a former Pony Express rider. During the siege, the station's occupants attached a wooden butter churn to a wagon axle and two wheels to make it look like a cannon, thus holding off the Indians until soldiers came to their rescue.

The soldiers chased away the Indians, who fled into Nebraska Territory. A reprieve followed in Colorado, but the Indians continued raiding in present Nebraska, Wyoming, and Montana. The fighting returned to the South Platte in 1869, culminating in the Battle of Summit Springs, near today's Atwood.

ATWOOD

Battle of Summit Springs

For the Cheyennes, it was the Moon of the Black Cherries when Maj. Eugene A. Carr, U.S. Fifth Cavalry, found them camped in a grassy area south of the South Platte River on July 11, 1869. The Southern Cheyennes, led by Tall Bull, had left their winter camp in Texas that spring, intending to travel north across the buffalo country and join the Northern Cheyennes and Lakotas in Wyoming and South Dakota. Crossing

Monument at Summit Springs, site of the last major encounter between the Cheyenne Indians and the frontier army in Colorado. The battle played out in the ravine behind the marker.

through Kansas, the elite Dog Soldiers raided Kansas Pacific Railroad construction camps and settlements in the Saline Valley. In a raid of a German community on May 30, the Indians kidnapped two white women, Susanna Alderdice and Maria Weichel, after killing Maria's husband and Susanna's baby.

At Fort McPherson in Nebraska, Major Carr got the order on June 7 to find the Indians and rescue the two white women. Carr was a New Yorker who had been cited for meritorious service during the Civil War and who would eventually (in 1894) be awarded a Medal of Honor. With eight companies of the Fifth Cavalry and 100 Pawnee scouts led by Frank and Luther North, Carr began pursuit on June 9.

The troops intercepted the Cheyennes and their Arapaho and Lakota allies and engaged them in skirmishes on July 3 and 4. Afterward Carr broke away, pretending to return to Fort McPherson for supplies and leading the Indians to believe they had eluded the soldiers. While Carr bided his time, Col. William B. Royall took some of the troops, with Buffalo Bill Cody as a scout, on a separate reconnaissance.

Tall Bull led his group into present Colorado. When the Indians reached the South Platte and found it running high, they retreated to Summit Springs and set up a temporary camp. In the early afternoon of July 11, Carr's scouts located the Indians' camp of eighty-five lodges about thirteen miles south of present Atwood. Carr sent a messenger to find Royall's party and led the remaining force of some 250 cavalrymen and 50 Pawnee scouts toward the camp.

A young Cheyenne horse herder spotted the troops and stampeded the horses toward the camp as an alarm. The troops killed him, but his warning allowed the Cheyennes to flee their lodges and mount a defense in the canyon. Nevertheless, the soldiers were able to kill Tall Bull and win the fight, which lasted only an hour. They found Susanna Alderdice and Maria Weichel, both of whom had been shot. Alderdice survived her wounds, but Weichel died. Besides Tall Bull, Cheyennes killed during the battle included Heavy Furred Wolf, Pile of Bones, Lone Bear, Black Sea, White Rock, Big Gap, Power Face, and forty-five other Cheyennes and Lakotas. The soldiers captured an additional seventeen Indians.

A dispute arose over which of two famous Indian fighters, Frank North or Buffalo Bill Cody, fired the shot that killed Tall Bull. Some maintained that Cody shot the Cheyenne chief from thirty yards away. But others, including his brother Luther North, claimed that Frank North was responsible for Tall Bull's death.

Cody biographer Robert A. Carter quoted Capt. George F. Price as saying that Cody "guided the Fifth Cavalry to a position whence the regiment was [able] to charge the enemy and win a brilliant victory." Carter also wrote that "in the Fifth Cavalry, credit was always given to Buffalo Bill." Cody himself claimed he killed Tall Bull, saying he did so because he wanted the chief's horse. He said he positioned himself in a ravine, and when Tall Bull rode by on his magnificent horse, Cody shot him. One of the soldiers caught the horse and turned it over to Cody. Tall Bull's wife later recognized the horse, confirming for Cody that he had indeed killed the Dog Soldier chief.

But other accounts say that Cody wasn't even present at the fight, that he was still out with Royall. These sources say it was Frank North who killed Tall Bull, doing so by tricking him. As Frank and Luther North rode toward the canyon, an Indian fired at Frank. Frank pretended he had been hit and fell from his horse, then motioned to his brother to take the pony and ride away from the scene. Believing that Frank had been mortally wounded, Tall Bull rode up, whereupon Frank shot and killed him.

The defeat of the Dog Soldiers spelled the end of the Cheyennes' free-ranging way of life. The Southern Cheyennes, who already had a reservation in Kansas, were eventually relocated to Oklahoma. The Northern Cheyennes were moved to the Whetstone Agency in South Dakota, far from their territory on the Colorado plains. Some of them engaged in battles on the northern plains before they, too, were sent to Oklahoma. They fled that agency in 1879 and ended up with a reservation in Montana.

MERINO

The community of Merino was settled by Michael Propst, who filed a timber claim on the site of the present town; some of Propst's ancestors still live in the area. Merino is just east of the site of the Godfrey's Ranch stage station, also known as Fort Wicked.

Fort Wicked

Holon Godfrey earned the name "Old Wicked" from the Cheyenne Indians after he and his family successfully defended their home on January 14, 1864, just a week after the Indians attacked Camp Rankin and Valley Station (see Julesburg and Sterling, earlier in this section). Throughout the three-day battle, Godfrey maintained a stream of instructions to his wife, Matilda, and children, Martha, Celia, and Cuba, as they held off about 130 attackers. Seeing the glow of a fire in the direction of nearby American Ranch, the Godfrey family knew that it had also been attacked, as had other stations along the South Platte. A man with the Godfreys made a nighttime escape from the besieged ranch to seek help. He reached Junction Station, and a wire was sent to Denver late that night:

> The American Ranch is burnt to the ground by Indians. About 100 made attack there yesterday morning. Inmates all destroyed. Valley Station burnt and Wisconsin probably destroyed. A messenger just got here after help. The Indians attacked Godfrey's ranch, two miles this side of the American, and are fighting there now. Messenger got away and is here after help now. Probably where line is down.
>
> I have my horse at door and will start down immediately and get line o.k. as soon as possible. All people in ranches attacked were killed.

The report that all were killed was inaccurate. Godfrey, his family, and others survived the attack. After the Indians bestowed the name "Old Wicked" on Holon Godfrey, it stuck, and his ranch became known as Fort Wicked. In July 1866, *New York Tribune* correspondent Bayard Taylor provided this description for his readers:

> Entering the fortress, we found a long adobe cabin, one part of which was occupied as a store, well stocked with groceries, canned provisions, and

*liquors. A bearded man with a good-natured but determined air, asked us if
we would stop for breakfast. [It] was Mr. Godfrey himself, the builder and
defender of the fort, which is known all along the [South] Platte as Godfrey's
Ranche.*

US 34
Fort Morgan—US 85
51 MILES

West of Fort Morgan, the Overland Trail continued along the South
Platte River to Latham (Greeley), roughly along what is now US 34.

FORT MORGAN

When you visit Fort Morgan, the first thing you are likely to learn is that
big-band orchestra leader Glenn Miller once lived here. Miller moved
to Fort Morgan with his family in 1918 and graduated from Fort Morgan
High School in 1921. He had become a world-famous musician by the
time he joined the Air Force in 1942. During the war, he put together a
radio show called *Sustain the Wings*, which became a huge success both
with the troops and at home. On December 15, 1944, heading to Paris
to play a concert for the troops, Miller boarded a single-engine plane in
London. In light rain and heavy fog, the plane took off. It never arrived
in Paris.

Although the cause of the crash is unknown, it is possible that the
Royal Air Force unwittingly struck it down. On the same day, following
an order to abort their mission and jettison their bombs, some members
of the RAF saw a plane go down in the English Channel. Later they
suspected it had been the one carrying Miller.

Of course, Fort Morgan was established long before Glenn Miller
came to town, during the height of the struggles between the Plains
Indians and white settlers on the South Platte. On December 11, 1864,
Col. John Chivington ordered that the Overland Stage line be rerouted
away from the river and instead cut across to the southwest toward Denver. The spot where the new stage trail turned off was called Camp Junction (or Fort Junction). Soon a group of volunteers known as the Tyler
Rangers moved to the area to fight the Indians, and they began to build
a fort, known as Camp Tyler, at this site.

On April 25, 1865, the post, now under federal control, was renamed Camp Wardwell, and permanent wooden structures were

Street scene, Fort Morgan, about 1905 —Courtesy Wyoming State
Archives, J. E. Stimson Collection

added. Companies G and H of the Third U.S. Volunteers (USV) were
stationed at Camp Wardwell for a time, and later, Company B of the
Sixth USV served there. These troops were "Galvanized Yankees," former Confederate prisoners who in exchange for their release agreed to
serve in the federal army in the West. The next year, Missouri Cavalry
troops moved in and the post received its final name, Fort Morgan, for
Col. Christopher A. Morgan.

Born in Cincinnati, Christopher Morgan fought for the Union during
the Civil War as a captain in the Thirty-ninth Ohio Volunteers before
being made a colonel. He died on January 20, 1866, from gas leaking out
of a stove in his room. Morgan never saw the fort on the South Platte
River that was named in his honor. The post was abandoned in 1868,
but the name stuck to the town that had grown up around it.

CROW CREEK

The first of a slew of hostile encounters between Cheyenne Indians and
the frontier army along the South Platte River occurred on Crow Creek,
north of present Kuner, on April, 12, 1864. Throughout the spring,

mules, horses, and cattle had been disappearing from area ranches and stage stations. Some Cheyennes told authorities that they'd "found" the missing livestock and would be glad to return the animals for a price. Lt. Clark Dunn, First Colorado Cavalry, and fifteen men confronted the natives, and a fight—which each side later claimed the other had started—broke out. Although it wasn't a major battle, Dunn was killed, and the skirmish set the stage for the deadlier actions that followed.

CO 14
Sterling—US 85
96 MILES

Small communities—Stoneham, Raymer, Buckingham, Keota, Briggs-dale, and Purcell—dot the region along CO 14. Farmers still grow some crops here, but much of the area north of the highway is now a jigsaw puzzle of private and public land. Among the public reserves is the Pawnee National Grassland.

PAWNEE NATIONAL GRASSLAND

In the 1930s the federal government bought up millions of acres of farmland throughout the West in response to the Dust Bowl. President Franklin D. Roosevelt established the Resettlement Administration in 1935 to pay destitute families for their homesteads and restore the damaged lands. The government purchases in Colorado were eventually developed as the Pawnee and Comanche National Grasslands, in the northeastern and southeastern part of the state respectively (see also Comanche National Grasslands in part 3). The Pawnee Grassland encompasses nearly 200,000 acres in two main areas, both with access from CO 14.

KEOTA

Indian translations for the name Keota include "gone to visit" and "the fire has gone out," according to Percy Eberhart in *Ghosts of the Colorado Plains*. Homesteaders settled this high plains grassland, claiming 160-acre plots under the Homestead Act. By 1920 the town had 129 residents, but a decade later, fully a quarter of them had departed. The exodus was the result of severe droughts that made eking out a living in this already dry area virtually impossible. The droughts devastated farmers throughout the West, turning homesteads into "dust bowls." During this time, the government's Resettlement Administration allowed many settlers to sell their land and move on to greener pastures. But some farmers stayed, and others moved back later, only to face further droughts in the 1950s and again in 2002.

When James Michener began the research for his 1976 novel *Centennial*, one of the places that particularly drew him was Keota. Michener had taught at the University of Northern Colorado in Greeley and had taken photographs in the area during the 1930s as drought forced homesteaders to abandon their dreams. It was not until the early 1970s that he set out to capture the region and its history in fictional form.

Michener spent years doing research for the book in Colorado. While in Keota, he struck up a friendship with longtime resident Clyde Stanley, who then operated the post office. Sitting in the post office—lined with books on one wall and abandoned P.O. boxes on another and with a retired printing press in one corner—Michener gleaned details from Stanley and his sister Faye, a retired schoolteacher, to flesh out the tale that became *Centennial*. In the book, the town of Line Camp resembles Keota, and the character of Walter Bellamy is based in part on Clyde Stanley.

US 85
Denver—Wyoming Border
90 MILES

During the fur trade era of the 1830s and early 1840s, twelve trading posts existed within what is now Colorado. Four of them—Forts Lupton, Jackson, Vasquez, and St. Vrain—stood along the South Platte River in the short stretch between the present towns of Fort Lupton and Greeley on US 85. Their location was strategic, midway between the two major trading centers of the region, Bent's Fort (near today's La Junta) and Fort Laramie, Wyoming. It was also where the Trappers Trail from Taos, New Mexico, crossed the South Platte on its way north. Although markers commemorate the sites of these forts, only one, Fort Vasquez, has been fully developed for public visitation.

This part of US 85 roughly parallels a section of the South Platte River and runs through what Indian agent Thomas "Broken Hand" Fitzpatrick in 1848 called "the best agricultural district in the country." In fact, Fitzpatrick suggested that the Indian agency be located along the South Platte. "The establishment of an agency house occupied by one or two men alone in the wilderness is seemingly a wild project, but it may shortly become a nucleus for the Indians to resort to, and may be the means of introducing many of them . . . to begin agricultural pursuits." In spite of Fitzpatrick's argument, the government placed the agency farther south, on the Arkansas River at Big Timbers.

FORT LUPTON

A marker on the west side of US 85, just north of the present town of Fort Lupton, is about half a mile from the site of the original Fort Lupton, originally known as Fort Lancaster. Both names came from a lieutenant of Col. Henry Dodge's First Dragoons, Lancaster Lupton, who founded the trading post in 1836. The post was the first permanent settlement in northern Colorado. Indians of the region sometimes gathered there for councils, so they never attacked it. The fort was abandoned in 1844, but it reemerged as a stage station on the Overland Trail, and a permanent town grew up a few miles south.

Six miles north of Fort Lupton is the site of Fort Jackson. Fur traders Peter Sarpy and Henry Fraeb started Fort Jackson in 1837. The post served as a center for trade with the Indians, as did other forts on the South Platte. An 1838 inventory from Fort Jackson listed these goods: looking glasses, powder horns, battle-axes, scalping knives, wristbands, finger rings, colored glass beads, vermilion, colored cloth, powder, lead, alcohol, brass kettles, and blankets.

Fort Jackson was a short-lived concern—Sarpy and Fraeb sold it to their rivals, the Bent, St. Vrain Company, in the fall of 1838, and the new owners closed it down a short time later. Sarpy eventually opened a trading post in Bellevue, Nebraska. Fraeb, who had begun a new trading venture with Jim Bridger in Wyoming, was killed by Indians in the Little Snake River country in 1841.

FORT VASQUEZ HISTORICAL SITE

Of the four forts built during the fur trade era in this part of Colorado, only Fort Vasquez has been reconstructed to give visitors a sense of what it looked like. The Colorado Historical Society re-created the post's adobe walls on the original site, though shifted about eight feet to accommodate US 85. The site, just south of Platteville, also has a museum offering information about all the South Platte forts, with displays of artifacts ranging from trade beads and weapons from the fur trade era to items recovered from the Sand Creek Massacre site.

Fort Vasquez was built in 1835 by Louis Vasquez and Andrew Sublette, agents for the Rocky Mountain Fur Company, to conduct fur trading. In 1840 two traders named Locke and Randolph bought the fort; two years later, Indians looted it and it was abandoned. While never

Visitors can get a sense of the fur trading era at at the reconstructed Fort Vasquez near Platteville.

fully rebuilt, the log structure served as an army base during the Indian wars of the 1860s.

Vasquez, a prominent trader, opened a post with Jim Bridger in far western Wyoming in 1842. That post, Fort Bridger, became one of the most important provisioning stops for emigrants on the Oregon-California Trail. Sublette returned to Missouri for a time, served with the Missouri Volunteers at Fort Kearny, and eventually moved to California, where he died of injuries from a grizzly attack.

Fort St. Vrain, the northernmost of the South Platte posts, stood near the mouth of St. Vrain Creek, about four miles west of present Gilcrest. Ceran St. Vrain and his partners William and Charles Bent built the adobe structure in 1837. The partners started the Bent, St. Vrain Company in 1831 and became the earliest successful entrepreneurs in Colorado. From their first trading house in Taos, New Mexico, they negotiated deals with Mexico, which at the time controlled the lands southwest of the Arkansas River. William Bent opened another operation, Bent's Fort, in 1833 (see Bent's Old Fort in part 3), and five years later, the company built the post here, originally known as Fort Lookout. Managed by Ceran St. Vrain's younger brother, Marcellin, the post soon took the St. Vrain name, as did the creek that flowed nearby.

Located along the old Trappers Trail, Fort St. Vrain operated successfully for six years, closing in 1844 after a steep drop in the demand for fur. A short time later, Ceran St. Vrain and another partner received a substantial land grant from the Mexican government. He spent his later years in New Mexico Territory, developing flour mills and cattle ranches. He died of apoplexy in October 1870.

The younger brother, Marcellin St. Vrain, whom most historians believe had two Indian wives, continued as a trader in Colorado. Fort St. Vrain had long since closed when the *Rocky Mountain News* reported, "Messrs. St. James and St. Vrain arrived with a large train of wagons, loaded with flour and a general assortment of goods, and opened a store . . . in the month of February, 1859. This was the first store opened in Denver." Eventually Marcellin left Colorado and returned to his family home of St. Louis.

Travelers on the trails to Denver passed by the abandoned Fort St. Vrain for decades. On a trip through Colorado in 1846, writer Francis Parkman described the site:

> At noon we rested under the walls of a large fort, built in these solitudes some years since by M. [Marcellin] St. Vrain. It was now abandoned and fast falling into ruin. The walls of unbaked bricks were cracked from top to bottom. Our horses recoiled in terror from the neglected entrance, where the heavy gates were torn from their hinges and flung down. The area within was overgrown with weeds, and the long ranges of apartments once occupied by the motley concourse of traders, Canadians, and squaws, were now miserably dilapidated.

In spite of its neglected state, in 1853 Fort St. Vrain was the site of a conference between Indian agent Thomas "Broken Hand" Fitzpatrick and the Cheyenne and Arapaho Indians. There, Fitzpatrick persuaded tribal representatives to take smaller annuities than those promised in the 1851 Fort Laramie Treaty, in which the Cheyenne and Arapaho Indians were given much of the land in present Colorado. Following this conference, which concluded on September 10, 1853, Fitzpatrick left the mountains for St. Louis, never to return.

Fitzpatrick believed that pushing Indians onto ever-smaller reservations would lead to their eventual demise, but the federal policy persisted. Just as he had predicted, starvation and disease proved to be greater weapons than soldiers' guns. (See also Great Sand Dunes National Park in part 2.)

PLATTEVILLE

The Platte River Land Company formed the agricultural town of Platteville in 1871, when it purchased several thousand acres from the railroad. Although similar to other farming colonies established in Colorado in the early 1870s, such as the one at Union Colony (see Greeley later in this section), Platteville was more a commercial enterprise than a communal settlement.

EVANS

A terminal point on the Denver Pacific Railroad, Evans was chosen as the site of an agricultural colony in 1871. Following the model of the Union Colony at Greeley, the Reverend Andrew C. Todd launched the St. Louis–Western Company to establish a communal farming enterprise. Crop production in Evans was never as good as at other area colonies, such as Greeley, but the fact that residents were allowed to visit taverns was a definite plus for those who chafed at the stricter rules of Union Colony.

An active rivalry churned between Evans and Greeley for the privilege of being the Weld County seat during the 1870s. The honor traveled back and forth several times before Greeley became the final winner in 1877.

GREELEY

Greeley started out as Union Colony, a cooperative farming community conceived by *New York Tribune* editor Horace Greeley. Nathan C. Meeker, agricultural editor of the *Tribune*, organized the project on December 23, 1869, in New York City, and in March 1870, the company selected a site near the confluence of the South Platte and Cache la Poudre Rivers. After purchasing 12,000 acres of land, primarily from the Denver Pacific Railway, the company filed on an additional 60,000 acres of public land and applied for incorporation under the territorial laws of Colorado.

Memberships in the Union Colony were available to "temperate men of good character" for a fee of $155, according to *A Colorado History*. In return, each member received a parcel of land suitable for farming plus one town lot. Meeker served as colony president.

The first fifty families arrived in May 1870, setting up tents and lean-tos. During the spring and summer, they dug irrigation ditches, plowed, sowed seeds, built structures, laid out streets, planted trees, and started a school. Before long, the colony had a tanning plant for buffalo hides, a farmer's club, a lyceum, a library, and a dramatics association. In his 1901 book *The Overland Stage to California*, Frank A. Root wrote about the colony, by that time called Greeley:

> The Greeley colony . . . *[started] with a fund of $150,000. This was judiciously invested in lands, irrigating canals, a mill power, and a 'colony fence,' enclosing the entire tract, thus for some time saving any further expense in building individual fences. . . .*
>
> *The region . . . is very fertile. It is pronounced unsurpassed for the production of wheat, rye, oats, barley, potatoes, and nearly all kinds of vegetables. The variety of potatoes known as the 'Greeley' practically has*

no equal in flavor and none can command the price it does in market. . . . The berries raised in that vicinity command enormous prices, for nothing can compare with them. . . .

Wheat has long been the great staple raised by the colony and its yield most of the time has been enormous, often as high as forty or fifty bushels per acre being realized, which has brought from ninety cents to $1.50 per bushel.

Not all settlers found the colony a utopia, however. Meeker ran the colony with an iron hand. As one man who left told anyone who would listen, "Don't go to Greeley, Colorado Territory! That is the last place on the face of this terrestrial ball that any human being should contemplate a removal to! Greeley, Colorado T., is a delusion, a snare—it is a fraud, a cheat, a swindle."

The colony ended its charter in 1880, but by then Greeley was firmly established, and it would come to be one of northeastern Colorado's most vital economic regions. Today it is one of the fastest-growing cities in the nation.

Agriculture continues to be the dominant industry. Since 1896 Greeley has held an annual event celebrating the area's potato farmers. Originally called Greeley Potato Days, the festival came to be known as the Spud Rodeo. It is still held every summer, now under the name Greeley Stampede.

Farming country near Greeley —Courtesy Wyoming State Archives, J. E. Stimson Collection

Cherokee City and Fort Latham

A stage station once stood just east of Greeley at the South Platte River Crossing of the Cherokee Trail (where US 34 crosses the river). At the first settlement here, known as Cherokee City, a few settlers formed the Cherokee Town Company and built several houses, a sawmill, and a stage station with livestock stables. In 1863 Cherokee City residents moved about a mile to the southwest, to the site of a busy stage station on the Overland Stage line. The station was called Latham, for California senator Milton S. Latham, who supported development of the Overland Trail.

The station was strongly built and often served as a fortress for settlers threatened by roving Indians. Also used as a post for army troops, it eventually became known as Fort Latham. Frank Root, the local mail agent at Latham, penned this description of the place in his book *The Overland Stage to California*:

> The stage station was the only house there. It was a substantially built one-and-one-half-story log structure, fronting south. There was a large one-story, rough-board addition built on the north side, fronting both east and west, in which were a large dining-room, kitchen, bedroom, and a storehouse. Its location was important. It was the junction of the branch stage line to Denver, and stages made close connections east and also with the main line to Salt Lake and California. Besides, it was a storehouse for supplies for three divisions, and this made it the most important way station on the overland route between Atchison [Kansas] and Placerville [California].

Trader Elbridge Gerry, who had come to Colorado in the 1830s, eventually settled with his family in Latham, where he operated the Gerry Trading Post. In August 1864, Gerry became the "Paul Revere of Colorado" after his Cheyenne Indian wife told him that Indians were planning raids along the South Platte from Fort Latham to Denver.

According to his wife's information, Gerry had only three days to spread the word. He saddled his horse and warned his neighbors near Fort Latham before heading upstream, toward Denver, alerting people all along the way. He got the message to the governor in Denver two days—and four horses—later.

By the time the Indians set out, the settlers had already fortified the areas west and south of Fort Latham, so the raiders focused their attention on the region east of the fort. They destroyed telegraph lines and harassed settlers and travelers. They also launched raids against Gerry's place, vandalizing property and stealing livestock. Gerry filed claims with the U.S. government for the damage but received only $13,200, a fraction of what he said he had lost. He eventually used the money to build the Gerry Block and the Gerry House Hotel in nearby Evans.

ROCKPORT

North of Greeley, US 85 runs through farm country and small towns such as Eaton, Pierce, Nunn, and Rockport. Due to its location near the Wyoming border, Rockport saw a boom of sorts after establishment of the Colorado Lottery. Because Wyoming has no state lottery, people from Cheyenne often drive the few miles south to Rockport for their chance to win some of Colorado's millions.

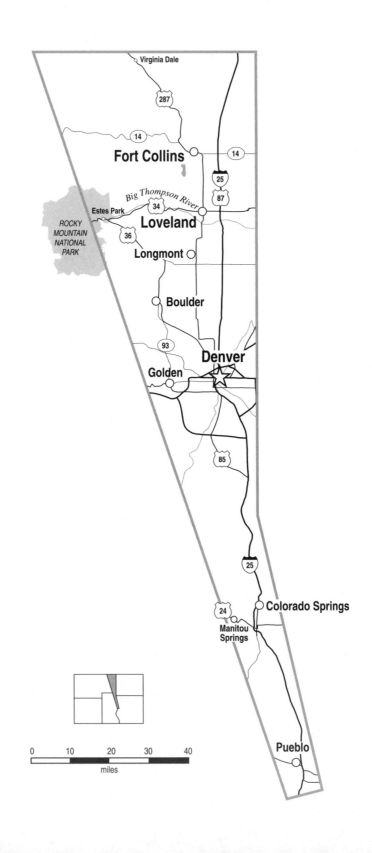

PART FIVE

North-central
THE FRONT RANGE

No place in the Rocky Mountains is more dynamic than Colorado's Front Range, which lies along the foothills of the Rockies, spilling out toward the plains. This region, which first drew gold seekers in 1859, still attracts new residents and visitors with its unequalled year-round recreational opportunities.

The Front Range contains Colorado's largest metropolitan areas and the majority of its population. Running north and south, the I-25 corridor traverses the Front Range from Pueblo to the Wyoming border, linking all the major communities, either directly or via intersecting highways. We will travel the region from south to north, beginning with I-25.

I-25/US 87
Pueblo—Wyoming Border
198 MILES

Interstate 25 from Colorado Springs to Denver roughly follows the route of the Cherokee Trail across Colorado, much of which incorporated the old Trappers Trail. The section of the Cherokee Trail between Denver and Virginia Dale ran approximately along what is now US 287 to the Wyoming border. Cherokee Indians (and others) forged the trail in 1849 as part of a route to the California gold diggings. It linked Bent's Fort (near La Junta) on the Santa Fe Trail with Fort Bridger (Wyoming) on the California Trail.

The Lewis Evans party was the first group of Cherokees to travel the route, thus it is sometimes referred to as the Evans Trail. Their route in Wyoming generally ran just south of today's I-80. In 1850 more Cherokee parties departed for California from Arkansas and Oklahoma. At Virginia Dale, near the Wyoming border, some of them took a new route, known as the South Branch of the Cherokee Trail, which roughly paralleled the present Wyoming border to Fort Bridger.

Over the next several years, the trail was used as a two-way route for gold rush travelers and commerce. It also served as a wagon road for emigrant families and was sometimes used for cattle drives. The trail had campsites roughly twelve to twenty miles apart, many of them at previously established campsites and posts. Later gold seekers also used the route during the Pikes Peak gold rush.

Horses saddled and ready to take visitors on a scenic ride on a snowy day at Aspen Lodge near Estes Park

Before the Evans party traversed the trail, government explorer John C. Frémont had traveled portions of the route in 1842 and 1844, as did Col. Stephen Watts Kearny in 1845 and Francis Parkman, who later became a recognized historian, in 1846. Mormon emigrants followed the trail from Pueblo, where some of them had spent the winter of 1846–47, to Fort Laramie before continuing to Salt Lake City (see Pueblo in part 2).

In the 1850s, several military commands also used the trail, including those of Maj. John Sedgwick and Col. William W. Loring. Portions of the North Branch became part of the Overland Trail, which Ben Holladay's stage company used after 1862. According to author Lee Whiteley, the trail went by many names over the years, including the Arkansas River Road, the Pueblo and Fort Lyon Road, the Arkansas Emigrant Trail, the Old Southern Road, the Old Laramie Road, and several others.

COLORADO SPRINGS

The original community at the site of Colorado Springs, Colorado City, was the first territorial capital. Not to be confused with Colorado City south of Pueblo, the historic district of Colorado Springs is referred to as Old Colorado City.

As miners rushed to the Colorado Rockies in 1859 seeking gold, the main travel route was over Ute Pass (now US 24), near Colorado Springs. On August 11, 1859, the Colorado City Town Company established itself on Fountain Creek, at the base of Pikes Peak, hoping the town would become the main supply base for the mining camps.

The new town, one mile wide and two miles long, immediately attracted residents, and before long there were 200 houses and businesses. Most of the buildings were wood, although some forward-thinking people built of quarried stone. During the winter of 1859–60, the town company began construction on a wagon road across Ute Pass to the South Park mining areas.

From the beginning, however, Colorado City had competition from both Denver City to the north and Canon City to the south. In addition, the outbreak of the Civil War hindered the fledgling town's growth as both men and government resources were funneled into the Union effort. Meanwhile, for various reasons, overland travel shifted to the South Platte route, with most of the Colorado traffic coming from the north and into Denver. These factors combined to dash Colorado City's hopes of becoming a supply center. The community sustained itself with agriculture, while a new neighbor, Colorado Springs, emerged. By the early twentieth century, the newcomer engulfed its predecessor.

City of Millionaires

William Jackson Palmer, a Civil War general and Medal of Honor recipient from Pennsylvania, is considered the "father" of Colorado Springs. Arriving here in 1870, he founded both the city and the Denver & Rio Grande Railroad. Palmer platted the city's streets and provided land for schools and churches. His own home was a sixty-seven-room castle known as Glen Eyrie.

Palmer promoted Colorado Springs as a health resort for the wealthy. It was near the mountains and boasted a dry, mild climate that was thought to be beneficial for tuberculosis. Many sanitariums were built, along with hotels and restaurants. Because of its proximity to the Cripple Creek gold mines, many mining tycoons moved to Colorado Springs, and it soon became known as the "City of Millionaires." Yet among the

The Pikes Peak cog railway still runs from Colorado Springs to the top of the mountain. —Courtesy Wyoming State Archives

luxury accommodations were the modest dwellings of local farmers and less successful miners.

In her journal of her travels through the West in 1881, Isabella Bird gave the town a mixed review:

> I then came to strange gorges with wonderful upright rocks of all shapes and colours, and turning through a gate of rock, came upon what I knew must be Glen Eyrie, as wild and romantic a glen as imagination ever pictured. The track then passed down a valley close under some ghastly peaks, wild, cold, awe-inspiring scenery. After fording a creek several times, I came upon a decayed-looking cluster of houses bearing the arrogant name of Colorado City, and two miles farther on, from the top of one of the Foot Hill ridges, I saw the bleak-looking scattered houses of the ambitious watering-place of Colorado Springs, the goal of my journey of 150 miles. . . . A queer embryo-looking place it is, out on the bare Plains, yet it is rising and likely to rise, and has some big hotels much resorted to. It has a fine view of the mountains, specially of Pike's Peak, but . . . to me no place could be more unattractive than Colorado Springs, from its utter treelessness.

Just as General Palmer sired Colorado Springs, Spencer Penrose nourished it. After making millions in gold and copper, Penrose helped fund the Pikes Peak and Cheyenne Mountain Highways and built the Cheyenne Mountain Zoo, the Will Rogers Shrine, and the fabulous Broadmoor Hotel.

During World War II, Colorado Springs became a center for military training. Both the Fort Carson Army Base and the Peterson Air Force Base were built in the early 1940s. Since then, several other military installations have joined the community: the U.S. Air Force Academy, the Schriever Air Force Base, the U.S. Army Space Command, and the North American Radar and Air Defense (NORAD, also known as the North American Aerospace Defense Command). NORAD, the most secretive installation of its kind in the country, is located deep inside Cheyenne Mountain. NORAD does participate in one public event, however—the Christmastime tracking of Santa Claus.

Although Colorado is the only place ever to reject the opportunity to host the Olympics (see Winter Park in part 6), Colorado Springs is the home of the U.S. Olympic Complex, which houses the headquarters for the U.S. Olympic Committee administration and the Olympic Training Center.

Garden of the Gods

The unique rock formations now known as Garden of the Gods, on the west side of Colorado Springs, were sacred grounds to the Ute, Arapaho, Kiowa, and Cheyenne Indians, who visited the site annually for spiritual ceremonies.

Some say that surveyors laying out the town of Colorado City in 1859 came upon the Indians' venerated site and suggested that it would make a good beer garden. But one of them, Rufus Cable, apparently had higher sensibilities. Declaring that the stunning natural beauty of the place befitted the gods, he dubbed it Garden of the Gods.

Twenty years later, Burlington Railroad president Charles Elliott Perkins bought 240 acres in the Garden of the Gods for a summer home. Later he purchased adjoining land, but he never built on any of the property. Instead, Perkins allowed free public access to the area. After his death in 1907, his children, honoring their father's wishes, gave the 480 acres that encompassed Garden of the Gods to the city of Colorado Springs. They stipulated that "it shall remain free to the public, where no intoxicating liquors shall be manufactured, sold, or dispensed, where no building or structure shall be erected except those necessary to properly care for, protect, and maintain the area as a public park."

DENVER

Some places are destined for greatness, and the Mile High City is one of them. Named for Kansas governor James W. Denver, as it was part of Kansas at the time, it quickly assumed its role as the biggest city in the Rocky Mountains. From its early days as a gold camp to its present status as a commercial, cultural, and transportation hub, Denver has dominated Colorado.

Pikes Peak or Bust!

On the first day of summer in 1850, John Beck, a Cherokee preacher en route to California's goldfields, stopped to do a little panning in Ralston Creek, near today's Arvada, a suburb northwest of Denver. He did find some color in his pan, but not enough to think the stream worthwhile, so he continued on to California.

A few years later, back in Oklahoma, Beck decided to try again. In the spring of 1858, he enlisted a partner, fellow Cherokee prospector Green Russell, and with a party of seventy men they made their way back to the cold streams of the eastern Rocky Mountains. By the time they started panning, the party had grown to 104 men. On June 24, the prospectors again found gold at Ralston Creek, and soon they were exploring other creeks in the region as well.

The big discovery came in August, when the Russell party found gold on Cherry Creek. On August 26, Kansas City's *Journal of Commerce* ran the headline: "THE NEW ELDORADO!!! Gold in Kansas Territory!! The Pike's Mines! First Arrival of Gold Dust in Kansas City!!!" Within days the story had run in papers in St. Louis and Boston, and the rush was on. Thousands of gold seekers loaded their wagons and headed to Cherry Creek, sporting signs saying "Pike's Peak or Bust!"

Several groups quickly formed to organize towns at the site of the gold find. The first was the Montana Town Site Company, which started plans for the town of Montana City in early September of 1858 but abandoned the project within a year. Hot on their heels, the St. Charles Association formed on September 24 to establish the town of St. Charles City on the South Platte River about five miles from the mouth of Cherry Creek. A month later another group, the Auraria Town Company, organized the town of Auraria on the other side of Cherry Creek. The Denver City Town Company set up shop a few weeks after that, on November 22, building Denver City right next to the St. Charles settlement. Before long, the vigorous Denver City had overtaken St. Charles.

Auraria and Denver City became strong rivals as repeated gold strikes attracted more throngs to the area. Recognizing that competition between them could end up harming them both, Denver City and Auraria agreed to consolidate as Denver in April 1860. The June 6, 1860, *Rocky Mountain News* ruminated on the infant city's amazingly rapid evolution:

A sketch of Denver City's early days by James F. Gookins (date unknown)
—From *Harper's Weekly*

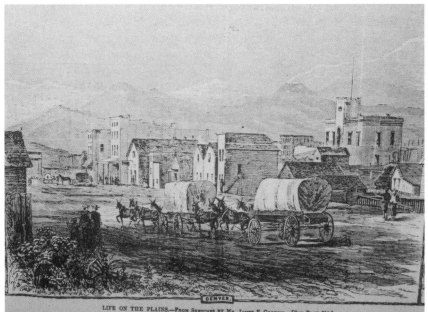

LIFE ON THE PLAINS.—From Sketches by Mr. James F. Gookins.—[See Page 654.]

> *Our city . . . in the spring of 1859 containing a motley collection of three hundred log huts, covered with mud, and on the first of July in that year having but one room with a plank floor, has in a few months increased to a city of six thousand people; with its fine hotels, stores, manufactories, and all the appliances, comforts and many of the luxuries of civilization. . . . Lofty buildings are rising on the business streets; solid and substantial edifices of which old cities might well be proud. . . . Great trains of huge Prairie freighters arrive and depart almost daily, and more than a thousand emigrant wagons arrive every week. With such a start and such a prospect what will be the future of Denver, the commercial emporium of the Rocky Mountains, the great city of the Plains?*

Besides its bustling daytime commerce, Denver had a thriving night-life as well. At the Denver Club, cattle barons and businessmen enjoyed fine food, wine, and entertainment. Another popular spot was Denver Hall, which newspaperman Libeus Barney wrote about in 1859:

> *Upon the first table as we entered, "Lasconette" was the game under consideration; on the next two Rouge-et-Noire, or "Red and Black," was being played; "Spanish Monte" occupied the next three; "French Monte" drew its worshippers around the seventh table; "Over and Under Seven," occupied two; "Chuck-a-Luck," three; "High Dice," one; "Van Tauma," three; "Roulette," one; and "Kansas Lottery," the balance. The tables rent from three to five dollars a night, and seldom a night passes but all are engaged.*

Some establishments were restricted to men. One female observer noted in 1871 that actresses were "in horrible undress, swinging and tumbling, and plunging heals [sic] over head out of their sphere. . . . Actresses coming to Colorado have been compelled, at a painful sacrifice to their modesty to 'shed the light frivolity of dress' in great measure."

Clearly, not everyone was impressed with the "great city of the Plains." In 1873 traveler Isabella Bird wrote this description of Denver: "There the great braggart city lay spread out, brown and treeless, upon the brown and treeless plain, which seemed to nourish nothing but wormwood and the Spanish bayonet."

Newspaper Wars

William H. Byers and Thomas Gibson began publishing Colorado's first newspaper, the *Rocky Mountain News*, on April 23, 1859, only thirty-nine hours after Byers arrived with his printing press. Because the publishers wanted to serve both Denver City and Auraria, they built their offices on piers in Cherry Creek.

Byers, an Ohio native, lived in Omaha, Nebraska, for a time and served as a member of the first Nebraska Territorial Legislature in 1854–55. In March 1859, he headed to Denver to start the *Rocky Mountain News*. He also invested in real estate, railroads, mining, and agriculture and built the first telegraph line between Denver and Santa Fe. Byers served at Colorado's first constitutional convention and was a prominent citizen of Denver for the rest of his life. A town east of the city is named for him.

Just twenty minutes after the first *Rocky Mountain News* hit the stands, another publisher, John Merrick, released the premiere issue of his *Cherry Creek Pioneer*. But the first issue was also the last. The very next day, Merrick sold his printing press to Byers's partner Thomas Gibson, who left the *Rocky Mountain News* to start the *Rocky Mountain Gold Reporter* and the *Mountain City Herald* in Gregory Gulch. But he soon returned to Denver, and on May 1, 1860, he released the *Rocky Mountain Herald*, the first daily newspaper in the Rocky Mountains. Gibson also issued another paper, the *Daily Mountaineer*, in August, but William Byers almost immediately bought it.

On August 27, 1860, the *Rocky Mountain News* became a daily. The Cherry Creek flood of 1864 wiped out the entire operation, but Byers quickly rebuilt in Denver City. Except for the few months after the flood, the newspaper has been continuously published from its first day to the present (although it has now merged with the *Denver Post*).

Words to the Wise

In their *Complete Guide to the Gold Districts of Kansas & Nebraska*, published in Chicago in 1859, Edwin R. Pease and William Cole outlined for prospective gold seekers the costs of the journey west:

> *A company of four can supply themselves with all necessary articles for mining, and provisions for from five and a half to six months, including two yoke of oxen and one wagon, for $140 per man, and a company of six for $120, including fares and freights from Chicago or St. Louis to [Leavenworth] City. Good oxen can be bought for from $65 to $80 per yoke and a good wagon from $75 to $80.*

The authors advised travelers to follow the northern route, where they would "find the principal streams bridged, and plenty of wood, water and feed, and good camping ground." One Pikes Peak miner, Joseph Baker, cautioned overlanders, "If you come in the Spring, beware of one thing. Don't overload your team, for there are some of the worst sand roads I ever saw."

Once at the camps, newly arrived miners found supplies limited and expensive. Much of the freight came up on the well-established Trappers Trail from Taos, New Mexico, 300 miles from Cherry Creek. Miner Alexander O. McGrew noted these prices at the early camps:

> *Mexican flour is worth from $10 to $12 a finagre, or Mexican measure of 145 lbs.; American flour is worth $15, $20 and $25 per cwt. . . . Beef is worth 15 cts. per lb; beans 20 cts. per lb; bacon 50 cts per lb; sugar 50 cts; coffee 80 cts; powder $1.50; lead 50c.; wool socks $1.00 per pair;*

*undershirts and drawers from $1.50 [to] $3.00, and other things in propor-
cion [sic]. Gold is taken at one dollar a pennyweight for all necessaries.*

While the high prices were tough for the miners, they were good for
the merchants. McGrew noted that would-be entrepreneurs would find
plenty of opportunities in the gold camps:

> *A good drug store, a hardware store with plenty of building materials, a
> printing office with a good job office attached, clothing and dry goods; in
> fact, a general assortment would do a good business. Sheet iron is in de-
> mand; lumber is worth fifty cents a foot, so that a good saw mill, shingle
> machine and lath cutter would do a good business. A daguerreotypist could
> make his fortune here at present. . . . Let mechanics who anticipate coming
> bring their tools, as wages will be high.*

Similarly, prospector E. C. Mather suggested that anyone with a
green thumb would be well advised to "come out in the spring as early as
possible, and be sure and bring a plow, and a supply of seeds; bring a light
plow as the soil is very loose and sandy, it is well adapted to raising wheat
and corn; there can be fortunes made in farming." Joseph Baker advised,
"As to driving beef I don't think it will pay, there are so many cattle here
now, and more to come in the spring. You will do well, however, to bring
milch cows. Money can be made at that."

Making a Mint

As might be expected, there were conflicts over the value of gold.
Generally, a pinch of gold dust was valued at twenty-five cents; larger
amounts were weighed on a scale. But gold dust stuck to scales, fingers,
and pouches. To resolve differences, Clark, Gruber & Company of Leavenworth, Kansas, established a banking house in Denver in 1860. They
soon began minting ten-dollar gold pieces. An advertisement for the
bank noted, "We have in connection with our Banking House, a MINT,
and are prepared to exchange our Coin for Gold Dust. The native gold is
coined as it is found, alloyed with silver. The weight will be greater, but
the value the same as the United States coin of like denominations."

The *Rocky Mountain News* reported on the first mintings: "A hundred
'blanks' had been prepared, weight and fineness tested and last manipu-
lations gone through with, prior to their passage through the press. . . .
The machinery was put in motion and 'mint drops' of the value of $10
each began dropping into a tin pail with the most musical 'chink.'"

The face of each coin was "a representation of the peak, its base surrounded by a forest of timber, and 'Pike's Peak Gold' encircling the summit. Immediately under its base is the word 'Denver.'" On the reverse
was a bald eagle encircled by the name of the firm, and beneath it the
date, 1860. Eventually the company also minted gold coins in denominations of $2.50, $5, and $20.

Other gold camps, however, established their own values. In Clear Creek, gold was worth $17 an ounce, but in Russell Gulch, it sold for $16 per ounce, although dirty or "common" gold might fetch only $12 an ounce.

Clark, Gruber & Company remained in business until 1863, when the federal government bought it out. The plan was for the government to continue minting coins, but instead it turned the business into an assay office. The federally operated Denver Mint did not open until 1906. In the meantime, two other private companies minted coins, and other entrepreneurs developed paper scrip in small denominations, which became known as "shin-plasters." Today, the Colorado Historical Society houses the machinery and dies of the pioneer Clark, Gruber & Company mint.

If You Don't Find Gold, Go-back!

Of the estimated 100,000 gold seekers who rushed to Pikes Peak after 1858, about 90 percent were disappointed. So many of them returned home that a name for them was coined: "go-backs." One of the go-backs, J. M. Newhall of Lawrence, Kansas, told of his misadventures in an 1873 article in *Kansas Magazine*:

> About the first day of March, AD 1859, four of us started for the Pike's Peak gold diggings, although we had been warned of the danger of making

A Frank Bierstadt drawing of a dejected group departing the gold country —From Harper's Weekly, August 13, 1859

so early a start in the season, and also sufficiently ridiculed about a "wild goose chase."

[After traveling for a time] we had slept two or three nights without [see-ing] the Smoky Hill [River]—then saw it again in the daytime—and finally we lost it altogether. . . . We had now only five days' provisions; no buffalo to shoot. . . . With no river and no game, some of us began to weaken a little . . . all because we couldn't see the mountains.

I happened to have a pocket-compass, we decided to travel south by that. . . . Sometimes there would be hardly anything to sight on.

After several days' traveling we reached Fountain City, quite near the mountains . . . [We found] only one, large log house. . . . There were no regular 'diggings'—nobody digging for gold—that we could see. . . . I shov-eled often in the river bed—got lots of shining stuff; but . . . all is not gold that glitters. . . . We wanted to stay because we were ashamed to go back home flat broke.

In the end, however, with his health suffering ("I was having the 'shakes,'" he said) Newhall did swallow his pride. He found "a little old wagon" and "with my two horses and affectionate dog, I started alone, back for home." On the way back, he met other gold seekers making their way to the peak, their wagons sometimes "chalked in letters more than a foot long across" with the famous slogan "Pike's Peak or Bust!" Soon, many of them would be turning back as well, the original slogan replaced with "Busted, by God!"

As Newhall encountered the hopeful, "Some would ask about the gold, and why I was going back. I would invariable [sic] answer, 'I got out of provisions, and there was no work going on; I had a hard time getting out, lost everything, got discouraged, and was going home.'" Neverthe-less, he did not discourage them. "I believe there is gold out there," he told them. "If you have plenty of provisions, go on by all means."

Disasters

The weather was still wintry on the morning of April 19, 1863, when a fire broke out in downtown Denver City. Before the volunteer fire companies could control the blaze, it had destroyed much of downtown, burning an estimated seventy buildings and supplies valued at $197,200. Like many other early western towns consumed by fire, Denver rebuilt, this time in brick and stone.

In 1880 destruction of a different kind hit the town. By that time, a substantial number of Chinese immigrants had settled in Denver. Throughout the West, Chinese railroad workers looking for new op-portunities in the mining camps were seldom allowed to stake claims of their own, so they often took jobs as cooks or doing laundry. In Denver's Chinatown, a downtown neighborhood between Fifteenth and Seven-teenth Streets along Wazee, other Chinese businesses thrived as well.

A network of underground passages provided access to opium dens, saloons, and Chinese brothels. Presumably because of the opium, the area became known as "Hop Alley."

On Halloween night in 1880, Hop Alley came apart at the seams. No one knows what started the riot—perhaps it was a disagreement over the price of some laundry, or maybe it was just another barroom brawl. While the cause isn't clear, the outcome changed Denver forever. During the night, rioters looted homes, burned businesses, and killed at least one man. City marshals eventually quelled the melee. Afterward, the city awarded $54,000 in damages to Chinese businessmen.

Capital City

In 1881 Denver became the state capital, permanently taking the designation away from Golden. Until that time, the two cities had vied for capital status, and the Colorado legislature went so far as to rotate where it held its annual sessions. The elegant state capitol building, with its gold-plated dome, was built in the 1890s.

With its role as capital assured, Denver accelerated its development in the late 1800s and early 1900s. The city got its first electric lights in

The Colorado State Capitol in the early twentieth century, when the building dominated downtown Denver. —Courtesy Wyoming State Archives, J. E. Stimson Collection

1883, and the first electric streetcars in the state began running here in 1885. Visitors could find a room for 25 cents on busy Lamimer Street or stay in the more upscale Hotel Albany.

Many educational and cultural institutions were built during this period, including the Denver Public Library, the University of Denver, the Denver Zoo, the Denver Museum of Natural History, and the Denver Stockyards, which became the largest sheep market in the country. The latter's National Western Stock Show still sponsors a rodeo each January, continuing a long tradition of rodeo in Colorado. The first known rodeo-style competition took place in Deer Trail, Colorado, on July 4, 1869, and the first major competition was held in Denver at the city's annual Festival of Mountain and Plain.

Denver held the first Festival of Mountain and Plain in 1895 as an attempt to boost the city's finances as well as its image and morale after the silver bust of 1893, which had taken a brutal toll on Denver's economy and population. The festival began as a carnival with exhibits, a parade, fireworks, and other activities. A few years later, after the first big public rodeo was held in Cheyenne, Wyoming, in September 1897, the festival added a major bronc-riding competition to its list of events. (See also Ovid in part 4.) The festival was discontinued in 1902, but Denver did eventually bounce back, primarily by expanding its agriculture-related industries.

The Unsinkable Molly Brown

One of Denver's most famous residents was Margaret Brown, known as the "Unsinkable Molly Brown" because of her survival of the *Titanic* disaster in 1912. Born Margaret Tobin in Hannibal, Missouri, she was called Maggie by her parents. At nineteen she moved to Leadville, Colorado, where she met and married Irish miner John Joseph "J.J." Brown. By 1887 J.J. was a mine superintendent and part of the Leadville social elite. The Browns hit it big with discovery and development of the Little Jonny Mine in 1893, which revived the faltering economy of Leadville. Eventually the Browns moved to Denver, buying a house at 1340 Pennsylvania Street.

It was her actions following the *Titanic* wreck that turned Margaret Brown into a legend. Shortly after the ship struck the iceberg, Brown—dressed in seven pairs of stockings, her warmest velvet suit, and layers of other clothing—joined her fellow passengers on the deck. She was thrust into a lifeboat and rowed through the cold darkness until she and the other survivors were picked up by the *Carpathia* the following day. After the rescue, Brown, who had been a first-class passenger, organized aid for the poorer survivors.

Denver's Larimer Street, early 1900s —Courtesy Wyoming State Archives

While lauded for her efforts, Brown was also criticized for her forth-right manner and her outspoken support of women's rights. In fact, she even protested the fact that the women were allowed into the lifeboats before the men during the *Titanic* disaster. "To me it is all wrong. Women demand equal rights on land—why not on sea?" Her estranged husband, J.J., said she was "too mean to sink."

Margaret lived in Denver until her death in 1932. Her story was eventually turned into a Broadway play, *The Unsinkable Molly Brown*, in which she was incorrectly portrayed as a vulgar former saloon girl who had struck it rich in Leadville. Her house in Denver is still standing, now operated as the Molly Brown House Museum.

Modern Denver

Since World War II, Denver has attracted energy, defense, and high-tech industries to support its economy. Tourism has also emerged as a major industry in Denver. In addition, with both the state capital and the regional headquarters for the federal government located here, thousands of Denver residents are employed in government jobs. While not immune to economic ups and downs, Denver has thrived and continues to thrive in the twenty-first century.

No discussion of modern Denver could be complete without mentioning the Broncos. Professional sports, particularly football, are a major source of entertainment and city pride for Denverites. In addition to the Broncos, several sports teams have had homes in Denver through the decades. By 1862 the city had several baseball teams and held regular local competitions; 130 years later, Denver acquired a Major League Baseball team, the Colorado Rockies. The city's national basketball team, the Denver Nuggets, and hockey team, the Colorado Avalanche, also have strong followings. But the main home team is the Broncos.

Formed in 1960, the Broncos have enjoyed years of faithful support from their fans. They finally won a Super Bowl in 1998, defeating the Green Bay Packers 31 to 24. The victory celebration and parade attracted an estimated 650,000 people to downtown Denver. The Broncos won again in 1999. The following year, Mile High Stadium hosted its last game, and the Broncos moved to their new home at Invesco Field.

CO 93
Golden—Boulder
30 MILES

GOLDEN

Nestled at the foot of the Rockies where I-70 begins its ascent to the Continental Divide, Golden was founded in 1859 as a supply center for the surrounding mining camps. From 1862 to 1867, Golden served as the territorial capital of Colorado, but the town lost its bid for becoming the state capital to Denver. Named for early miner Tom Golden, the town retains its mining roots with the Colorado School of Mines, a top engineering college that still holds field studies at mines in the Colorado Rockies.

Railroad Crossings
One of Golden's founders and most dedicated boosters was entrepreneur W.A.H. Loveland. In the early 1860s, Loveland, along with early Colorado explorer Edward L. Berthoud and another partner, got a charter to construct a wagon road up Clear Creek Canyon. But before they could build it, the Civil War broke out and resources were diverted to other areas.

Undaunted, Loveland soon started planning a railroad to connect Golden with area mining districts, knowing that a rail line through the town would ensure its prosperity for decades to come. In 1865 the territorial legislature granted him a charter for the Colorado & Clear Creek Railroad, later renamed the Colorado Central. The plan included a tunnel under the Continental Divide to create a vital east-west link.

Unfortunately for Golden, wrangling among railroad interests delayed construction of the line, allowing Denver to acquire its own rail line a few months before Golden's Colorado Central line was completed in September 1870. Amid legal, political, and corporate struggles with Union Pacific, the Colorado Central pushed west for the next several years, but progress was slow. Nevertheless, the railroad supported significant commerce and helped Golden and other communities prosper.

Continuing railroad wars and a national economic slump hindered further expansion of the Colorado Central, and it took until 1878 for Loveland to complete the line between Black Hawk and Central City. Finally, in 1879, Loveland was forced to sell out his interests to Jay Gould, who then made a deal with the Union Pacific in what one historian called "the boldest steal in railroad history."

Beer Money

Although Golden ultimately lost its competition with Denver to be Colorado's capital and major city, the town grew steadily. One of the local economy's major industries was, and still is, the Adolph Coors Brewery, founded in 1873. Coors markets its beers as being made from, as the trademarked label puts it, "pure Rocky Mountain spring water." It is the largest single-source brewery in the world, and tours of the operation are a popular attraction.

BOULDER

Prospectors founded the town of Boulder, but not as a mining camp. In 1858 Thomas Aikens and a dozen prospectors rode out from Fort St. Vrain, originally bound for the gold diggings at Cherry Creek. Liking the looks of the mountains west of the fort, however, the prospectors saw the site's potential as a supply center for area mining camps and built a dozen crude log cabins at what would soon be Boulder City. As Alfred A. Brookfield, one of the men with Aikens, put it, "We thought as the weather would not permit us to mine we would lay out and commence to build what may be an important town." There were sixty shareholders in the Boulder City Town Company, which included 4,044 lots to be sold at $1,000 each.

Boulder's growth was slow at first, but one of the events that secured the town's fate was legislation signed on November 7, 1861, that designated Boulder as the site for a state university. Still, it took more than a decade for construction to begin. In 1872 several Boulder

View of Pearl Street in Boulder, 1902 —Courtesy Wyoming State Archives, J. E. Stimson Collection

residents donated land for the university, but the territorial legislature demanded that residents raise some cash as well. The legislature would donate $15,000 for the university only if residents matched the amount.

The funding was secured in 1874, and the university opened in 1877. The first building, Old Main, was used for classrooms, an auditorium, a library, and laboratories. Later a residence for the university president was added. Today the Boulder campus, one of four University of Colorado campuses, serves nearly 30,000 students.

In part due to the presence of the university, Boulder became a center for education as well as for scientific research and development. In 1898 the Texas-Colorado Chautauqua Association formed to "promote educational, literary, and scientific undertakings, the promotion of arts and the maintenance of a summer school in the state of Colorado." The Boulder laboratories of the National Bureau of Standards began operating in 1901.

By the 1950s, technology companies were setting up shop in Boulder. The Ball Brothers Research Corporation, now called the Ball Aerospace & Technologies Corporation, was founded in 1956 to develop rockets and other technologies. Within a decade the company employed more than 500 scientists, engineers, and other workers and had contracted

University of Colorado, Boulder, 1902 —Courtesy Wyoming State Archives, J. E. Stimson Collection

with NASA to work on the Orbiting Solar Observatory program. Beech Aircraft Corporation established a plant in Boulder in 1955; the National Center for Atmospheric Research started operations in 1960; and IBM was in operation here by the mid-1960s.

US 287
Longmont—Wyoming Border
84 MILES

The general route of US 287 linking Fort Collins with Laramie, Wyoming, has long been a travel corridor. No doubt Indians used it for centuries, as there is a natural pass around the mountains at its north edge. In 1825 Gen. William H. Ashley's second expedition to the Green River Valley of western Wyoming passed through with supplies for the first-ever trappers' rendezvous.

LONGMONT

Founded by the Chicago-Colorado Colony in the spring of 1871, on land grants from the Denver Pacific and Kansas Pacific Railroads, Longmont had 400 colonists by June of that year. Soon there were forty to fifty buildings, including a town hall and library. Many of the early settlers were sponsored by New York philanthropist Mrs. Elizabeth Thompson, who became known as the colony's "fairy godmother." The abundance of water from St. Vrain, Left Hand, and Boulder Creeks assured the town's agricultural success.

LOVELAND

Fort Namaqua, at the western edge of present Loveland, was settled in 1858 by Mariano Medina, who built a toll bridge across the Big Thompson River and operated a general store serving the stage line. The fort was also a campsite on the Cherokee Trail and later a station on the Overland Stage route. Loveland was founded in 1877 with the arrival of the Colorado Central Railroad, which ultimately linked most of the Front Range communities. The town was named for the man responsible for the Colorado Central, W.A.H. Loveland (see Golden, earlier in this section).

Since 1947, Loveland has been known as the "Sweetheart City" thanks to a clever Valentine's Day program that plays off the town's name. Postmaster Elmer Ivers, Chamber of Commerce president Ted Thompson, and Thompson's wife, Mabel, came up with the idea of re-mailing valentines from the town to give them a Loveland postmark. Since then, Loveland has had one of the busiest post offices in the country come February, and millions of cards have been sent to sweethearts all over the world. The Thompsons are commemorated with a bronze relief at Thompson Park, just one of many public sculptures you'll find throughout this community.

FORT COLLINS

The origin of Fort Collins can be traced to July 22, 1862, when the Ninth Kansas Cavalry was sent to establish a post at present Laporte to protect travelers on the Cherokee and Overland Trails. Camp Collins was named for the commanding officer, Lt. Col. William O. Collins. Colorado troops replaced the Kansas unit in the fall and remained there until May 1864, when Company F of the Eleventh Ohio Cavalry replaced the Colorado troops.

A flood of the Cache la Poudre River on June 9, 1864, surged through Camp Collins, washing away tents, supplies, and even some of the cabins. With advice from local farmer Joseph Mason, the soldiers relocated the camp to a site on the Cache la Poudre less prone to flooding, on present Willow Street in Fort Collins. The army was careful to build the new fort in a place that would leave land open for future farms. The new post was referred to as Fort Collins, and after evacuation of the post in 1866, the community that remained kept the name.

In 1872 a private town company organized by Gen. Robert A. Cameron, the Fort Collins Agricultural Colony, took over the Fort Collins military reservation. Memberships in the colony were offered to people of "good moral character" for fees ranging from $50 to $250. In return they received a lot in town and farmland. The town developed irrigation systems with water from the Cache la Poudre.

The arrival of the Colorado Central Railroad assured the future of Fort Collins. In 1873 the Colorado Central was built to connect Front Range communities from Golden to Longmont. Soon it pushed into the mountains to Berthoud and finally stretched along the range to Loveland and Fort Collins in 1877. At the same time, another line was being built from Cheyenne. The first Wyoming Line train steamed into Fort Collins on October 8, 1878.

Early residents of Fort Collins got fresh water from the Cache la Poudre River. In a 1923 article for the *Fort Collins Express*, longtime resident George H. Glover remembered, "The Poudre River was a pretentious stream in those days and flowed not far away. Water was delivered to

Parade in downtown Fort Collins, 1906 —Courtesy Wyoming State Archives

householders at 50 cents a barrel. There was a well just north of the main [Colorado State University] building and water was drawn by buckets, which however, was really not fit to drink."

Ansel Watrous also discussed the town's domestic water supply in his 1911 *History of Larimer County*, but cited the cost of a barrel at 25 cents. "The people were supplied with water for cooking and drinking purposes from what was known as the 'water wagon,' consisting of a tank on wheels. From this primitive system of water works, people were able to supply their needs at a rate of 25 cents a barrel or 5 cents a pail full. The water was dipped up from the river near College Avenue bridge and peddled out through the town. . . . Water needed for the laundry and cleaning purposes was obtained from the irrigation laterals that traversed the town."

Colorado State University, which began as Colorado Agricultural College, was established as a land-grant university in the fall of 1879. The university helped early Fort Collins prosper. Today it serves some 17,000 students and remains a vital part of the city's economic base—in fact, it's the town's biggest employer. Agriculture, too, remains an important part of the regional economy. Other major employers include Anheuser-Busch, which has a brewery at the eastern edge of the city, and high-tech companies such as Hewlett-Packard.

Lindenmeier Archaeological Site

Anyone who has studied archaeology is aware of the Lindenmeier site, north of Fort Collins near the Wyoming border. When the Smithsonian Institute conducted site excavations here in 1935, archaeologists uncovered evidence of occupation from around 10,000 years ago, the earliest artifacts in the world known at the time. About two years later, archaeologists near Folsom, New Mexico, discovered artifacts of the same age. Because the operations at Folsom were on a larger scale, this early civilization was named the Folsom culture.

The Lindenmeier site is on a former cattle ranch, which the city of Fort Collins bought in 2004. Plans to develop the area for public access—possibly as a national monument—are currently under way. An exhibit at the Fort Collins Museum includes artifacts from and information about the Lindenmeier site.

VIRGINIA DALE

During the 1849 gold rush, the Evans party forged the Cherokee Trail through Colorado, which subsequently became part of the emigrant trail system. This well-used trail passed through the spot that became known as Virginia Dale, just south of the Wyoming border. Although little remains of Virginia Dale today, it was once an active stagecoach

Photo of the Virginia Dale stage station in 1870, taken by William Henry Jackson —Courtesy Wyoming State Archives

station. It is the only station on the entire Overland Mail line that remains standing in its original location.

The Virginia Dale station was built in 1862 as the headquarters of the Fourth Division of Ben Holladay's Overland Mail. Named by superintendent Joseph A. "Jack" Slade for his wife, Maria Virginia Slade, it became one of the best-known stations. An undated WPA report described the Virginia Dale station:

> [The] commodious building had a cellar approached by an incline down which the station horses might be led to sanctuary when Indian attack threatened. The roof was sheathed with shingles freighted from St. Louis, Missouri, at an expense of $1.50 a pound.
>
> The immunity from Indian attacks upon his stages which Holliday [sic] hoped to enjoy on the Overland trail was not realized, and almost constantly throughout its career as a stage station, Virginia Dale was a refuge from hostile bands of Sioux, Cheyennes, Arapahoes, Southern Utes and even the erstwhile friendly Shoshones.

Overland Mail superintendent Jack Slade had a famous ongoing feud with Jules Beni, the man for whom Julesburg is named. It began with an argument over the loss of some of Slade's mules, then escalated when Beni wounded Slade with a shotgun. Slade recovered and Beni left the region for a while. One unpublished account, which acknowledges that the story is a mix of fact and legend, offered this scenario of how the feud played out:

> *After Slade was transferred to Virginia Dale, Jules came back to the coun-*
> *try, rumbling threats and making boasts as to what he intended to [do] with*
> *Slade. Slade put the case before military authorities and received a sort of*
> *unofficial permission to protect himself. [Later, Slade] sent out some of his*
> *men and they captured Jules, bringing him bound, hand and foot, to Vir-*
> *ginia Dale. The Frenchman was tied up to a post in the corral and there*
> *left over night. The next morning Slade went out and mercilessly shot him*
> *twice, killing him without giving him a chance.*

As the legend goes, after killing Beni, Slade made good on an earlier threat to cut off Beni's ears and carry them in his pocket. A local cowboy is said to have claimed he witnessed Slade "gravely entertaining a small girl who had stopped with her emigrant family in the Dale, with one of the ears, in which he had placed a couple of pebbles, [which,] dried as it was, served as an excellent rattle."

Slade, who had a wild, unpredictable nature that was enhanced by alcohol, engaged in numerous other escapades. Once he shot up a store in Laporte, and another time he fired shots through the roof of a stage as the driver raced by. Eventually he was removed from his duties. Later, while living in Virginia City, Montana, Slade was hanged by vigilantes.

US 34
Loveland—Estes Park
38 MILES

Between Loveland and Estes Park, US 34 follows the Big Thompson River along the route of an early Indian trail. Inside Rocky Mountain National Park, the highway is known as Trail Ridge Road (see Rocky Mountain National Park in part 6). It is the highest elevation highway in the nation, offering spectacular views of the Colorado Rockies and ranges to the north in Wyoming.

By 1902 increasing tourism in the Estes Park area had caught the attention of a group of Loveland merchants, who invested $24,000 to build a road through Big Thompson Canyon. Completed in 1904, the one-lane dirt road had "corduroy" bridges made from logs tied closely together. At first, the trip between Loveland and Estes Park took two days. In 1908 the state of Colorado got involved, making improvements to the road to accommodate stagecoaches and, soon, automobiles. Finally, in 1938 it became US 34. The highway had two lanes of blacktop, high bridges, and in the section known as the Narrows, embankments to provide flood protection.

Big Thompson River

The Arapaho Indians called the Thompson River the "Pipe River," or more literally, "the Place Where Pipes Are Made," because they carved pipes in the area. Its current name likely comes from David Thompson, the famous fur trader and explorer.

From the early days of settlement, the Big Thompson River has been key in the industrial and agricultural production of the eastern plains of Colorado. In 1911 Loveland city councilman Charles Viestenz proposed building a hydropower plant on the river to supply electricity to the town. Although the city denied his proposal, Viestenz believed in the project and purchased land for a future plant site. The power plant was finally completed in 1925 with service to Loveland. The development also included canals and reservoirs for irrigation around Loveland and Fort Collins.

Through the years, residents along the river saw periodic flooding. A flood in 1894 spread over a mile wide in Loveland, and in 1919, flooding destroyed several bridges. In 1951, seven people died and five families lost their homes when heavy rains caused a breach in a reservoir on Buckhorn Creek, causing an estimated $200,000 in damage. But the worst was yet to come.

A 1971 Corp of Engineers study warned of potential flooding along the Big Thompson, but nobody was prepared for what happened on July 31, 1976. A massive thunderstorm that evening dropped an estimated twelve inches of rain in only four hours. Capt. William Thomas of the Colorado State Patrol said in an interview, "This was the darndest rain I was ever in. Raindrops as big as the end of the average man's thumb, coming straight down, lukewarm, not an ounce of wind. . . . It was hard to breathe, incidentally, there was so much water in the air."

The National Weather Service issued a warning to area residents and travelers, but by the time the word went out, the disaster had already begun. The Big Thompson River rose nineteen feet above its normal level, and the wall of water rushed through Estes Park, down the canyon, through Loveland, and onto the plains. Colorado Highway Patrol officer Tim Littlejohn later described the scene to the *Loveland Reporter-Herald*: "It was like boiling, muddy water down a dry gulch with boulders that sounded as big as my patrol car; houses and cars were floating like corks."

The *Fort Collins Coloradan* and the *Denver Post* reported that as the flood rose, another officer, William Miller, had to abandon his patrol car, telling his dispatcher, "The whole mountainside is gone. We have people trapped on the other side. I'm going to have to move out. I'm up to my doors in water! Advise, we can't get to them. I'm going to get out of here before I drown!"

Through that awful night, people tried to climb the canyon walls to reach safety, but some perished. By early the next morning, governor Richard Lamm had called out all available Colorado troopers and the National Guard. U.S. Army helicopters from Wyoming and Colorado, Forest Service workers, and other emergency personnel were also summoned to the scene.

The Big Thompson flood demolished 418 homes and 52 businesses and damaged many others, causing $35.5 million in damage. It also destroyed a major section of US 34. Even worse, it killed 145 people; 6 of the bodies were never found. Most of those who died were visitors to the region. There were so many bodies that the Union Pacific Railroad, a meat-packing company called Monfort of Colorado, and Timple Trucking supplied refrigeration cars to store them.

Larimer County was declared a federal disaster area by President Gerald Ford, and the region received $21 million in federal aid. Signs warning folks to "Climb to Safety" during heavy rains are now posted throughout the canyon.

ESTES PARK

Known for its scenic beauty and recreational opportunities, Estes Park is the eastern gateway to Rocky Mountain National Park (see Rocky Mountain National Park in part 6). Joel Estes, for whom the city was named, was the first settler in the area. After moving here from Kentucky in 1860, Estes found the area less than ideal for raising cattle, so he sold his herd and in 1867 converted the family home into an inn.

In 1874 a British earl, Lord Dunraven, started a land-purchasing scheme in Estes Park. He paid people from the Denver region to file on homestead land then transfer the land to him. Before authorities could stop him, Dunraven had control of 15,000 acres. He also built the Estes Park Hotel to serve the growing number of visitors coming to the region via a stage line from Longmont.

As it became clear that the area was attractive to tourists, more hotels, shops, and restaurants began to spring up. Among them was the impressive Stanley Hotel, which still stands on the hill overlooking Estes Park. Freelan Oscar Stanley, known as F.O., moved to Estes Park in 1903 after developing tuberculosis. He and his twin brother, Francis Edgar (F.E.) Stanley, had founded the company that developed the Stanley Steamer automobile, and F.E. took over management of the company when F.O. left for the Rockies. In 1909 F.O. built the luxurious Stanley Hotel. It was the first fully electric-powered hotel in Colorado, running on electricity generated by the Stanley Power Plant. To transport his hotel guests, F.O. developed the Model 88 Mountain Wagon autobus, which could seat a dozen passengers. The Mountain Wagon was a success, providing reliable transportation between Loveland and Estes Park.

The immensely enterprising Stanley also helped establish the Estes Park Protective and Improvement Association to improve roads and trails while protecting local wildflowers and wildlife. "Those who pull flowers up by the roots will be condemned by all worthy people, and also by the Estes Park Protective and Improvement Association," the association warned.

The Stanley Museum at the Stanley Hotel in Estes Park is dedicated to the history of the famous establishment, which is still in operation, and to F.O.'s many other contributions to the town.

The imposing Stanley Hotel in Estes Park, built in 1909, is still in business.

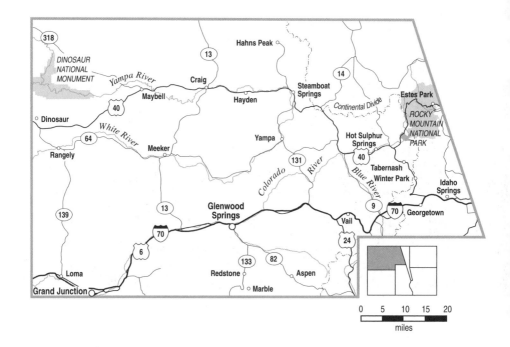

PART SIX

Northwest
MOUNTAIN PARKS
AND DINOSAUR COUNTRY

The northwestern section of Colorado, as defined here, is bordered on the north by Wyoming, on the west by Utah, on the south roughly by I-70, and on the east by the Front Range. The Colorado River runs through this part of the state, and the far northwest corner has a desertlike landscape. This region also has several of the broad mountain valleys known as parks. Locals know these as Browns Park, Middle Park, and North Park. All were home to large cattle ranches, and Browns Park (sometimes called Browns Hole) was a hangout for outlaws such as Butch Cassidy and the Sundance Kid.

That dinosaurs roamed this land eons ago is evidenced by the numerous remains found in Dinosaur National Monument, along the Colorado-Utah border. To the east, the high desert of the Western Slope is where one of Colorado's legendary Indian uprisings—the Meeker Massacre of 1879—took place. Further east and south are some of the world's best-known skiing meccas: Steamboat Springs, Aspen, and Vail.

North Park is cattle country and has been since the first settlers arrived. In this area, ringed by mountains that are nearly always snow-capped, known as the Never Summer Range, some ranchers still use horse-drawn equipment to harvest hay and feed the herds. Middle Park is unique in that it was not included in either the Louisiana Purchase of 1803 nor the Treaty of Guadalupe Hidalgo in 1848. Instead, it remained under the control of the Ute Indian tribe until they relinquished their claim in 1881, and it did not actually become an official part of the United States until in 1936.

John Charles Frémont "discovered" both North and Middle Parks, along with South Park, on his expedition of 1842. Frémont's father-in-law and mentor, Missouri Senator Thomas Hart Benton, described the area in an 1854 speech:

> . . . large, beautiful mountain coves . . . delightful in summer, and tempered
> in winter, from the concentration of the sun's rays; and sheltered by the

Hay rake at the Never Summer Ranch in Rocky Mountain National Park

> *lofty rim of mountains, forever crowned with snow, which wall them in, and break off the outside storms. The . . . buffaloes not only feed, but lodge there, and make them places of their immense congregation; attended by all the minor animals—elk, deer, antelopes, bears.*

We begin our tour near the Utah border and continue east, following in turn the highways through Browns Park, Middle Park, and North Park, and ending just west of the Denver metropolitan area.

CO 139
I-70 at Loma—Rangely
73 MILES

CANYON PINTADO

Traveling across western Colorado in 1776, Fathers Francisco Silvestre Vélez de Escalante and Francisco Domínguez followed the approximate route of today's CO 139 between Loma (at I-70) and Rangely (off US 40 via CO 64). South of what is now Rangely, the friars began to see Indian drawings, or pictographs, on the sandstone walls of nearby cliffs. The images included handprints, horses, white birds, and trapezoidal human figures, later dubbed "carrot men." Some of the pictures depicted crop plants like corn and wheat, indicating that the people who drew them may have been farmers.

On September 9, Escalante wrote in his journal, "Halfway through this canyon toward the south there is quite a lofty rock cliff on which we saw, crudely painted, three Shields, or Apache Shields, and a spearhead. Farther down on the north side we saw another painting, which supposedly represented two men in combat."

A number of rock art sites in Canyon Pintado (Painted Canyon) have been developed, and today the public can view the same pictographs the two padres saw more than two centuries ago. The Bureau of Land Management has placed interpretive signs at many of the sites, and signs along the highway mark the turnoffs.

Horse pictograph in Canyon Pintado

When Spanish priests Domínguez and Escalante traveled through Canyon Pintado in 1776, they noted pictographs such as these white bird images and other symbols.

RANGELY

Like other towns in this area, Rangely started as a ranching community. At the junction of CO 64 and CO 139, Rangely is just south of Dinosaur National Monument, and where there are dinosaur bones, there are fossil fuels. Coal has been mined in this area since the first homesteaders arrived. In the late 1940s, oil was found, starting a boom. A few decades later, natural gas resources began to be developed here.

The town's economy is still based primarily on its energy resources. The Rangely Outdoor Museum preserves many of the town's historic buildings and houses Indian artifacts, pioneer-era items, and old coal-mining and oil-drilling equipment.

CO 64 and FLAT TOP ROAD
US 40 at Dinosaur—Yampa
158 MILES

CO 64 passes through Rangely and follows the White River to Meeker. From there, travelers can pick up the Flat Top Road, a scenic byway that meanders east to Yampa, skirting the Flat Tops Wilderness. This preserve encompasses 235,000 acres of the White River and Routt National Forests. Out of Meeker the route follows County Road 8; later it becomes Forest Service Road 16. About half of the road is paved and half is gravel, and it is closed in the winter, but in good weather the entire route is accessible for any vehicle.

MEEKER

The White River Utes lived in northwestern Colorado for centuries, but a violent episode in 1879 led to their permanent removal from the region. The event became known to the whites as the "Meeker Massacre"; the Utes refer to it as the "Meeker Incident."

Nathan C. Meeker became the agent for the White River Indian Agency in 1879. His wife, Arvilla, and daughter, Josephine, joined him soon after his arrival at the agency. In one of his first acts as agent, the sixty-four-year-old former newspaper editor relocated the agency to Powell Bottom, about four miles down the White River, unconcerned that it was the place where the Utes grazed their horses and held races. Meeker had previously helped organize the Union Colony, a successful Christian farming settlement on the South Platte River, in present Greeley, and he was determined to run the Indian agency the way he

White River Ute leader Colorow was thought to be in-volved in the 1879 Ute uprising. —Courtesy Grand Encampment Museum

had the colony, emphasizing agricultural development and community cooperation (see Greeley in part 4).

In April Meeker hired several people, including farmers from the Union Colony, to begin plowing in Powell Bottom. But the farmers had to stop their work when Indians fired shots at them. By the middle of the summer, reports of Utes burning hay, meadows, and forests were flooding the region. But the accusations may have been false, as even ranchers agreed that the fires could have been started by lightning.

Meanwhile, in southern Wyoming, the Utes traded some pelts with local ranchers for butter "and killed enough game for their own immediate use," according to rancher Taylor Pennock. The Indians then headed south toward North Park, "but did no damage nor made no threats." Back at the agency, however, Meeker had a conflict with a Ute named Johnson, also known as Canalla. Afterward Meeker wrote to the army for support, setting off a fatal chain of events.

Nathan C. Meeker
—Courtesy Colorado
Historical Society

Milk Creek Battle

Meeker's request for help came to Maj. Thomas Tipton Thornburgh, the commanding officer at Fort Fred Steele, near Rawlins, Wyoming. Thornburgh organized a command of some 200 soldiers and 16 civilians, and the troops headed south on September 19. At Fortification Creek, just south of the Wyoming border, Thornburgh left some men at a supply camp and proceeded south with the rest of the command.

Hesitant to take his troops to the agency without an express request from Meeker, Thornburgh sent messages to the agent. Receiving no reply, he advanced slowly. By then the Utes had moved their women and children from the agency to a camp on Piceance Creek, twelve miles south of the agency, and established themselves near Milk Creek Canyon, south of Craig. The Indians told Thornburgh not to bring all his troops onto the reservation, but they said he could bring in a small party.

On the night of September 28, Thornburgh's scout Charlie Lowry met with Meeker. According to M. Wilson Rankin's account, Lowry found Meeker "nervous" and "suffering from the effects of a beating administered by Johnson." But there was no sign of trouble. Later that night, eight Utes came in from Milk Creek, reporting the approach of the soldiers.

The next morning, Lowry and agency worker E. W. Eskridge rode out to meet with Thornburgh, accompanied by a small group of Utes.

Eventually the Indians sent Lowry to continue on alone, keeping Eskridge with them. Meanwhile, Thornburgh's troops moved south from Williams Fork. Before they reached Milk Creek, considered the boundary line for the reservation, they met up with Lowry. Despite his agreement with the Utes, Thornburgh decided to move forward with all his troops, following a shortcut trail, the Morapos, that his guide Joe Rankin knew.

Lt. George Paddock, escorting the supply wagon train two miles back, later described what happened next: "When nearing the head of sarvisberry draw, which the trail followed, [guides] Rankin and Secrist saw about twenty-five mounted Indians leave other Indians on the second ridge . . . and make a dash as though to head them off on the trail, a short distance ahead. [Rankin and Secrist] turned back to the command and Rankin noted they were in for a fight." In fact the Indians, having expected the soldiers to take the main road, were surprised to find them on the shortcut trail.

Thornburgh ordered Lt. Samuel A. Cherry to take ten of Capt. Joseph J. Lawson's men within hailing distance of the Indians, while Lawson and the rest of his men followed 600 yards behind and awaited developments. When Cherry got in range, he waved a hat in a gesture of peace, but the Indians shot at him. He pulled back and Lawson advanced. The soldiers quickly retreated, however, when the Indians went on the offensive.

Thornburgh sent Rankin back to the wagons to tell wagon master William McKinstry to form a corral. They arranged the wagons in a three-quarter circle facing the banks of Milk Creek. Thornburgh retreated his troops toward the wagons, but on the way there, he was shot and killed. Many other troopers were also killed or wounded. Those who made it to the wagons dug trenches and bolstered their barricade with supplies and dead horses and mules.

With Thornburgh dead, Capt. J. Scott Payne was the officer in charge. Though wounded himself, he kept up his men's courage. Doctor R. M. Grimes was also wounded but continued treating the injured. Surrounded, the troops could do nothing more than try to defend themselves. Later in the afternoon, the Indians set fire to the grass near the wagons in an attempt to rout the soldiers from their position. The men fought the fire with burlap sacks and clothing, and even dug dirt with their knives to throw on the flames.

That night, Rankin, civilian John Gordon, and two corporals mounted the strongest remaining horses and rode for help. Rankin traveled alone, following the Morapos Trail north. Riding almost without a stop, except to trade horses when possible, Rankin reached Rawlins about 2 a.m. on October 1, having ridden some 150 miles in around twenty-seven hours. There, he wired Gen. George Crook, who ordered Gen. Wesley Merritt

*Major Thomas
Tipton Thornburgh*
—Courtesy Colorado
Historical Society

at Fort D. A. Russell near Cheyenne, Wyoming Territory, to go to the aid of Thornburgh's men.

Heading in a different direction, John Gordon and the corporals also found help. They took the agency road north to a ranch on the Bear River (Yampa River), where they ran into a courier from the White River Agency. The courier said he was on his way to find Capt. Francis Dodge and the Ninth Cavalry, who were somewhere to the southeast waiting for word about whether they were needed at the agency. Gordon's party enlisted a local man to go to Steamboat Springs and send a message to Dodge about the siege.

News of the attack at Milk Creek spread quickly through the region. Soon residents from as far north as Saratoga, Wyoming Territory, gathered at central points to prepare defenses should the uprising spread. Dodge received word the day the battle began, September 29. By daybreak on October 2, he and his Buffalo Soldiers were nearing the battle site. He sent a few men ahead to let Payne's men know they were there.

Dodge's troops made it through the hostile lines to join Payne and the remains of the command. But Dodge, now the ranking officer, could not advance because the terrain was too steep. Thus, rather than rescuing the Thornburgh command, the Buffalo Soldiers became trapped with them. By noon on October 4, most of the cavalry horses were dead. The stench of dead men and animals was becoming unbearable and the soldiers were exhausted. Around 175 to 200 Utes remained in the hills surrounding the battle site.

Fortunately for Dodge and Payne, Merritt's relief column was on its way. The new troops reached Milk Creek early on October 5. Upon their arrival, the Utes began withdrawing. One Indian, waving a white flag, approached the soldiers. The Uncompahgre Ute chief Ouray, a man respected by most Utes, had sent a message to the White River Utes urging them to abandon their attack. The messenger told Merritt that the White River Utes wanted a new agent. Merritt agreed, and the Indians withdrew. Merritt moved the men to a new camp, and thirty-eight wounded soldiers were transported to Fort Steele on October 7.

Visitors may see the Milk Creek battlesite and monuments to those who fought there off Yellowjacket Pass Road between Craig and Meeker. One marker lists all the army casualties of the battle.

Monuments at the Battle of Milk Creek

Meeker Massacre

While the troops at Milk Creek were under siege, another crisis had unfolded. Nathan Meeker was dead. A group of Utes had attacked the White River Agency, killing Meeker, blacksmith E. Jasper Price, agency worker E. W. Eskridge, seven other employees, and several freighters. On October 11, marching south from Milk Creek to establish a fort at the White River Cantonment, Merritt and the troops found the bodies. The Indians had ransacked and burned most of the buildings, but as M. Wilson Rankin, who was with the troops, later reported, "The agency flag pole, from which the stars and stripes floated, representing a government institution, was not molested." Surveying the grisly scene, the soldiers realized that the raiders had also taken captives: Arvilla and Josephine Meeker along with Price's wife Sophronia and her two small children were missing.

After retreating from Milk Creek, the Utes went to the Piceance Creek camp for their families and moved south, taking the captives with them. Rescuers were dispatched from the Uncompahgre Agency, and after twenty-three days of captivity, Arvilla and Josephine Meeker,

Drawing of Arivella Meeker, left, Sophronia Price, and her two children —From *Frank Leslie's Illustrated Newspaper*, November 22, 1879

Worker at the White River Museum in Meeker raising the flag

Sophronia Price, three-year-old Mae Price, and baby John Price were released. On June 8, 1880, the United States Senate ratified an agreement to buy the Ute Reservation in Colorado. The White River Utes were relocated to the Uinta Reservation in Utah.

After the Meeker Massacre, General Merritt established a military post on the White River some four miles above the ruined agency. The fort had adobe, brick, and log structures surrounding a square parade ground. Three years later, the army left the post and sold the buildings to settlers. The town that evolved, christened Meeker, was incorporated in 1885. When Rio Blanco County was organized in 1889, Meeker became the county seat.

Today, the fort structures are part of the White River Museum. The museum has information about the 1879 Ute uprising and the Meeker massacre, as well as exhibits related to the area's early settlers.

YAMPA

Yampa, which you can also—and more easily—reach via CO 131, is the eastern endpoint of the scenic Flat Top Road. Yampa was once a shipping point for goods from Denver to the small settlements in the area, including Pinnacle, a ranching community about seventeen miles north. Later, when the timber industry set up shop in this part of Colorado, Yampa became the site of several sawmills. Like its neighbors, Yampa is now a ranching community whose economy is supplemented by summer recreationists. Pinnacle no longer exists.

In the late 1800s, settlements in this area were quite isolated. In an unpublished manuscript written in the 1930s, one early settler in Pinnacle, Beryl Morten, painted a vivid picture of what life was like in those days:

> It was in June of 1897 that I came to Colorado, an immigrant English girl seeking a higher altitude. Four months later I was married. Such a fine-looking lad Billy was, tall and slender, a picture of health, so sweet and kind. In July of 1898 Eileen, our darling baby girl was born. . . .
>
> [We moved into] a little one-room log cabin set in the middle of a large meadow. . . . I often thought of what my dear old mother in England would have thought, could she have seen my one little room, papered with British newspapers, curtained off with coarse drapes, red geraniums blithely blooming from tomato cans in the windows. My babies would not need books to read; they could read the walls. . . .
>
> [Billy] carried the mail from Pinnacle to Yampa to meet the stagecoach from Denver, then brought the mail back to Pinnacle that same afternoon. Then, after a chat with Old Aunty Williamson, postmistress, he would return home in time for supper.

When the snows began to fall, Billy carried the mail in a sled pulled by a team of gray horses, Smoky and Fanny, while Beryl and baby Eileen stayed home in the cabin. "I spent the greater part of my time reading and embroidering clothes for my baby," she recalled.

One winter day "the big snowstorm of the year" hit, and Billy did not return home that evening. Beryl sat in fear not only for him, but also for herself. She heard an ominous scratching at the door but was afraid to open it. The next morning, Billy came home. He identified tracks in the snow around the cabin as those of a mountain lion. He also described his ordeal of the previous night.

As he drove toward the cabin, the horses and sled had pitched over a twenty-foot-high drift, knocking him unconscious. When he roused himself, he cut the horses loose. "With almost superhuman effort he had lifted the mail bags to the horses' backs and finally gotten back up the drift onto the road." It took him several hours to reach the nearest ranch, two miles away, where he spent the night. The sled remained in the drift until spring.

Billy began making his daily run on snowshoes, packing the mailbags over the seventeen-mile route on his back. In the meantime, Beryl and Billy, fearing that their isolated cabin was not a safe home for them and their baby, decided to move to Yampa. The post office granted Billy's request to reverse his route, allowing him to start and end in Yampa, but they still faced the problem of how to get through the deep snow to their new home.

We started about eleven o'clock at night on the eleventh of February. It was about thirty below zero. We had to leave then so that the snow would be crusted firmly enough to hold us up. Billy made a little sled for Eileen and nailed a box to the top of it. I slit several pillows and lined the bottom and sides of the box with feathers. Then, after wrapping her in all the warm flannels I possibly could, I laid Eileen in this bed of feathers. After feeding her, I heated a bottle almost scalding hot and placed it, together with several hot water bottles, down among the feathers. Then I covered her with half of another pillow. She would be just as warm as toast in her bed of feathers.

Leaving everything behind except for a few clothes, they prepared to set out. Beryl donned her high overshoes and snowshoes, and Billy wrapped gunnysacks around her legs. Then they took off into the frigid but brightly moonlit night.

It seemed impossible. Oh, how high those drifts were. Billy would go to the bottom, then call to me. It seemed I could never get down. Billy would say, 'Can you do it?' I had to, or stay there. I would shut my eyes and plunge down, down, down. When I became very tired we would stop to rest, but only for a few moments. When the baby stirred or began to whimper, I would get down on my knees and talk to her. I couldn't uncover her because of the intense cold.

Around five o'clock in the morning they stopped at a ranch. Once inside in the warmth of the rancher's home, Beryl fainted from exhaustion. She was put to bed along with the baby. Later the rancher took them the rest of the way to Yampa in his sled.

Billy continued his mail run for the remainder of the winter, but "he grew thinner each day and by spring looked more like a ghost than a man," Beryl recalled. Finally, "with a feeling of thankfulness," the family moved to Denver in early May.

US 40
Utah Border—Steamboat Springs
131 MILES

CRAIG AND HAYDEN

The region north of the Yampa River between Craig and Hayden has long been ranch country. Cattle ranches were well established by the early 1890s, when sheep ranchers, mostly from Wyoming, started moving their herds onto northwestern Colorado ranges. The area became a war zone as the cattlemen and sheepmen clashed.

In the late 1800s, battle lines were drawn between sheep ranchers and cattlemen in north-western Colorado. Eventually, the sheepmen prevailed, and sheep still graze in this area.

Most of the sheep herds that spent the winters in Wyoming moved south into the valley of the Little Snake River in the spring. Cattle ranchers in the Yampa River Valley, then called the Bear River Valley, were concerned the sheep would move east into their range and wanted to keep them out. They believed that the sheep's sharp hooves ruined the grasses and that their smell kept the cattle away from the range.

By 1894 Colorado cattlemen were determined to define the areas where sheep could and couldn't go, and they met with the sheepmen to discuss the situation. On April 21, 1894, Wyoming's *Carbon County Journal* said that the two sides had reached an agreement: "The country reserved [for cattle] is about fourteen miles wide, on the average, while the country open to sheep surrounds this little patch on every side. The sheepmen profess to be satisfied with this arrangement."

But the peace did not last long. On September 14, the *Craig Courier* reported on new developments:

> *Thirty-eight hundred sheep were stampeded over a bluff into Parachute Creek on September 10th while their owners were at the Peach Day celebration in Grand Junction. One of the herders, Carl Brown, resisted and*

was shot in the hip. . . . A posse from Parachute found a mass of dead sheep at the foot of a thousand-foot bluff and climbing up the narrow trail found a wounded herder. The owners are residents of Parachute with rights to the adjacent range and the posse made a futile race to apprehend the raiders.

The sheepman at the center of the conflict was J. G. (Jack) Edwards, who owned some 60,000 head. In the spring of 1895, Colorado cattlemen braced for a showdown with Edwards. On May 23 the *Cheyenne Leader* wrote of the escalating situation:

On the night of the nineteenth, riders were sent out to scour the country and warn the settlers that sheepmen now holding their flocks on Snake River at the Wyoming line, were contemplating an invasion of the Bear River cattle ranges. The effect was electrical, and by noon today fully three hundred-fifty cattlemen and feeders were assembled to decide upon positive action to keep the sheep back, in the event of their not being withdrawn from the cattle territory.

Due to "the danger to cattle and ranchers by a sheep invasion," the *Leader* reported, a mass meeting of citizens in Craig unanimously adopted resolutions that had been set forth by the Stock Feeders Association. The resolutions were also approved in Hayden and other nearby communities. The cattlemen's proclamation aimed to prohibit sheep from grazing or being herded in "the country drained by the Bear River, which includes all the territory from the Continental Divide west to Utah"—in essence, anywhere in northwestern Colorado. Furthermore, the document stated, "If sheepmen will not respect our rights, we will be compelled to resort to such means as will protect us in what we believe to be our just and equitable rights."

The cattlemen knew, however, that Edwards and the other sheep ranchers were unlikely to accept their terms. As the *Leader* noted, "It is believed that the sheepmen will disregard the warning of the stock raisers, and attempt to drive through the forbidden territory, fattening their mutton as they approach the railroad, depending on state aid in the protection of their rights." The article said that "a force of eight hundred to a thousand" cowboys and stockmen, hoping to forestall such action, were "holding themselves in readiness forcibly to resist any advance made south of Hahns Peak by the sheep owners. A war is imminent and unless the more conservative heads prevail, the rifle will figure a conspicuous part in a Routt County sheep war."

On June 1, armed men in Hayden prepared to defend their range. The cattlemen organized in military fashion, electing a "general" and ten "captains" to command the companies. Wagon trains of supplies were also put together for the campaign. The June 2 *Cheyenne Leader* covered the unfolding story:

During the day fully two hundred armed men, representing the ranching and cattle industries, arrived in town, soon to disperse and scatter for the night among the ranchmen in the vicinity of Hayden. . . . About fifty men are in bivouac in an open field near town, and sitting about camp fires in the midst of stacked guns.

The following morning, the "marching force" made its way toward the sheep camp, where some 40,000 animals were believed to be grazing at the headwaters of Elkhead Creek. The cattlemen had sent a message to the sheep camp warning the sheepmen to leave the area. If they refused, the reporter predicted, "a bloody battle will occur in the Elkhead Mountains."

Tensions soon abated, however, when the cattlemen found that the sheep pushing up against their territory, at Fortification Creek, did not belong to the hated Jack Edwards. The owner was allowed to depart in peace after agreeing not to cross the state line again. On June 12, 1895, the *Leader* wrote, "The sheep war for the time being has been declared off and, unless the sheepmen disregard the warning that has been given by the settlers, no blood will flow."

Even so, sheepmen in Wyoming made constant threats to cross the boundary. Edwards wanted to drive his sheep to Denver & Rio Grande railheads in Colorado for shipping. Colorado freighters were already gladly hauling his wool to the Union Pacific railhead in Rawlins. On March 21, 1896, the *Cheyenne Leader* reported that "Jack Edwards . . . has hinted that he may protect his interests with militia."

On May 23, the *Courier* reported that Edwards was just north of the state line and moving his sheep toward Colorado. A month later, the long-anticipated violence erupted, but only briefly. The cattlemen killed two of Edwards's herders and scattered his sheep. Then "a party of masked men" confronted Edwards and warned him to move his sheep within ten days. He agreed but asked that they allow him to keep his 8,000 wethers in California Park until fall. Thus the bargain was made and further conflict was averted.

Although he upheld his agreement, the next January Edwards told a reporter that cattlemen were still threatening him. "I have an armed force of about fifty ready for the clash when it comes. I am compelled to keep a small army about my place all the time." Over the next several years, Edwards and other sheepmen continued to push into Colorado and the cattlemen continued to push back. In 1899 Edwards sold his sheep to the Geddes Sheep Company and moved to Oregon, but the range disputes continued.

The sheep war wound down around 1905, when National Forest Reserves were established, regulating boundaries, but conflicts still erupted into the 1920s and beyond. Cattlemen continued to threaten sheep owners and workers. They scattered herds and fed the sheep grain laced with strychnine. In spite of all this, sheep still range in northwestern Colorado today.

STEAMBOAT SPRINGS

The first settlers in Steamboat Springs were James Crawford and his family. On May 1, 1873, James, his wife Margaret, and their three children, Lulie, Logan, and John, left Missouri bound for Denver in a wagon train with four other families. After thirty-five days on the road, the wagons hit an impasse in Empire. James Crawford pressed on alone over Berthoud Pass to explore the possibilities farther west. The following year he took his family to Hot Sulphur Springs and established a cattle ranch.

Still unsatisfied, Crawford soon set out on another exploratory trip. A traveler he met along the way told him about some mineral springs to the north known as Steamboat Springs, apparently because one of the springs sounded like a steamboat chugging. Crawford went there and, liking what he saw, claimed a homestead in 1875.

Crawford and four other homesteaders built the first five cabins in Steamboat Springs. But due to its isolation, the settlement did not grow quickly enough for Crawford. After the Ute Indians were removed from Colorado in 1879, making the state more attractive to settlers, Crawford stepped up his campaign to incorporate the town. Enticing investors from Boulder, Crawford raised $160,000 and on January 14, 1884, formed the Steamboat Springs Company.

The Crawfords remained in Steamboat Springs throughout their long lives, celebrating fifty years of marriage on May 25, 1915. James died on June 24, 1930, and Margaret died nine years later. Both are buried in the city cemetery under a monument inscribed "The End of the Trail."

Ski Town USA

In its early days, Steamboat Springs was primarily a cattle- and sheep-ranching community. Then, in the late 1940s, residents began to promote the true wealth of the region: snow. Calling itself "Ski Town USA," the town actively sought to entice winter visitors. The first world-champion ski-jumping contests were held here, and Steamboat has become one of Colorado's best-known ski destinations. Skiing became such a big part of the local tradition that the high school marching band performed on skis.

The first skiing facilities in Steamboat were built in the early 1900s. Norwegian ski jumper Carl Howelson, a former circus performer known as the "Flying Norseman," moved to Steamboat Springs to work as a stonemason. But when he wasn't working on buildings, he was zipping down the mountains and jumping off mounds of snow. In 1914 Howelson helped organize Steamboat's first winter carnival. For that event, he built a ski jump on Woodchuck Hill. The following year, a bigger, better jump was built on an adjacent hill, which has since become known as Howelson Hill. This jump became the site of early world-record ski jumps, and it is still used by world-class ski jumpers. By the 1930s, skiers were training in Steamboat for the Olympic games. Among the town's dozens of homegrown Olympians were Gordy Wren, who participated in the 1948 games at St. Moritz, and Buddy Werner, a two-time Olympian and the first American skier to win a major European event, the Hahnenkaam in Austria.

Even so, Steamboat's Storm Mountain wasn't developed as a downhill ski area until the 1960s. Under the watchful eye of rancher John Fletcher—who more than once mortgaged his cattle herd to keep the project going—and with support from three Denver businessmen and local skiers Buddy Werner and Marvin Crawford, the Steamboat Ski Area opened on January 12, 1963. The following year, Storm Mountain was renamed for hometown hero Werner after he died in an avalanche.

Steamboat has produced dozens of Olympic competitors over the years. Sixteen ski jumpers trained here for the 2002 Winter Olympics in Salt Lake City, as did the U.S. women's hockey team and the U.S. freestyle team. Steamboat Springs snowboarder Shannon Dunn was the first American to medal in the snowboard half-pipe at the 1998 Nagano games; she also competed in the Salt Lake Olympics.

CO 318
Utah Border—US 40
62 MILES

BROWNS PARK

The remote valley known as Browns Park, in the far northwestern corner of Colorado and extending into Utah and Wyoming, comprises mostly government land around the Green River. The only highway through the area is CO 318, and the only town to speak of is Maybell, population around 300. Some would say that only hardy people would want to live where the chance of being bitten by a rattlesnake is probably greater than the chance of a good rain. Over the years, this high-desert country has attracted fur trappers for the beaver, ranchers for the grazing, and outlaws for the isolation.

The namesake of Browns Park is uncertain, but an account by M. Wilson Rankin written in 1937 suggests that it was named for Baptistie Brown, a Hudson's Bay Company fur trapper who came to the area in 1827. Another man who trapped with Baptistie Brown in Browns

Hole for three years was also called Brown. Rankin wrote, "Because of his pious or quiet disposition, his stooping shoulders and his living at Baptistie's camp, he was named 'Bibleback Brown.'" Baptistie Brown left Browns Hole about 1842, but Bibleback Brown reportedly stayed behind, trapping along the Little Snake and Bear (Yampa) Rivers.

From 1836 until around 1839, Americans Philip Thompson, William Craig, and Previtt Sinclair operated a fur trading post in Browns Hole called Fort Davy Crockett. The exact site is unknown, but it was somewhere near the confluence of Vermillion Creek and the Green River (upstream from the Gates of Lodore), in far northwestern Colorado. The post was a popular place for beaver trappers, Indians, and travelers to obtain supplies, in spite of the fact that its shoddy structure, muddy floors, and ill-kempt condition earned it the nickname "Fort Misery."

The next significant visitor to Browns Park was Maj. John Wesley Powell. In 1868 his Rocky Mountain Expedition spent time camped near Meeker at a place later known as Powell Bottom. The expedition then moved north and launched its first trip down the Green and Colorado Rivers in May 1869 from Green River City, Wyoming, a terminus of the Union Pacific Railroad. Powell wrote, "The good people of Green

The Green River widens as it enters the Gates of Lodore, a canyon named by John Wesley Powell while he explored the area in 1869.

River City turn out to see us start. We raise our little flag, push the boats from the shore, and the swift current carries us down."

A week or so later, the expedition entered Browns Park and explored the area, including what is now Dinosaur National Monument. It was Powell who named the "Canyon of Lodore," a reference to the poem "The Cataract of Lodore" by Robert Southey. It is now called the Gates of Lodore. Later in the journey, Powell's party became the first to successfully navigate the Colorado River through the Grand Canyon. After a three-month journey through previously unexplored territory, Powell and his men arrived in northwestern Arizona.

Ranchers and Rustlers

The abundant natural grass in Browns Park attracted cattlemen to the region, beginning in the early 1870s. Two ranchers from Evanston, Wyoming Territory, were the first to settle in this broad valley. Their ranch manager, J. S. Hoy, started his own ranch in 1875. Other ranchers and homesteaders soon followed.

Among the most successful of these ranchers was Ora Haley. Haley had already made a fortune in cattle in Wyoming when he established his Two Bar Ranch in Browns Park in early 1880. A part of the Haley Livestock & Trading Company, the Two Bar soon ranged some 7,000 head of cattle. Before long, Haley brought in another 6,000 head, quickly establishing his ranch as the largest in the region.

Ora Haley had been a butcher in Black Hawk, Colorado, and Laramie, Wyoming. He made a nice profit supplying beef to the Union Pacific Railroad crews, and in 1871 he purchased his first ranch, about twenty miles southwest of Laramie. Five years later, he drove a herd of shorthorn and Hereford cattle to Oregon, netting his first bundle in the livestock business. Investing in more land and cattle, he soon had some 36,000 deeded acres stretching along the Laramie River. Then, pushing his operation into Colorado, he established a headquarters on the Little Snake River and claimed rangeland in Browns Park to fatten the calves from his Wyoming operation.

Through the years, Haley employed many good cowboys, but undoubtedly the best in his Colorado operation was Hi Bernard, foreman of the Two Bar Ranch. A Texan who started cowboying at age twelve with Charlie Goodnight, Bernard brought a herd north when he was only seventeen. He found work with Haley's Laramie River outfit, then moved to the Colorado holdings. Some reports say that Bernard made Haley around $1 million a year during the eight years he ran the Two Bar. But the relationship went sour in 1904 when Bernard married "Queen" Ann Bassett, a fiery woman who passionately hated Ora Haley. Because the feeling was mutual, Haley soon fired Bernard.

Without Bernard at the helm, the Two Bar faltered. Haley lost a fortune and eventually sold most of his Colorado holdings. He died in 1919 at age seventy-four, leaving an estate valued at $2 million. In the meantime, Ann Bassett had been making a legacy of her own.

The cultured daughter of Browns Park ranchers Herbert and Elizabeth Bassett, Ann appreciated Shakespeare and Chaucer but could also rope and ride with the best men—and the worst. She may have thrown a wide loop a time or two, and she is believed to have consorted with various outlaws, including Butch Cassidy and the Sundance Kid. There are some who claim that the mysterious Etta Place, who married Sundance and accompanied him to South America, was none other than Ann Bassett, but this theory has pretty much been debunked.

In Browns Park, Bassett made bitter enemies, notably Ora Haley, who considered her a rustler. She is known to have claimed a few head of his stock, and he fought back with midnight riders, among them the notorious Tom Horn, who probably killed Bassett's fiancé, Matt Rash. She evened the score with Haley by marrying Hi Bernard. The couple had a rocky relationship, however, which eventually ended in divorce.

In the fall of 1911, Bassett found herself facing rustling charges from Haley. She eventually won an acquittal, which was a landmark decision for the region's small cattlemen, who resented the dominance of Haley's giant operation. Small ranchers celebrated the verdict for days. Bassett remarried in 1923, staking her claim with cattleman Frank Willis. Eventually they moved to Leeds, Utah, but returned to Browns Park for summer holidays until Ann's death in 1956.

Butch Cassidy
—Courtesy Wyoming State Archives

Others who spent time in Browns Park in those days included a motley assortment of rustlers and outlaws. Members of the Wild Bunch—Butch Cassidy, the Sundance Kid, and Elzy Lay—found work and sometimes sanctuary with the ranchers of Browns Park, a convenient hideaway situated between their known haunts in central Wyoming and in Utah around Price and Circleville.

CO 82
Glenwood Springs—US 24
84 MILES

GLENWOOD SPRINGS

In July 1860, former Indiana railroad contractor Richard Sopris explored Colorado's western mountains, making his way down what he called the Thunder River, now known as the Roaring Fork River. At its confluence with the Grand River (now the Colorado) he came upon the hot springs he named Grand Springs, in the heart of present Glenwood Springs.

The first white settler at Grand Springs was John M. Landis, who arrived here in 1878 and returned the next year to build a log cabin. Word of mineral deposits in the region attracted other settlers to the area, and a mining camp known as Dotsero sprang up on the border of the Ute Indian reservation. Although the miners encountered no problems with the Indians, they build a log fort called Fort Defiance.

In 1880 Landis filed a land claim for 160 acres at the river junction. Even though the land was still in Ute territory at the time, the region was about to open for settlement thanks to the Ute uprising of 1879. Meanwhile, area coal mines prospered and Defiance grew. In 1883 the settlement was renamed Glenwood Springs for Glenwood, Iowa. Later that year, the town became the Garfield County seat, which drew additional business to the area. Before long, the Denver & Rio Grande Railroad arrived, and in November 1884, a U.S. Land Office opened in Glenwood Springs to deal with the ever-increasing number of claims made on the former Indian lands.

Doc Holliday at the Hotel Glenwood
During the growth spurt, businessman Walter Devereaux created the Glenwood Light & Water Company and, equally important, the Colorado Land & Improvement Company. Under the latter enterprise he developed the hot springs into a resort. The plan called for

a 150-by-600-foot pool, with a bathhouse and a "vapor cave." By 1886 the four-story Hotel Glenwood was housing guests.

Many prominent people stayed at the Hotel Glenwood over the next few decades. The arrival of the legendary John Henry "Doc" Holliday in 1887 attracted much attention in town. Suffering from consumption (tuberculosis), Holliday may have come to Glenwood Springs to take advantage of the hot mineral pools. Having made his reputation at the shoot-out at the OK Corral in Tombstone, Arizona, in 1881, Doc settled into his room at the Hotel Glenwood, dealing some poker and faro, perhaps performing some dentistry, and no doubt drinking quite a lot. Holliday died in his hotel room on November 8, 1887, probably with his paramour, Big Nose Kate, by his side. He was buried in town.

South Canyon Fire

One of the most horrific wildfires in Colorado history occurred on Storm King Mountain, seven miles west of Glenwood Springs, on the evening of July 2, 1994. The South Canyon Fire, spawned by lightning, did not appear to be large at first, and a small Forest Service crew headed up the mountain to tackle it. But as the blaze spread, BLM firefighters and smoke jumpers were called in. By July 6, the flames were engulfing the piñon, cedar, and Gambel oak trees that covered the mountain. An expert firefighting crew from Prineville, Oregon, arrived on the scene, and it was thought that with their support, the fire would be manageable.

Around 3 p.m., a cold front swept over the area, changing the situation drastically. In the high winds, the fire simply exploded. A huge cloud of smoke obscured the sun as flames rocketed up the mountainside, climbing around 1,900 feet in just two minutes, at an estimated eighteen miles per hour. The firefighters and smoke jumpers above the fire line simply could not outrun the blaze. Fourteen men and women, mostly from the Prineville crew, died in the South Canyon Fire.

Glenwood Springs residents mourned along with the firefighters' families. Within hours people had wrapped purple ribbons around their arms in remembrance. The city council met the next day to plan the Storm King Fourteen Monument, which was later installed in Two Rivers Park. Although there were no further fatalities, the fire was not completely contained until early August. This fire changed the way the Forest Service conducted future firefighting training and operations, redoubling its efforts to maximize crew safety.

In addition to the monument, the trail up Storm King Mountain serves as another memorial to the South Canyon firefighters. The steep and rugged trail reminds hikers how difficult the terrain was for those who fought the fire, and at an observation point on the mountain, fourteen crosses stand in honor of the fallen heroes.

Glenwood Canyon Highway

Glenwood Springs became embroiled in controversy in the mid-1970s when Glenwood Canyon, east of the city, was slated to become a corridor for I-70. Although a two-lane highway had already been built between the canyon's massive granite walls, opponents argued that four lanes of traffic would pose too much risk to the fragile environment. But proponents, including the Federal Highway Administration and the U.S. Department of Transportation, stressed the need for a better, safer highway.

After much debate and nearly ten years of planning, work on the massive project started in 1983. Using special construction techniques, crews built forty bridges and viaducts and several tunnels, including the 4,000-foot-long Hanging Lake Tunnel. In places where the canyon is narrow, the westbound lanes were built on a viaduct directly above the eastbound lanes.

The Glenwood Canyon Highway was officially opened on October 14, 1992. At a construction cost of nearly $500 million, it is one of the most high-tech highways in Colorado. Cameras along the route allow officials to monitor traffic and react to emergencies. Some sections even have electronic monitoring strips that can track individual vehicles. Among its other awards, the highway was named the Outstanding Civil Engineering Achievement of 1993.

ASPEN

Prospectors from the Leadville region took a tortuous route over the Continental Divide in the late 1870s to look for gold and silver, and they eventually found it in the Roaring Fork Valley. As this was in Ute Indian territory, the miners called their camp Ute City, but before long it was renamed Aspen. With backing from wealthy eastern capitalists, by 1890 Aspen's silver production had eclipsed that of Leadville. A brothel district emerged on Durant Street, and saloons, gambling houses, and theaters sprang up on Cooper Street. In 1887 Aspen became the first city in Colorado to provide electricity to all its residents. By 1893 the town had a population of 12,000, with six newspapers, three banks, four schools, an opera house, and two theaters. But the prosperity did not last long; silver production began to decline that same year, and by 1935, only around 700 people lived in Aspen.

Yet just as Aspen's future looked bleakest, a new resource emerged: snow. International ski enthusiasts began scouting Colorado and other areas in the United States for development, and the steep slopes of Aspen Mountain put a gleam in their eyes. Swiss avalanche expert André Roche was building a ski area in nearby Ashcroft when World War II erupted, putting a damper on the project. Roche, along with members of

Vintage trolley car on display in Aspen

the newly organized Aspen Ski Club, pressed on in Aspen, however. They outlined a racecourse on Aspen Mountain and rigged two sleds to a boat tow attached to a motor-powered mine hoist to get skiers to the top.

Although World War II delayed resort planning, Aspen actually benefited from the war. The Tenth Mountain Division, headquartered at Camp Hale, brought men to this part of the Rockies to train for winter warfare (see Camp Hale in part 2). Soldiers on leave also skied here recreationally. By the time the war ended, Aspen had become internationally known for skiing.

After the war, Austrian Friedl Pfeifer, with support from Chicago industrialist Walter Paepcke, began building a full-scale resort in the town. Pfeifer wanted to see a ski area comparable to those in Europe, saying "Aspen was made by God with skiers in his mind." Paepcke, on the other hand, envisioned a summer resort, "a mountain community where people could fulfill themselves in body, mind and spirit—the trinity of the 'Aspen Idea,'" according to Heritage Aspen. While Pfeifer drew international skiers to Aspen, Paepcke brought in cultural events, such as the Goethe Bicentennial Convocation in 1949. Their combined efforts created the year-round, international hot spot that Aspen is today.

In the 1970s a young singer named John Denver brought a new kind of attention to Aspen. His megahit "Rocky Mountain High" became an anthem for young people wanting to escape the stress of urban life and connect with nature. Hundreds of these counterculturalists—considered hippies by longtime residents—invaded Aspen, which quickly developed a reputation as a party town with loose law enforcement.

But John Denver's impact on Aspen was miniscule compared to that of condominiums. These housing units were built primarily for people who came to Aspen to play for a few weeks or months, not to live. The part-time residents irrevocably changed Aspen's character. One condo development quickly led to another in former mining and agricultural lands all along the Roaring Fork Valley. Real estate prices skyrocketed. By the early twenty-first century, it was being said that the billionaires were pushing out the millionaires.

INDEPENDENCE

On July 4, 1879, prospectors discovered the Independence gold lode on the west side of Independence Pass. The town that grew up beside the new gold mines went by numerous names: Chipeta, Farwell, Hunter's

Remains of the mining town of Independence are preserved by the Aspen Historical Society, which offers tours to the area.

Pass, Mammoth City, Mount Hope, Sparkill, and the one that stuck, Independence. The remains of the boomtown can still be seen just south of CO 82.

By 1880 around 300 people called Independence home. Within a year the Farwell Mining Company had control over all the major mines, including the Legal Tender, the Last Dollar, the Dolly Varden, and Independence Nos. 1, 2, and 3. Independence soon grew to around 1,500 residents and had forty businesses. In October 1881 the *Independence Miner* began publication.

Like nearly all mining booms, the boom of the upper Roaring Fork region went bust, taking Independence down with it. Mining revenues dropped suddenly and dramatically, from more than $190,000 in 1881 and 1882 to only about $2,000 in 1883.

Although most people left Independence with the bust, a few hardy souls stayed on. At an elevation of 10,900 feet, Independence was not an easy place to live. In the winter of 1899, Independence residents became stranded by snows. Undaunted, they used wood from town buildings to construct seventy-five pairs of skis, on which they set off in a group to Aspen.

Independence is now a ghost town, but the Aspen Historical Society has breathed new life into it, stabilizing and restoring some of the original structures for visitors.

CO 133
CO 82 at Carbondale—Marble
28 MILES

CO 133 is the northern "handle" of the West Elk Scenic Loop Byway, connecting to the main "loop" part south of the Paonia Reservoir, near Somerset.

REDSTONE

Redstone is a picturesque village full of art galleries and upscale shops, surrounded by spectacular mountain scenery. The town, on the Crystal River, was built in the early 1900s by coal mogul John Cleveland Osgood as an unusually luxurious company town for his workers. Osgood's idea was to provide superior living conditions for miners in the hope of avoiding the labor problems that other coal towns were having at the time. Bachelors lived in rooms at the Redstone Inn, and workers with families had small houses; all housing had indoor plumbing and electricity. Though they were comfortable in Redstone, the miners were required to live by their employer's strict rules, which some resented.

Osgood himself resided in an opulent, forty-two-room mansion called Cleveholm, where he entertained such luminaries as President Theodore Roosevelt. By 1903 Osgood had lost his coal mines and much of his fortune, but he remained a millionaire until his death in 1926.

The Redstone Inn still stands as a hotel, and Cleveholm Manor, or Redstone Castle, has been used intermittently for events. The Coke Oven Historic District has remnants of the old brick coal ovens.

MARBLE

Mining engineer George Yule discovered high-quality marble in this area in the 1880s. The town of Marble was established in 1899, growing to more than 1,500 residents by 1915. Blocks of marble from the Yule Marble Quarry, opened in 1905, were used in both the Tomb of the Unknown Soldier and the Lincoln Memorial. After various ups and downs in the marble market, the quarry finally closed in 1941. It was later reopened, but production has never reached its former heights.

I-70
Glenwood Springs—Idaho Springs
108 MILES

VAIL

Walking through Vail is like being transported to a European ski village. No motorized vehicles other than delivery trucks are allowed inside the village, and bicycles abound. Shops offer fur coats and hats, the newest styles in skiwear, and gourmet foods. Outdoor bronze sculptures adorn what seems like every corner. But before the development of the slopes that made it world famous, Vail was a small town in a narrow valley, surrounded by sheep and cattle ranches.

Uranium prospectors with Geiger counters came to search the mountains around Vail in the 1950s. One of them, Earl V. Eaton, saw potential in Vail Mountain, but not for a uranium mine. In 1954 Eaton invited Pete Seibert of the Loveland Basin ski area to take a look. To disguise their intentions from land speculators, they formed the Transmontane Rod and Gun Club while quietly securing a permit from the U.S. Forest Service to build a ski area.

Once the project was under way, the partners no longer kept it a secret. Launching a massive advertising campaign to attract investors, they soon won support from Sears, Roebuck & Co.; Federated Department Stores; Upjohn; Schlitz Brewing Co.; and Quaker Oats, among others. The Vail ski area, which opened to the public on December 15, 1962, featured the first gondola lift in the nation, and soon two double chairlifts were added. Vail would eventually become the largest skiing complex in the United States.

As the resort took off, the surrounding valley practically exploded with development. Condominiums sprang up in East Vail, West Vail, and Beaver Creek, from which buses transported skiers to the slopes. The walking, jogging, and biking paths around Vail became cross-country ski trails in the winter. In the 1970s, Vail received a significant amount of free publicity when President Gerald Ford spent his vacations there.

Although skiing in Colorado did not begin in Vail, the town's popularity certainly gave the state its first major push as an international ski destination. Throughout its development, Vail has successfully competed with other resort communities in the region, such as Crested Butte, Breckenridge, Winter Park, and the granddaddy of Colorado's ski industry, Steamboat Springs. By the 1980s it had eclipsed them all, even giving the glamorous Aspen a run for its money.

GEORGETOWN

Spread along the banks of Clear Creek, Georgetown was the site of several important mining strikes in Colorado. More than $90 million in gold, copper, silver, lead, and zinc were mined in the region up until 1939.

The town is named for George Griffith, who with his brothers and other family members worked nearby gold claims starting in 1859. The following year Griffith brought in the first stamp mill to process the gold ore. He and his brothers ignored the silver they found because they had no way to process it. The Griffiths also spent $1,500 to build a toll road between the Griffith Mining District and Eureka Gulch, west of Central City, charging a dollar per person. The Griffiths' gold production peaked in 1861; two years later they sold their claim and the stamp mill to Central City businessman Stephen F. Nickolls.

Though the gold petered out, Georgetown continued to prosper from its rich silver deposits. In addition, area settlers came to town for supplies, especially around Christmas. Merchants catered to the demand, as the *Georgetown Miner* reported in 1872:

> *Monti & Guanella, agents of Santa Claus in Georgetown, are preparing to fill all orders for Christmas goods promptly, and to the entire satisfaction of their customers. The [merry] old gentleman flashing over the country*

With its solid brick buildings, Georgetown still looks much the same as it did during the mining boom of a century ago.

with his capacious freight teams, has crammed the large store of his favorite agents with turkies and chickens, gobbling and crackling, to grace Christmas feasts. And then such quantities of vegetables, fruit confectionary, cake and toys for little girls, blushing maidens, stately dames, little boys and old boys, as the jolly old elf has on exhibition at his headquarters at Monti & Guanella's is a sight entertaining and highly satisfactory to the inhabitants of the "Silver Queen."

In 1879 Georgetown was connected to Silver Plume via the Georgetown Loop, whose engineers cleverly suspended railroad tracks over Devils Gate Canyon. Over the years, the Colorado Historical Society has sponsored special tourist trains over this stunning and historic rail route.

IDAHO SPRINGS

Remnants of Idaho Springs's mining days—the Dixie Gold Mill, the Argo Mill, and the mill wheel on the waterfall that tumbles from Flirtation Peak—remain on the hills on both sides of I-70. Much of the town was built on tailings and dumps from the mines.

In February 1858 William Green Russell and his brothers left Georgia to seek gold in Colorado. The party of nine had grown to over a hundred by the time the men reached Cherry Creek in May. The miners, many of them Cherokee Indians, prospected along the Front Range for about a month. Having little success, most of them quit, leaving only William Russell and about a dozen others. Then in early July, Russell and company found gold dust in Dry Creek near Englewood—the best find of the year in that region. Six months later, prospectors hit three major strikes in the area, and the rush was on.

Birth of a Gold Rush

Following gold discoveries in the Denver area, independent miners struck gold in three new locations in January 1859. The first was on January 7, 1859, when, while hunting for deer, George A. Jackson found gold in Chicago Creek near Clear Creek at present Idaho Springs. Within ten days, two more discoveries were made, one at Black Hawk, just north of Idaho Springs, the other at Gold Hill, west of Boulder.

Jackson's claim became known as Jackson's Bar. After he sold out, it was renamed Payne's Bar, later becoming Sacramento and finally Idaho Springs. The town shares its mining history with Black Hawk and its neighbor Central City, both now small casino towns on CO 119. In early 1859, Black Hawk's Gregory Gulch was the epicenter of the gold rush. Horace Greeley, among the first journalists to arrive in Gregory Gulch after the gold discovery, described the scene:

> *There are said to be five thousand people already in this ravine [Gregory Gulch], and hundreds pouring into it daily. Tens of thousands more have been passed by us on our rapid journey to this place, or heard of as on their way hither by other routes. . . .*
>
> *As yet the entire population of the valley sleeps in tents or under booths of pine boughs, cooking and eating in the open air. I doubt that there is as yet a table or chair in these diggings, eating being done around a cloth spread on the ground, while each one sits or reclines on mother earth.*

Miners used whatever conveyance they could to reach the goldfields. One interesting form of transportation was the prairie wind wagon, invented for the express purpose of taking gold seekers to Colorado, described in the *Daily Missouri Republican* in 1859: "The affair is on wheels which are mammoth concerns, about twenty feet in circumference. . . . It is to be propelled by the wind, through the means of sails. As to the wheels, it looks like an overgrown omnibus; and as to the spars and sails, it looks like a diminutive schooner. It will seat about Twenty-four passengers . . . and travel an average of over 100 miles per day."

Transportation through Colorado's challenging terrain was indeed an urgent issue. Horace Greeley reported on the problem:

Nearly every pound of provisions and supplies of every kind must be hauled by teams from the Missouri river some seven hundred miles distant, over roads which are mere trails, crossing countless unbridged water-courses, always steep-banked and often mirey, and at times so swollen by rains as to be utterly impassable by waggons. Part of this distance is a desert, yielding grass, wood and water only at intervals of several miles, and then very scantily. To attempt to cross this desert on foot is madness—suicide—murder.

In Black Hawk in 1868, Nathaniel Hill erected Colorado's first smelter, replacing placer mining with hard-rock methods in the region. As the mining industry grew, more camps popped up in the area. Within fifteen years, many of them had evolved into stable communities. One of these was Nevadaville, just west of Central City, of which Frank Fossett wrote in 1876, "The mines on either side of it have been extremely productive and have been worked more or less since the country was first opened. There are several quartz mills, here; also churches, and a public school with 150 pupils, population nearly 1,000."

While many mining towns developed in the region, it was Idaho Springs that emerged as the center of activity. In the early days of the boom, travelers coming from the east could take the railroad to Golden but had to switch to a stagecoach for the rest of the journey. Thus it was inevitable that Idaho Springs would begin to clamor for a railroad of its own. A line known as the Floyd Hill branch of the Colorado Central reached Idaho Springs on June 12, 1877, establishing it as a major hub for the region.

Argo Tunnel

By 1893 mining production had begun to slow down around Idaho Springs, but the construction of the Argo Tunnel brought hope for new prosperity to the region. Initially known as the Newhouse Tunnel, the project provided access to gold veins deep in the mountains. Eventually, more than 100 miles of tunnels were built, and production increased significantly. The success brought additional investors into the area, benefiting many towns besides Idaho Springs, such as Silver Plume and Georgetown.

Violence at the Sun and Moon Mine

A labor dispute in 1903 led to one of the great tragedies of the Idaho Springs mining region. Around 11 p.m. on July 28, R. A. Powell, a watchman at the Sun and Moon Mine, noticed a flicker on the hillside above the mine. Before he knew it, someone was firing shots at him. He shot back, then saw a keg tumbling his way. The keg was one of several that union saboteurs had filled with dynamite to send down the hill toward the mine. The first one rolled past Powell, struck the shaft house, and exploded. In the meantime, one of Powell's bullets had hit another keg, injuring one of the saboteurs, Philipo Fuoco. In great pain, Fuoco was taken to a hospital in Georgetown, where he died without naming his accomplices.

After the attack, twenty members of the Western Federation of Miners were jailed in Idaho Springs, and three others, including former union president William Bates, were jailed in Georgetown. When talk began to spread that the union men would likely beat the charges, enraged townspeople stepped in. On the night following the explosion, residents rang the bell at the Sun and Moon, and before long around 500 people had gathered in Idaho Springs. They marched to the jail and demanded the keys. Taking fourteen of the accused men to the edge of town, the citizens told the union miners to keep walking until they were out of Colorado. Their families, the group said, would be sent behind them.

Calling itself the Citizens' Protection League, the group also "invited" other union members to leave town. Thirteen of the accused union men eventually returned to Idaho Springs and Georgetown to face trial for conspiracy; all were acquitted. Charges against the Citizens' Protection League were dismissed.

A New Era

By the mid-1900s, due to a sharp downturn in mining, many former boomtowns in this area were nearly abandoned. Then, in the 1990s, Colorado legalized limited-stakes gambling, which rejuvenated the area. These days, gold seekers gather in Central City and Black Hawk once again, but instead of pans and sluice boxes, they use cards and dice to mine for their fortunes.

COUNTY ROAD 129
Steamboat Springs—Hahns Peak
25 MILES

South of Steamboat Springs, CO 131 runs through ranch country. North of Steamboat, a county and Forest Service road (129) leads to Steamboat Lake State Park and Hahns Peak before ending at the Wyoming border. Once an active mining and timber area, this part of the state is now mostly government land, maintained for recreation.

Hahns Peak —Courtesy Wyoming State Archives

HAHNS PEAK

Hahns Peak, just northeast of Steamboat Lake, was named for prospector Joseph Hahn. Hahn and his partner George R. Way came to Colorado from Illinois in 1860 to prospect on the east slope of the Rockies, then on the west slope. At the peak that subsequently took Hahn's name, they found gold in the gulches, but they had to abandon their diggings before winter set in. Eventually returning to Illinois, they recruited another partner, William Doyle, who agreed to accompany them back to their gold claims in the spring. But before they could leave, the Civil War broke out. Way and Doyle enlisted in the army and served for the next three years.

The three finally made the trip to Colorado in the fall of 1866. It was already late in the season when they reached Hahns Peak. Running low on supplies, Hahn and Doyle sent Way to Empire, nearly 100 miles away. Way never returned. Heavy snows had blocked the passes, and he may have been unable to get through. Whatever the reason, he spent the winter in Empire.

In March, Hahn and Doyle made their own attempt to go to Empire. But after about forty miles, Hahn collapsed from exhaustion and illness near Rabbit Ears Pass. Doyle remained with Hahn for a time but eventually decided he had to continue, leaving his sick friend behind. Finally spotting a trapper's camp in upper Middle Park, Doyle "stumbled in, completely exhausted from cold and hunger," according to an account by M. Wilson Rankin. After recovering his strength, Doyle proceeded to Empire. Hahn's body was eventually found and buried beneath a mound of rocks, with a snowshoe marking the grave. Way and Doyle never returned to Hahns Peak.

The next prospectors to work the peak were William Slater and his partner, Bibleback Brown, in 1869. Slater had been trapping in the Hahns Peak area when he found mining tools left by Hahn and Way. He asked Brown to join him in prospecting the area, and the two found several promising sites. They left before winter set in but returned the next spring with two additional partners and began mining in earnest.

Within a few years, John V. Farwell had moved in on the mining operations at Hahns Peak. By July 1877, the Farwell Mining Company had established company offices, a store, a hotel, and other buildings. The settlement was christened "Bug Town," later changed to International Camp.

Needing a link to the railroad, Farwell began building a road to Laramie City, Wyoming Territory, along the old Laramie Trail. Later, beginning in 1898, John M. "Jack" Ellis developed much of Farwell's route as a freight trail. Now called the Ellis Trail, it is used as a hiking trail through the Routt National Forest.

In the early 1900s, mining gave way to timber. The Carbon Timber Company had an extensive network of tie-cutting camps in both Colorado and Wyoming. When the company was found to be illegally cutting timber on the Park Range Forestry Preserve (now the Routt National Forest), it was required, as part of its penalty, to construct the eighteen-mile-long Fireline Stock Driveway. The trail, begun in 1907, was later used heavily for moving sheep herds.

US 40
Steamboat Springs—Idaho Springs
132 MILES

MIDDLE PARK

US 40 slices through Middle Park, which lies mostly in western Grand County, from Rabbit Ears Pass to Kremmling and east to Tabernash. Middle Park was not formally part of the United States until 1936.

Outside the scope of both the Louisiana Purchase and the land ceded by Mexico in 1848, it remained Ute Indian territory until 1881, when the tribe was forced out of northern Colorado. Finally, on August 9, 1936, Colorado Governor Edwin C. Johnson formally claimed this "no-man's-land" as part of Colorado at a ceremony in Breckenridge.

Like its adjacent parks, Middle Park was first settled by ranchers. It remains a prime ranching area, but due to the ski areas around Winter Park, tourism has eclipsed agriculture as the biggest industry.

HOT SULPHUR SPRINGS

The hot mineral water at what is now Hot Sulphur Springs attracted Ute Indians for decades. In 1864 *Rocky Mountain News* editor William N. Byers used Indian scrip to purchase the springs from an Indian woman. Byers developed the main pools for visitors in the 1870s, and the town became and has remained a modestly popular spa resort. In 1874 Hot Sulphur Springs became the seat of Grand County.

TABERNASH

Before the town of Tabernash, named for a Ute chief, was founded as a railroad camp in 1905, it was the site of the Junction Ranch, so named because it was at the junction where the roads to Empire and Black Hawk converged. The stage station here was known as Junction House.

In August 1878, a band of Utes rode into Middle Park after killing a white man in far eastern Colorado. At or near the Junction House station, they threatened a horse tender, who rode to Hot Sulphur Springs to spread the alarm. The sheriff there quickly organized a posse and rode back to Junction House, where the posse confronted the Indians and killed one of them. The Indians dispersed and headed west.

On the Blue River in present Kremmling, the Utes came across homesteader Abraham Elliott cutting wood and killed him. According to one account, the Indians disliked Elliott because he had refused to give them food a year earlier. The news of Elliott's death spurred area settlers to organize another party to chase down the Utes. The posse caught up with the Indians at their camp near present Meeker. They recovered seven stolen horses but never apprehended the Indians who killed Elliott.

WINTER PARK AND MOFFAT TUNNEL

The Moffat Tunnel runs east from Winter Park and connects to a Forest Service road to Rollinsville. It was originally conceived as part of a rail route between Denver and Salt Lake City. In the early 1920s, the Moffat Tunnel Improvement District, comprising Denver, Grand, Moffat, and Routt Counties and portions of other counties, was created by a special legislative session. The tunnel commission sold bonds to raise funds, and work started in 1923.

The construction crews soon discovered that, in some places, the seemingly solid rock wasn't solid. In these cases, the workers had to install supports of steel and concrete. The excavation was a dangerous job—twenty-nine people were killed during the tunnel's construction. The most serious accident happened on July 30, 1926, when a 125-ton cave-in crushed six members of a timber crew.

Builders ran into another serious problem when water from Lower Crater Lake, some 1,100 feet overhead, began to leak into the tunnel. In February 1926 workers dug a smaller "pioneer" tunnel next to the main tunnel, then cut a fissure to let the lake drain into it. Eventually the entire lake emptied into the pioneer tunnel, which was then used as an aqueduct. In the end, the project ran about $11 million over budget.

The railroad tunnel was "holed through" on July 17, 1927, and the first regular train passed through on February 26, 1928. The six-mile tunnel cut only twenty-three miles from the distance between Denver and Salt Lake City, but going through the mountain rather than over it significantly improved the safety and comfort of the crossing and reduced costs for the Denver & Rio Grande.

The cabins at West Portal, overlooking Middle Park, that formerly housed the tunnel construction crews were soon renovated into quarters for the Arlberg Club of Denver, a group of wealthy ski enthusiasts who forged the first ski runs at Winter Park. By the mid-1930s, skiers routinely headed to the new resort, taking the train through the Moffat Tunnel.

Denver residents further developed Winter Park in 1938 with support from Denver Parks and Improvements manager George Cranmer. This program, along with federal public-works funds and private donations, provided the first $50,000 needed to begin full-scale development at Winter Park. Improvements included more trails and a T-bar lift. The Civilian Conservation Corps, the U.S. Forest Service, and volunteers from Denver all pitched in on the labor.

In 1967 Colorado organized an Olympics committee to prepare a bid to host the 1976 Winter Olympics at either Winter Park, Vail, or Steamboat Springs. But environmental concerns coupled with trepidation about costs—originally estimated at $14 million but soon ballooning to $25 million—led to growing opposition to Colorado's Olympic bid. By the time the Olympic Committee gathered in Sapporo, Japan, in 1972 to choose the host for the 1976 games, the Colorado-site opponents were well organized. After a public squabble between the two sides, voters in Colorado overwhelmingly rejected hosting the Olympics, passing resolutions that bannned using additional public funds for Olympic planning. The 1976 games took place in Innsbruck, Austria.

BERTHOUD PASS

At more than 11,000 feet, Berthoud Pass was a tough climb. Journalist Bayard Taylor wrote of his 1866 ascent by stagecoach: "It was, indeed, a terrible pull. . . . Our horses stopped, almost gasping for breath . . . our knees tottered, our bodies were drenched with sweat, our eyes dim, heads giddy, and lungs utterly collapsed."

Berthoud Pass, on US 40, was named for engineer and Civil War veteran Edward L. Berthoud, who crossed it in 1861, with Jim Bridger as his guide, to survey a mail route between Denver and either Salt Lake City or Provo, Utah. Berthoud, born in Switzerland, came to America in 1830. After engineering railroad lines in the Midwest, he settled in Golden. He and W.A.H. Loveland, one of the founders of Golden, were the first to initiate serious discussions about building a railroad into the mountains to connect rail lines with area mining districts. Berthoud subsequently became chief engineer for Loveland's Colorado Central Railroad (see Golden in part 5).

Later, Berthoud served as the first registrar and secretary of the Colorado School of Mines in Golden, where he taught both geology and civil engineering. He was also a member of the Colorado legislature and was elected Golden's mayor in 1890. In addition to the mountain pass, the town of Berthoud, just south of Loveland, was also named for him.

CO 14
US 40—US 287
132 MILES

CO 14 roughly follows the route of the first improved road connecting Fort Collins and North Park, the Cache la Poudre Canyon Toll Road, begun in 1879. Work on the road was already well under way when news of a mining discovery in North Park came in the spring of 1880. The builders, the Cache la Poudre and North Park Toll Road Company, rushed to finish the job. Immediately upon its completion, Luke Voorhees's Cheyenne & Black Hills Stage Company established a stage line over the new road, and hotels and other businesses soon sprang up along the route.

Voorhees's stage line carried passengers and mail between Fort Collins and the mining towns of North Park each day. It had four seventeen-passenger coaches and eight six-passenger buckboards. Other carriers followed, and traffic on the toll road was steady as area mining towns continued to sprout and grow. The tolls were two dollars for each vehicle drawn by one horse, ox, or mule, and one dollar for each additional team animal. A riding horse was one dollar, loose horses and cattle were forty cents per head, and sheep were twenty cents each. The toll road became a public highway in 1902.

NORTH PARK

Several small communities make up the region known as North Park, including Gould, Rand, and Walden, the Jackson County seat. Encircled by mountains, this wide valley is range and hay country, as it has been since the first white settlers arrived. It was once home to buffalo herds, but the last free-ranging animals were gone by the early 1870s. Since then, cattle have grazed on this land watered by the headwaters of the Michigan, North Platte, and Laramie Rivers.

According to M. Wilson Rankin, D. J. Fordyce and W. H. Pinkham were the first settlers in North Park, arriving in 1877. Pinkham later ran the Pinkhampton Post Office and Road Ranch. Another early homesteader was J. A. Mendenhall, who in 1879 brought in 3,000 cattle and 600 horses and established a ranch on the east side of the park. At the same time, additional prospectors came to look for minerals in the surrounding mountains, but few found ore, and most left in 1879 after the Ute Indian uprising.

The ranchers, however, stuck around. They pastured cattle on the valley grass during the summer and allowed the herds to roam freely around the high country in the winter. It worked pretty well until the winter of 1883–84, when heavy snows covered the grazing lands. After serious losses, some ranchers began harvesting hay for winter feeding. Those who did not take the lesson to heart soon faced a harsher one. After the killer winter of 1886–87, known as the "Great Die-Up" from Montana to Texas, ranchers learned that they had to provide their cattle supplemental feed to keep them in the high country through the winter.

By 1897 the ranchers were intent on finding better, faster, easier ways to harvest hay. One North Park rancher designed a breakthrough method, which Stephen Payne described in *Where the Rockies Ride Herd*:

> The idea was to shove or pull the hay up a slanting framework constructed of poles and let it fall straight down from the top of this slide onto the stack. . . .

Jack Green . . . built the first slide stacker and then experimented with various block-and-tackle methods of pulling the hay up the incline. These methods, however, proved so slow, cumbersome and unsatisfactory that it was not until another North Parker, Joe Lawrence, invented the 'pusher' that ranchmen began to realize that the slide stacker, plus the pusher, plus home-made two-wheel sweeps, was the answer to their hay-stacking problem.

Across the West, family ranches are becoming rare. Many of them have been consolidated into larger holdings under corporate ownership. Nevertheless, tradition dies hard in North Park, where some ranchers still use teams of horses and slide stackers to harvest hay.

US 34
US 40 at Granby—
Rocky Mountain National Park
17 MILES

From US 40 at Granby, US 34 heads past Lake Granby to Grand Lake, near the border of Rocky Mountain National Park. The highway, called Trail Ridge Road inside the park, continues north along the western border of the park, through the Kewuneechee Valley toward the Never Summer Mountains. Several hiking trails can be accessed from the road. One of the trails follows Timber creek, the headwaters of the mighty Colorado River.

GRAND LAKE

Grand Lake started as a supply center for gold seekers in the 1870s. Little gold was found, so the prospectors moved on, but Grand Lake survived and prospered as a lakeside resort town. It is also the western gateway to Rocky Mountain National Park, although the eastern entrance, near Estes Park, is by far the more popular one (see Estes Park in part 5).

ROCKY MOUNTAIN NATIONAL PARK

Perhaps 10,000 or 11,000 years ago, people first made their way through the area that is now Rocky Mountain National Park. American Indians hunted in the region, leaving behind tipi rings and markers from vision quests. As early as 1840, mountain man Kit Carson traveled in the region, camping near present Estes Park.

A Report of a 1914 Pack Trip by Oliver W. Toll provides some early names for various sites in the area. Among the Arapahos, the Estes

Park basin was called "the Circle," and Longs Peak and Mount Meeker were known as the "Two Guides." The mountains from McHenrys Peak to Stones Peak were the "Bald Mountains," the Mummy Range was the "White Owls," Thatchtop Mountain was called "Buffalo Climb," Hallett Peak was "Thunder Peak," and Prospect Mountain was "the Shirt." Trail Ridge, or Tombstone Ridge, was called the "Child's Trail"

Headwaters of the Colorado River in Rocky Mountain National Park

Trail rides into the mountains from Grand Lake sometimes hold up traffic in town.

because Indian children would dismount their horses and walk on its steep terrain.

Enos Mills, who first visited this area in 1884 at age fourteen, became the primary force in lobbying for the preservation of what is now Rocky Mountain National Park. Mills, a dedicated naturalist and writer, owned the Longs Peak Inn, from which he led wilderness trips. In 1909 he proposed setting aside the area around Longs Peak as a national park. In countless lectures, letters, and articles, he touted this special landscape, generating support from the Colorado Mountain Club, the Denver Chamber of Commerce, and others. In spite of opposition from agriculture, logging, and mining interests, the region was set aside as Rocky Mountain National Park on January 26, 1915. Through the years, the park has expanded to some 416 square miles and now hosts about 3 million visitors annually.

Longs Peak

Longs Peak, the primary landmark in Rocky Mountain National Park, was named for Maj. Stephen H. Long, who first saw it on his 1819–20 Yellowstone Expedition. Long's nineteen-member expedition traveled west from the Missouri River with topographers, a naturalist, a cartographer, a zoologist, a painter, and a physician who was also a botanist and geologist. Seeking the source of the Platte, Arkansas, and Red Rivers, Long's company followed the Platte River across present Nebraska then went along the south branch into Colorado. The men were miles away when they first viewed the mountain they believed was Pikes Peak, which was in fact much farther south. The peak the men saw would eventually be named for Long himself.

Long and his party traveled west for a bit through the South Platte Valley, having a gill of whiskey to celebrate the Fourth of July, before continuing south along the Front Range. They camped below the real Pikes Peak, which scientist Edwin James and two companions successfully climbed, the first known white men to do so (see Pikes Peak in part 2).

From the peak, the expedition continued south to the Arkansas River. After traveling west for a while, they saw the Royal Gorge and turned back east, then headed south in search of the Red River. Like the Zebulon Pike expedition years before, they failed to find it, nor did they find the source of the Platte or the Arkansas. The Long Expedition did, however, create a new map showing the region east of the Rockies as the "Great American Desert." This misnomer would have an impact on the region for decades, as hundreds of thousands passed through but few stopped to live on the plains.

In his final report, Long compared the area to the African Sahara, writing, "I saw in my route, in various places, tracts of many leagues, where the wind had thrown up the sand . . . and on which not a speck of vegetable matter existed." Long advised that the region should "remain the unmolested haunt of the native hunter, the bison, and the jackall."

In July 1868, Maj. John Wesley Powell's expedition of the Rocky Mountains left from Cheyenne, Wyoming, traveling south along the Front Range. Among Powell's goals was to climb Longs Peak. One of his men wrote of the excursion, "After a pretty hard climb we did it, built a monument on the top, raised a flag, threw some wine on the monument." Careful to guard his temperate reputation, the soldier added, "the little that remained in the bottle was drank by 5 of the party, 2 of us withstanding all entreaties did not drink on Longs peak, whatever the papers may say to the contrary." After investigating the peak, the party headed into western Colorado. They explored the upper Colorado River and the Grand Canyon the following year.

Never Summer Ranch/ Holzwarth Historic Site

Off Trail Ridge Road is the trailhead for the short hike to the Never Summer Ranch/Holzwarth Historic Site, one of several historic homesteads in Rocky Mountain National Park. The National Park Service has preserved the original log home and outbuildings and offers daily tours of the ranch, which was established in 1917.

Cabin at the Holzwarth Historic Site

Bibliography

Abbott, Carl, Stephen J. Leonard, and David McComb. *Colorado: A History of the Centennial State*. Boulder: Colorado Associated University Press, 1982.

Arps, Louisa Ward. *Denver in Slices: A Historical Guide to the City*. 2nd ed. Athens, OH: Swallow Press, 1998.

———. *High Country Names*. Denver: Colorado Mountain Club, 1966.

Aschermann, Arla. *Winds in the Cornfields of Pueblo County Colorado. Ghost Towns and Settlements, 1787–1872*. 3rd ed. Pueblo, CO: Pueblo County Historical Society, 1994.

Atherton, Lewis. *The Cattle Kings*. Lincoln: University of Nebraska Press, Bison Books, 1961.

Baker, Dick. "The Beginning of the Cache la Poudre Canon Road," *Fort Collins Shopping Guide*, January 1, 1954.

Bancroft, Caroline. *Famous Aspen*. Boulder: Johnson Books, 1967.

Barney, Libeus. *Letters of the Pike's Peak Gold Rush*. San Jose, CA: Talisman Press, 1959.

Bartlett, Richard A. *Great Surveys of the American West*. Norman: University of Oklahoma Press, 1926.

Beasley, Conger, Jr. *Spanish Peaks: Land and Legends*. Niwot: University of Colorado Press, 2001.

Bebe, Lucius, and Charles Clegg. *Narrow Gauge in the Rockies*. Berkeley, CA: Howell-North, 1958.

Bird, Isabella. *A Lady's Life in the Rocky Mountains*. New York: G. P. Putnam's Sons, 1879–80; Sausalito, CA: Comstock, 1977.

Blevins, Terry, ed. *Tri-County History: A Centennial*. Limon, CO: Eastern Colorado Printery, 1989.

Bright, William. *Colorado Place Names*. Boulder: Johnson Books, 1993.

Brotemarkle, Diane. *Old Fort St. Vrain*. Boulder: Platteville Historical Society, 2001.

Brown, Dee. *The Gentle Tamers*. New York: Bantam, 1958.

Brown, Robert L. *Colorado Ghost Towns Past and Present.* Caldwell, ID: Caxton Printers, 1993.

Buchholtz, C. W. *Rocky Mountain National Park: A History.* Boulder: Colorado Associated University Press, 1983.

Byers, William N. *Encyclopedia of Biography in Colorado.* Chicago: Century, 1901.

Cafky, Morris. *The Colorado Midland.* Denver: Rocky Mountain Railroad Club, 1965.

Cannon, Brian Q. *Remaking the Agrarian Dream: New Deal Rural Resettlement in the Mountain West.* Albuquerque: University of New Mexico Press, 1996.

Carey, Raymond G. "Colonel Chivington, Brigadier General Connor, and Sand Creek." In *The 1960 Brand Book . . . of the Denver Posse of the Westerners,* edited by Guy M. Herstrom. Boulder: Johnson Publishing Company, 1961.

Carothers, June E. *Estes Park: Past and Present.* Denver: University of Denver Press, 1951.

Carter, Robert A. *Buffalo Bill Cody: The Man Behind the Legend.* New York: John Wiley & Sons, 2000.

Casement, Frances. Letter to Mrs. C. C. Jennings. June 30, 1867. John Stephen and Francis Jennings Casement Papers, Accession No. 308. American Heritage Center, University of Wyoming.

Cassells, E. Steve. *The Archaeology of Colorado.* Boulder: Johnson Books, 1983.

Chronic, Halka. *Roadside Geology of Colorado.* Missoula, MT: Mountain Press, 1980.

Colton, Ray C. *The Civil War in the Western Territories.* Norman: University of Oklahoma Press, 1959.

Conard, Howard Louis. *"Uncle Dick" Wootton.* Chicago: W. E. Dibble, 1890.

Coolican, Frank. "Historic Virginia Dale Station and the Overland Mail." Unpublished manuscript written September 4, 1937. WPA Subject File 142: Stage Stations. Wyoming State Archives, Cheyenne.

Crum, J. M. *Rio Grande Southern Story.* Durango, CO: Railroadiana, 1957.

Crutchfield, James A. *Eyewitness to American History.* Boise, ID: Tamarack Books, 1996.

———. *It Happened in Colorado.* Helena, MT: Falcon Press, 1993.

Crutchfield, James A. *The Santa Fe Trail*. Plano, TX: Republic of Texas Press, 1996.

———. *Tragedy at Taos*. Plano, TX: Republic of Texas Press, 1995.

Cunningham, Ruth, ed. *Homesteaders and Other Early Settlers, 1900–1930: History of Western Cheyenne County, Colorado*. Vol. 1. Kit Carson, CO: Kit Carson Historical Society, 1985.

Danielson, Clarence L., and Ralph W. Danielson. *Basalt: Colorado Midland Town*. Boulder: Pruett Publishing, 1965.

Dary, David. *Seeking Pleasure in the Old West*. New York: Alfred A. Knopf, 1995.

Davis, Richard Harding. *The West from a Car-Window*. New York: Harper & Brothers, 1892; 1903 reprint.

Drago, Harry Sinclair. *The Great Range Wars: Violence on the Grasslands*. Lincoln: University of Nebraska Press, Bison Books, 1985.

Duffus, Robert L. *The Santa Fe Trail*. New York: Longmans, Green, 1930.

Eberhart, Perry. *Guide to the Colorado Ghost Towns and Mining Camps*. Denver: Sage Books, 1959.

Eichler, George R. *Colorado Place Names*. Boulder: Johnson Books, 1977.

Fay, Abbott. *A History of Skiing in Colorado*. Ouray, CO: Western Reflections Publishing Co., 2000.

Feitz, Leland. *Alamosa: A Quick History*. Colorado Springs: Little London Press, 1976.

———. *Conejos County: A Quick History*. Revised edition. Colorado Springs: Little London Press, 1995.

———. *A Quick History of Creede*. Colorado Springs: Little London Press, 1969.

Fetter, Richard L., and Suzanne Fetter. *Telluride*. Caldwell, ID: Caxton Printers, 1979.

Fisher, John. *A Builder of the West*. Caldwell, ID: Caxton Printers, 1939.

Fletcher, Patricia K. A., Jack Earl Fletcher, and Lee Whiteley. *Cherokee Trail Diaries*. Vols. 1 and 2: Caldwell, ID: Caxton Printers for the Fletcher Family Foundation, n.d. Vol. 3: Sequim, WA: Fletcher Family Foundation, 2001.

Foscue, Edwin J., and Louis O. Quam. *Estes Park: Resort in the Rockies*. Dallas: University Press, 1949.

Frazer, Robert W. *Forts of the West*. Norman: University of Oklahoma Press, 1965; 1972 reprint.

Frazier, Deborah. *Colorado's Hot Springs*. Boulder: Pruett Publishing, 1996.

Frink, Maurice. *The Boulder Story: Historical Portrait of a Colorado Town*. Boulder: Pruett Publishing, 1965.

Frison, George C. *Prehistoric Hunters of the High Plains*. New York: Academic Press, 1978.

Fritz, Percy Stanley. *Colorado, the Centennial State*. New York: Prentice-Hall, 1941.

Fry, Eleanor. *Colorado Travel 1846–1880*. Pueblo, CO: Pueblo County Historical Society, 1981.

Gillette, Ethel Morrow. *Idaho Springs: Saratoga of the Rockies*. New York: Vantage Press, 1978.

Goodykoontz, Colin B., ed. *Colorado: Short Studies of Its Past and Present*. Boulder: University of Colorado Press, 1927.

Greeley, Horace. *An Overland Journey*. New York: C. M. Saxon, Barker, 1860; New York: Knopf, 1969.

Green, Stewart. *Scenic Driving Colorado*. Helena, MT: Falcon Press Publishing Co., 1994.

Gregg, Josiah. *Commerce of the Prairies*. New York: Henry G. Langley, 1844; Lincoln: University of Nebraska Press, Bison Books, 1967.

Gregory, Marvin, and P. David Smith. *The Million Dollar Highway: Colorado's Most Spectacular Seventy Miles*. Ouray, CO: Wayfinder, 1986; Ouray, CO: Western Reflections Publishing Co, 1997.

Grinnell, George B. *The Cheyenne Indians*. 2 vols. New Haven: Yale University Press, 1923; Lincoln: University of Nebraska Books, Bison Books, 1972.

———. *The Fighting Cheyennes*. New York: Charles Scribner's Sons, 1915; Norman: University of Oklahoma Press, 1956.

———. *Two Great Scouts and Their Pawnee Battalion*. Cleveland, OH: Arthur H. Clark, 1928.

Hafen, LeRoy R. *Broken Hand*. Denver: Old West Publishing Co., 1973.

———. *Colorado: The Story of a Western Commonwealth*. Denver: Peerless Publishing Co., 1933.

———, ed. *Mountain Men and the Fur Trade of the Far West*. 10 vols. Glendale, CA: Arthur H. Clark, 1964–72.

Hafen, Leroy R., ed. *Pike's Peak Gold Rush Guidebooks of 1859*. Glendale, CA: Arthur H. Clark, 1941; Philadelphia: Porcupine Press, 1974.

Hafen, LeRoy R., and Ann W. Hafen. *Colorado: A Story of the State and Its People*. Denver: Old West Publishing Company, 1947.

Haines, Francis. *The Buffalo: The Story of American Bison and Their Hunters from Prehistoric Times to the Present*. Norman: University of Oklahoma, 1970.

Hall, Frank. *History of Colorado*. 4 vols. Chicago: Blakely Printing Co., 1891–95.

Heap, Gwinn Harris. *Central Route to the Pacific, from the Valley of the Mississippi to California: Journal of the Expedition*. Philadelphia: Lippincott, Grambo and Co., 1854.

Heitman, Francis B. *Historical Register and Dictionary of the United States Army from Its Organization, September 29, 1789, to March 2, 1903*. 2 vols. Washington, DC: U.S. Government Printing Office, 1903.

Hogan, Marion A. *Kit Carson, Colorado*. Kit Carson, CO: Kit Carson Historical Society, 1974.

Hoig, Stan. *The Sand Creek Massacre*. Norman: University of Oklahoma Press, 1961.

Hollister, Ovando J. *History of the First Regiment of Colorado Volunteers*. Denver: Thomas Gibson, 1863. Reprint: *Colorado Volunteers in New Mexico, 1862*. Chicago: R. R. Donnelley & Sons, The Lakeside Press, 1962.

Holt, R. D. "The Proposed National Cattle Trail," *Cattleman*, 1943.

Irwin, Henry, and William F. Cody. *The Great Salt Lake Trail*. Topeka, KS: Crane, 1913; Williamstown, MA: Corner House Publishers, 1978.

Iverson, Kristen. *Molly Brown: Unraveling the Myth*. Boulder: Johnson Books, 1999.

Jackson, Helen Hunt. *Bits of Travel at Home*. Boston: Little, Brown, 1878.

James, Edwin. *An Account of an Expedition from Pittsburgh to the Rocky Mountains*. Philadelphia: Carey & Lea, 1823; Cleveland, OH: Arthur H. Clark, 1905.

Jocknick, Sidney. *Early Days on the Western Slope of Colorado*. Denver: The Carson-Harper Co., 1913; Ouray, CO: Western Reflections Publishing Co., 1998.

Josephy, Alvin M. *The Civil War in the American West*. New York: Alfred A. Knopf, 1991.

Kelly, Charles. *Outlaw Trail*. Salt Lake City: published by the author, 1938; Lincoln: University of Nebraska Press, Bison Books, 1996.

Kessler, Ron. *Anza's 1779 Comanche Campaign*. Monte Vista, CO: published by the author, 1994; Monte Vista, CO: Adobe Village Press, 2001.

———. *Old Spanish Trail North Branch and Its Travelers*. Santa Fe, NM: Sunstone Press, 1998.

Kings, John. *In Search of Centennial: A Journey with James A. Michener*. New York: Random House, 1978.

Kohlman, Oley. *A Tough 100 Years: A History of the North Park Stockgrowers Association*. Walden, CO: North Park Stockgrowers Association, 2000.

Kouris, Diana Allen. *The Romantic and Notorious History of Brown's Park*. Basin, WY: Wolverine Gallery, 1988.

Lavender, David. *Bent's Fort*. Garden City, NY: Doubleday, 1954.

———. *The Big Divide*. Garden City, NY: Doubleday, 1949.

———. *The Great West*. New York: American Heritage, 1965; New York and Boston: Mariner Books, 2000.

Leckenby, Charles Harmon. *The Tread of Pioneers*. Steamboat Springs, CO: *Steamboat Pilot*, 1945.

Lecompte, Janet S. *Pueblo, Hardscrabble, Greenhorn: The Upper Arkansas, 1832–1856*. Norman: University of Oklahoma Press, 1978.

Lee, Mabel Barbee. *Cripple Creek Days*. New York: Doubleday, 1958.

Lee, Wayne C. *Trails of the Smoky Hill*. Caldwell, ID: Caxton Printers, 1980.

Leyendecker, Liston E. *The Griffith Family and the Founding of Georgetown*. Niwot: University Press of Colorado, 2001.

Lippincott, Sarah [Grace Greenwood]. *New Life in New Lands*. New York: J. B. Ford & Co., 1873.

Litvak, Dianna. *Colorado Travel-Smart Trip Planner*. Santa Fe, NM: John Muir Publications, 1996.

Luchetti, Cathy, and Carol Olwell. *Women of the West*. New York: Orion Books, 1982.

Marcy, Randolph B. *Thirty Years of Army Life on the Border*. New York, 1886.

Marshall, John B., and Temple H. Cornelius. *Golden Treasures of the San Juan*. Denver: Sage Books, 1961.

McCook, Edward M., contributor. *Annual Report of the Commissioner of Indian Affairs to the Secretary of the Interior for 1870*. Washington, DC: Government Printing Office, 1871.

Metz, Myrtle D. *Of Haviland and Honey: A Colorado Girlhood 1924–1947*. Boulder: Pruett Publishing, 1992.

Miller, Mark. *Hollow Victory*. Niwot: University Press of Colorado, 1997.

Mills, Enos. *The Story of Estes Park*. Estes Park, CO: published by the author, 1917.

Monnett, John H., and Michael McCarthy, *Colorado Profiles: Men and Women Who Shaped the Centennial State*. Niwot: University Press of Colorado, 1987.

Morten, Beryl. "Pinnacle." Unpublished manuscript, n.d. WPA Subject 230. Wyoming State Archives, Cheyenne.

Moulton, Candy. *Roadside History of Nebraska*. Missoula, MT: Mountain Press, 1997.

———. *Roadside History of Wyoming*. Missoula, MT: Mountain Press, 1995.

———, and Flossie Moulton. *Steamboat: Legendary Bucking Horse*. Glendo, WY: High Plains Press, 1992.

Mumey, Nolie. *Creede: The History of a Colorado Silver Mining Town*. Denver: Artcraft Press, 1949.

Nankivell, John H. *History of the Military Organizations of the State of Colorado*. Denver: W. H. Kistler Stationery Co., 1935.

Nelson, Jim. *Glenwood Springs: The History of a Rocky Mountain Resort*. Ouray, CO: Western Reflections Publishing Co., 1999.

Noel, Thomas J. *Denver Landmarks and Historic Districts*. Niwot: University Press of Colorado, 1996.

Noel, Thomas J., and John Fielder. *Colorado 1870–2000 Revisited: The History Behind the Images*. Englewood, CO: Westcliffe Publishers, 2001.

Noel, Thomas J., and Cathleen M. Norman. *A Pikes Peak Partnership: The Penroses and the Tutts*. Niwot: University Press of Colorado, 2000.

O'Connor, Richard. *Gould's Millions*. Garden City, NY: Doubleday, 1962.

Olsen, Rex T. *Return to Cottonwood Draw*. Irvine, CA: Olsen Press, 1995.

O'Neal, Bill. *Historic Ranches of the Old West*. Austin, TX: Eakin Press, 1997.

Oppelt, Norman T. *Guide to Prehistoric Ruins of the Southwest*. Boulder: Pruett Publishing, 1981; second edition, 1989.

Otero, Miguel Antonio. *My Life on the Frontier 1864–1882*. New York: Press of the Pioneers, 1935; Albuquerque: University of New Mexico Press, 1987.

Pabor, W. E. *Greeley in the Beginning*. Greeley, CO: Greeley Museum, 1973.

Papanikolas, Zeese. *Buried Unsung: Louis Tikas and the Ludlow Massacre*. Logan: University of Utah, 1982; Lincoln: University of Nebraska Press, Bison Books, 1991.

Payne, Stephen. *Where the Rockies Ride Herd*. Denver: Sage Books, 1965.

Pendley, William Perry. *War on the West: Government Tyranny on America's Great Frontier*. Washington, DC: Regnery Publishing, 1995.

Perkin, Robert L. *The First Hundred Years: An Informal History of Denver and the "Rocky Mountain News."* Garden City, NY: Doubleday, 1959.

Pike, Zebulon Montgomery. *The Journals of Zebulon Montgomery Pike*. Edited by Donald Jackson. Vol. 1. Norman: University of Oklahoma Press, 1966.

Preuss, Charles. *Exploring with Frémont: The Private Diary of Charles Preuss, Cartographer for John C. Frémont on the First, Second, and Fourth Expeditions to the Far West*. Norman: University of Oklahoma Press, 1958.

Propst, Nell Brown. *Forgotten People: A History of the South Platte Trail*. Boulder: Pruett Publishing, 1979.

Rankin, M. Wilson. *Reminiscences of Frontier Days Including an Authentic Account of the Thornburgh and Meeker Massacre*. Denver: Smith-Brooks, 1935.

Reyher, Ken. *Antoine Robidoux and Fort Uncompahgre*. Montrose, CO: Western Reflections Publishing Co., 1998; revised edition, 2002.

———. *Silver and Sawdust: Life in the San Juans*. Ouray, CO: Western Reflections Publishing Co., 2000.

Rideing, William H. *A-Saddle in the Wild West*. London: J. C. Nimmo and Bain, 1879.

Rinehart, Frederick R. *Chronicles of Colorado*. Boulder: Roberts Rinehart, 1984.

Rohrbough, Malcolm J. *Aspen: The History of a Silver Mining Town, 1879–1893*. New York: Oxford University Press, 1986; Boulder: University Press of Colorado, 2000.

Root, Frank. *The Overland Stage to California: Personal Reminiscences and Authentic History of the Great Overland Stage Line and Pony Express from the Mississippi River to the Pacific Ocean.* Topeka, KS: published by the author, 1901.

Rumsey, Becky. "Court Rains on Title to Colorado Land Grant," *High Country News,* Western Roundup, May 16, 1994.

Ruxton, George F. *Adventures in Mexico and the Rocky Mountains.* New York: Harper & Brothers, 1848.

Sage, Rufus G. *Scenes in the Rocky Mountains, Oregon, California, New Mexico, Texas and Grand Prairies.* Philadelphia: Carey & Hart, 1846. Reprint: *Rocky Mountain Life.* Lincoln: University of Nebraska Press, Bison Books, 1982.

Sanford, Mollie Dorsey. *Mollie: The Journal of Mollie Dorsey Sanford in Nebraska and Colorado Territories, 1857–1866.* Lincoln: University of Nebraska Press, 1959.

Scher, Zeke. "Land for Sale: Bodies Included," *Empire Magazine, Denver Post,* November 21, 1976.

Schlissel, Lillian. *Women's Diaries of the Westward Migration.* New York: Schocken Books, 1982.

Shoemaker, Len. *Roaring Fork Valley.* Denver: Sage Books, 1958.

Shwayder, Carol Rein, comp. *Weld County—Old and New: People and Places.* Volume 5, *Historical Gazetteer, Dictionary of Place Names, Weld County, Colorado, Pre-historic Indians to 1992.* Greeley, CO: Unicorn Ventures, 1992.

Simmons, Virginia McConnell. *San Luis Valley: Land of the Six-Armed Cross.* Boulder: Pruett Publishing, 1979; Niwot: University Press of Colorado, 1999.

———. *The Ute Indians of Utah, Colorado, and New Mexico.* Niwot: University Press of Colorado, 2000.

Smith, Duane A. *The Birth of Colorado: A Civil War Perspective.* Norman: University of Oklahoma Pres, 1989.

———. *Silverton: A Quick History.* Ouray, CO: Western Reflections Publishing Co., 1997.

———. *Song of the Hammer and Drill: The Colorado San Juans, 1860–1914.* Niwot: University Press of Colorado, 2000.

Smith, P. David. *Ouray: Chief of the Utes.* Ouray, CO: Wayfinder Press, 1986. Revised edition: Ouray, CO: Western Reflections Publishing Co., 1998.

———. *A Quick History of Ouray.* Fort Collins, CO: First Light Publishing, 1996. Revised edition: Ouray, CO: Western Reflections Publishing Co., 1999.

Standish, John K. "Up the Texas Trail," *The Producer: The National Livestock Monthly,* 1932.

Stevenson, Thelma V. *Historic Hahn's Peak.* Fort Collins, CO: Robinson Press, 1976.

Stewart, Elinore Pruitt. *Letters of a Woman Homesteader.* Lincoln: University of Nebraska Press, Bison Books. 1989.

Stiger, Mark. *Hunter-Gatherer Archaeology of the Colorado High Country.* Niwot: University of Colorado Press, 2001.

Stokowski, Patricia A. *Riches and Regrets: Betting on Gambling in Two Colorado Mountain Towns.* Niwot: University Press of Colorado, 1996.

Taylor, Morris F. *Trinidad, Colorado Territory.* Pueblo, CO: O'Brien Printing & Stationery Co., 1966.

Toll, Oliver W. *A Report of a 1914 Pack Trip.* N.p., 1962.

Trento, Salvatore M. *Field Guide to Mysterious Places of the West.* Boulder: Pruett Publishing, 1994.

Ubbelohde, Carl, Maxine Benson, and D. A. Smith. *A Colorado History.* Boulder: Pruett Publishing, 1982.

———, eds. *A Colorado Reader.* Boulder: Pruett Publishing, 1962.

U.S. Congress. House of Representatives. *The Chivington Massacre.* Reports of the Committees, 39th Cong. 2nd sess., 1867.

U.S. War Department. *The War of the Rebellion: A Compilation of the Official Records of the Union and Confederate Armies.* Four series, 128 vols. Washington, DC: Government Printing Office, 1880–1901.

Van Dorn, Perry. *Flickering Lights in Vacant Windows: A History of the J. W. Hugus & Co.* Grand Junction, CO: Pyramid Printing, 1992.

"Virginia Dale Stage Station." Unpublished manuscript; no author, n.d. WPA Subject file, 142: Stage Stations. Wyoming State Archives, Cheyenne.

Voynick, Stephen M. *Climax: The History of Colorado's Climax Molybdenum Mine.* Missoula, MT: Mountain Press, 1996.

———. *Colorado Gold: From the Pike's Peak Rush to the Present.* Missoula, MT: Mountain Press, 1992.

———. *Leadville: A Miner's Epic.* Missoula, MT: Mountain Press, 1984; revised edition, 1988.

Warner, Ted J., ed. *The Domínguez-Escalante Journal, 1776.* Provo, UT: Brigham Young University Press, 1976.

Wentworth, Edward N. "Sheep Wars of the Nineties in Northwest Colorado." In *1946 Brand Book: Twelve Original Papers Pertaining to the History of the West*, ed. Virgil V. Peterson. Denver: The Westerners, 1947.

West, Elliott. *The Saloon on the Rocky Mountain Mining Frontier*. Lincoln: University of Nebraska Press, Bison Books, 1979.

White, David A., ed. *News of the Plains and Rockies, 1803–1865*. 9 vols. Spokane, WA: Arthur H. Clark, 1996–2001.

Whiteley, Lee. *The Cherokee Trail*. Boulder: published by the author, 1999.

Whitford, William C. *Colorado Volunteers in the Civil War*. Denver: Colorado State Historical Society, 1909; Golden, CO: Pruett Press, 1963.

Wilson, Elinor. *Jim Beckwourth*. Norman: University of Oklahoma Press, 1972.

Wishart, David J. *The Fur Trade of the American West, 1807–1840*. Lincoln: University of Nebraska Press, 1979; Bison Books edition, 1992.

Works Progress Administration. State of Colorado Writer's Program. *Colorado: A Guide to the Highest State*. American Guide Series. New York: Hastings House, 1941.

Worster, Donald. *A River Running West: The Life of John Wesley Powell*. Oxford, NY: Oxford University Press, 2001.

Newspapers

Bennington Banner (Bennington, Vermont)

Carbon County Journal (Rawlins, Wyoming)

Cheyenne Leader (Cheyenne, Wyoming)

Craig Courier

Daily Missouri Republican (Westport, Missouri)

Denver News

Denver Post

Empire Magazine (*Denver Post*)

Fort Collins Coloradan

Fort Collins Express

Fort Collins Shopping Guide

Frank Leslie's Illustrated Newspaper and *Frank Leslie's Illustrated Weekly Newspaper* (New York)

Georgetown Miner

Grand Junction Daily Sentinel

Harper's Weekly (New York)

High Country News (Paonia, Colorado)

Journal of Commerce (Kansas City, Missouri)

Kansas Herald of Freedom (Lawrence, Kansas)

Kansas Magazine (Topeka, Kansas)

Loveland Reporter-Herald

Missouri Intelligencer (Franklin, Missouri)

New York Tribune (New York City)

Rocky Mountain News (Denver, Colorado)

Santa Fe Gazette (Santa Fe, New Mexico)

Steamboat Pilot

Trinidad Chronicle-News

Western Journal (St. Louis, Missouri)

Index

About the Author

An avid student of western history, Candy Moulton carries her camera and notebook everywhere she travels. She is the author or coauthor of a dozen western history books, including two previous books in the Roadside History series-*Roadside History of Nebraska* (1997) and *Roadside History of Wyoming* (1995). Her latest title is *Chief Joseph: Guardian of the People*, published by Forge Books.

In addition to writing books, Moulton has worked on films. She was a writer and associate producer for "Footsteps to the West" and other film exhibits at the National Historical Trails Interpretive Center in Casper, Wyoming. She also contributed to the BBC documentary "Seven Journeys to the West" and the History Channel's *Investigating History* series.

Moulton makes her home near Encampment, Wyoming, where she edits the Western Writers of America's *Roundup Magazine* and the Oregon-California Trails Association newsletter, *News from the Plains*. She also contributes regularly to several periodicals, including *True West*, *American Cowboy*, *Wild West*, *Persimmon Hill*, the *Casper Star-Tribune*, and the *Rawlins Daily Times*.

We encourage you to patronize your local bookstore. Most stores will order any title they do not stock. You may also order directly from Mountain Press, using the order form provided below or by calling our toll-free, 24-hour number and using your VISA, MasterCard, Discover or American Express.

Some other Roadside History titles of interest:

_____Roadside History of Arizona, Second Edition	paper/$20.00	
_____Roadside History of Arkansas	paper/$18.00	cloth/$30.00
_____Roadside History of Colorado	paper/$20.00	
_____Roadside History of Montana	paper/$20.00	
_____Roadside History of Nebraska	paper/$18.00	cloth/$30.00
_____Roadside History of Nevada	paper/$20.00	
_____Roadside History of New Mexico	paper/$18.00	
_____Roadside History of Oklahoma	paper/$20.00	
_____Roadside History of Oregon	paper/$18.00	
_____Roadside History of South Dakota	paper/$18.00	
_____Roadside History of Texas	paper/$18.00	cloth/$30.00
_____Roadside History of Utah	paper/$18.00	
_____Roadside History of Vermont	paper/$15.00	
_____Roadside History of Wyoming	paper/$18.00	cloth/$30.00
_____Roadside History of Yellowstone Park	paper/$10.00	

Please include $3.00 per order to cover shipping and handling.

Send the books marked above. I enclose $_____

Name_____

Address _____

City/State/Zip _____

☐ Payment enclosed (check or money order in U.S. funds)

Bill my: ☐ VISA   ☐ MasterCard ☐ Discover ☐ American Express

Card No. _____ Exp. Date:_____

Signature _____

MOUNTAIN PRESS PUBLISHING COMPANY
P.O. Box 2399 • Missoula, MT 59806 • Order Toll-Free 1-800-234-5308
E-mail: info@mtnpress.com • Web: www.mountain-press.com